FAMILY DISOR-GANIZATION

An Introduction to a
Sociological Analysis

By ERNEST R. MOWRER, Ph.D.

*A*RNO *P*RESS & *T*HE *N*EW *Y*ORK *T*IMES

New York   1972

Reprint Edition 1972 by Arno Press Inc.

Reprinted from a copy in
The University of Illinois Library

LC# 74-169396
ISBN 0-405-03873-9

Family in America
ISBN for complete set: 0-405-03840-2
See last pages of this volume for titles.

Manufactured in the United States of America

FAMILY DISORGANIZATION

THE UNIVERSITY OF CHICAGO PRESS
CHICAGO, ILLINOIS

———

THE BAKER & TAYLOR COMPANY
NEW YORK

THE MACMILLAN COMPANY OF CANADA, LIMITED
TORONTO

THE CAMBRIDGE UNIVERSITY PRESS
LONDON

THE MARUZEN-KABUSHIKI-KAISHA
TOKYO, OSAKA, KYOTO, FUKUOKA, SENDAI

THE COMMERCIAL PRESS, LIMITED
SHANGHAI

FAMILY DISOR-
GANIZATION

*An Introduction to a
Sociological Analysis*

By ERNEST R. MOWRER, Ph.D.

THE UNIVERSITY OF CHICAGO PRESS
CHICAGO · ILLINOIS

Composed and Printed By
The University of Chicago Press
Chicago, Illinois, U.S.A.

FOREWORD

Astonishing as it may seem, very little is known about the nature and organization of the modern family. Except for a few impressionistic sketches in fiction, no pictures of it exist. The biological, psychological, and sociological sciences yield only fragmentary findings from their haphazard and desultory incursions into this new field.

Our ignorance of the life of the present-day family is none the less colossal because of the vast and increasing literature upon sex and marriage and the family. For much of this literature deals with family life of other societies than our own, the best of it with marriage and the family among preliterate peoples, and the remainder of it with the large patriarchal family, the type of familial organization of the ancient Israelites, Romans, and Greeks—the type which still prevails in contemporary China, Japan, and India.

Indeed, the greater part of the increasing annual output of books on marriage and the family is devoted, not to any systematic and disinterested description of the modern family, but to vivid, always intense, and often embittered indictment of its defects, real or alleged. Conservatives and radicals alike condemn the family as it is, but on different grounds; the first seeking to modify it gradually in conformity with traditional standards, the latter to destroy it entirely, or completely to reconstruct it on newer and freer lines.

There are, of course, volumes on family life, such as Westermarck, *A History of Human Marriage;* Helen Bosanquet, *The Family;* Howard, *A History of Matrimonial*

Institutions; Flügel, *The Psycho-Analytic Study of the Family;* Calhoun, *A Social History of the American Family*, which present from different angles disinterested accounts and interpretations of familial organization. Although each of these volumes makes a contribution to our knowledge of the family, no one of them, nor all of them together, supplies anything approaching an adequate description, not to speak of a satisfactory explanation, of the family under the changing conditions of modern life.

While no systematic study of the modern family has been essayed, many practical problems related to it and bound up with it, such as divorce and desertion, juvenile delinquency, and the conflict between the older and the younger generations, have led to individual studies by social workers, statisticians, and, more recently, by psychiatrists and sociologists. Although these inquiries had their origins largely in common-sense observation and reflection, they gradually developed different technique of investigation and more critical and orderly methods of recording findings. In consequence there now exists a considerable literature upon the problems of the modern family, and, what is still more significant for social research, a great accumulation of concrete materials, in the records of social agencies, in the archives of courts, in the reports of the United States Census Bureau, and in the files of institutes for psychiatric research.

This literature and these materials upon different phases of family disorganization furnish the reason for this study by Dr. Mowrer. Its purpose was to make a systematic survey of the methods of research now in use in the investigation of the problems of the modern family. The natural expectation was that a critical and comprehensive examination of methods employed upon individual projects would not only contribute to raising the standards of research on family life, but might also offer a new and unifying and fundamental conception of the family as a center of orientation for all further work.

How far this volume has achieved both these objectives may be left to the future to decide. In any event, all studies in this field for some time to come must reckon with the acute analysis of the statistical and the case-study methods presented here. Of even more significance, perhaps, for fruitful research are the chapters on ecology, on social forces, on behavior sequences, and on socio-analysis, which present exhibits of the most recent approaches to the study of the family.

This present volume does not undertake a complete analysis of modern family organization. But it has assembled and tested the tools of research requisite for the task. It has, indeed, gone further and presented samples of products from the use of these various techniques. These exhibits of family disorganization in its different aspects—comparative statistics of divorce for United States and foreign countries, and for rural and urban areas, the distribution of divorce and desertion by local communities in a metropolitan city, family disorganization in relation to the social forces of modern life, the analysis by family tensions and behavior sequences of individual cases of family disintegration—taken together give the reader an appreciation of the factors and forces affecting the family under modern conditions. One tends to be forced to the conclusion, not only that the family is in a transition period, but that much of its disorganization as it finds expression in divorce, in escape from family responsibility, and in the revolt of youth is inherent in the present-day conception of marriage and the family.

Dr. Mowrer points out that since modern marriage in the United States is, more than anywhere else in the world, in the hands of young people themselves, it, therefore, is organized upon the basis of romantic love. But the romantic impulse in and of itself is not always, and perhaps never, a sufficient guaranty of the permanence of marriage. With the rapid decline, especially in cities, of the older community and neighborhood control over family relationships, there is an increasing demand for a constructive program of family reorganization.

This raises the question, then, of the relation of the study of familial disorganization to the control and treatment of the problems of family life. The answer given in the final chapter will disappoint many, probably most of the readers, but it is the only honest reply: "Further research." From child-guidance centers, institutes of juvenile research, and the so-called "family clinics" as well as from independent studies, especially of normal families, promising results may be awaited.

This volume makes one unique contribution to our understanding of family disorganization which merits special attention. For the first time, cases of both divorce and desertion in a metropolitan city have been spotted upon a map in such fashion as to show the distribution of family disorganization by local communities. Desertion is "the poor man's divorce." When it is taken into account, it gives us a truer index of the actualities of family disorganization than that presented by divorce alone. The divorce and desertion rates vary widely and independently throughout the different local districts of the city, showing both the hetero-

geneity of social life within a modern metropolitan area and
the correlation of the stability or instability of family life
with the state of local community organization or disorganization. The problems of family life are evidently correlated
with all the other social problems of the city: juvenile delinquency, recreation, vice, housing in its widest implications,
poverty. This makes it fitting and significant to give this
work a place in the series of studies of which several volumes
have already been published dealing with the organization
and problems of the city.

ERNEST W. BURGESS

November 15, 1926

AUTHOR'S PREFACE

The problem of family disorganization has engaged the attention of reformers for several generations. Within the last two decades it has come to the attention of the public through the newspapers and magazines. Reams of paper have been wasted and quarts of ink spilled in the discussion of remedies. But the volume of family disorganization constantly increases if one can believe the story told in divorce statistics.

But can one believe the story told in divorce statistics? Must not such statistics be supplemented with statistics of desertion, non-support, and separation? Are these measures anything more than formal expressions of something more fundamental? What are the causes of all this confusion in family life? How can one get at the fundamental factors? What is the value of past studies in understanding and appreciating the subtle tendencies of human nature as they find expression in modern family disorganization? These are only a few of the questions implicit in the writings of social workers, reformers, publicists, journalists, sociologists, church men, etc. Such questions represent also only a few of those which the author has attempted to discuss objectively in this book.

Obviously, not all of these questions will appeal to everyone. Neither will all sections of this book be as interesting to one reader as to another. But somewhere, if he is interested in this problem at all, he will find something which will provoke him to further thought upon the problem and lead, it is hoped, to a more objective understanding of some phase of family disorganization—whether in terms of control or of appreciation.

The organization of the book falls naturally into four parts: "I. Introduction," "II. Statistics and Statistical Methods," "III. The Case-Study Methods," and "IV. Conclusions." The reader should not be frightened, however, with the introduction of statistics in the early part of the discussion, for it is only in terms of an understanding of statistical analysis that he can appreciate fully the more vital comprehension of the problem which case-studies give him. It is to be hoped that he will find himself well compensated by the human-interest appeal of the case-study section for whatever "mental agony" the statistical section may occasion.

The writer cannot acknowledge his indebtedness, unfortunately, to everyone who has aided directly and indirectly in the preparation of this book. The origin of ideas is often lost long before one gets the ideas themselves into print. Undoubtedly, however, the careful reader will recognize in the discussion the writer's indebtedness for his theory to Professors Albion W. Small, Ellsworth Faris, Robert E. Park, and Ernest W. Burgess, of the University of Chicago; to Professor Charles Horton Cooley, of the University of Michigan; to Professor Victor E. Helleberg, of the University of Kansas; and to Dr. William I. Thomas, of the New School for Social Research.

In addition there are those who have aided more directly, chief among whom are Professor Burgess, who read the manuscript and contributed many valuable suggestions; Messrs. August W. Miller and Samuel E. Erickson, clerks of the Circuit and Superior courts of Cook County, respectively, who allowed the divorce records in their charge to be consulted; Judge Timothy D. Hurley, who interceded in behalf of the writer in getting access to certain records; Miss Irene Inderrieden, of the Court of Domestic Relations, who allowed the records in her charge to be used; Dr. Richard Lord, who placed his statistical machinery at the disposal of the writer; the United States Bureau of the Census, from whom the latest statistics of divorce were secured; Miss Ruth Shonle, who read the manuscript and offered many suggestions leading to the improvement of the English; and, finally, Harriet R. Mowrer, who contributed to the case-study section both in analysis and materials. The writer also desires to make acknowledgment to the Local Community Research Committee of the University of Chicago for assistance in the making of the study and in preparing the manuscript for publication.

ERNEST R. MOWRER

CHICAGO, ILLINOIS
September 15, 1926

CONTENTS

PART I.   INTRODUCTION

PART II.   STATISTICS AND STATISTICAL METHODS

PART III.   CASE-STUDY METHODS

PART IV.   CONCLUSIONS

PART I
INTRODUCTION

CHAPTER I

FAMILY DISORGANIZATION AND THE CONFUSED IDEALS OF THE MODERN FAMILY

Almost within the last generation the family has come into public consciousness as the matrix of a growing social problem. It is not alone an increase in the more obvious forms of family disorganization, such as divorce, separations, and desertions, which causes concern; these explicit forms are recognized as but the overt expressions of a new conception of the family, uneasily felt but as yet largely undefined. As the family has seemed about to disintegrate, programs and plans for its rehabilitation have appeared in numbers. Some seek to counteract the disintegrating forces with new rules of conduct and new ideals; others advocate clearing the ground for an entirely new institution. Few coincide either in analyses or causes or in remedies suggested. They are, nevertheless, a reflection of current attitudes toward the family and hence may serve as a point of departure for more scientific study.

The family is not merely a group of individuals living in close proximity, as formal studies of divorce and desertion often seem to assume. It is also an organization of attitudes and ideals which each family develops independently and which characterizes the family as a cultural group. Family pride, family prejudice, the jokes and proverbs intelligible to no outsider, and the hopes and ambitions that distinguish families from one another help to make up what may be called the "family complex." It is this identification of in-

3

terests which makes of the family a co-operating unit, felt by its members and recognized by the community

The establishment of a family is the process of building up organized attitudes in which all concur. Family disorganization represents the converse process in which the family complex breaks up and the ambitions and ideals of the individual members of the family become differentiated.

The legal aspects of marriage and divorce are recognition by the community or state that family attitudes have been established or discontinued, i.e., disintegrated. Marriage and divorce do not make or dissolve the family in any fundamental sense. The family runs its course in the interaction of its members, and at appropriate times the state takes formal cognizance of the status of family affairs.

It is obvious that if the ideal of the corporate family which exists in the American mores was upheld in its entirety there would be little family disintegration and hence few legal divorces. The public interest in marriage and divorce and the efforts to discover panaceas for family disintegration are indicative of a wavering of the old ideal of divorceless marriage and at the same time of a failure to comprehend fully the forces at work.

THE TRIPLE ROOTS OF THE MODERN FAMILY

The historical antecedents of the modern family and of the disorganization which is part of it are both recent and definite. Twentieth-century family disorganization is a part of the great movement toward individualization which has characterized Western civilization in the last four hundred years. This movement has been strongest in the cities where there is greater opportunity to escape the restraints of established custom, but even the most remote rural districts have not escaped its force. Industry, education, religion, and social organization as well as the family have been affected by this general movement to free the individual from his previous unquestioning submission to traditional group control. Family disorganization is thus but a fractional part of results which are rooted in the Reformation, the Romantic movement, and the Industrial Revolution.

It is true, of course, that certain types of family disorganization antedate modern individualism. Death and circumstance, always as now, have disrupted the family as a group. Nearly every society, preliterate and ancient as well as modern, has made provision under certain conditions for divorce. But in the past, family disorganization was incidental to family life. It rarely entered into the conscious calculations of husband or wife that marriage could be less long than life itself, and all members of the family suppressed individual wishes—if, indeed, they had them— which if expressed might have tended toward the disruption of the corporate family group. In its present forms, however, family disorganization is the direct and natural manifestation of a changed conception of the family; for the modern family, as an institution, is the organized expression of attitudes and values widely different from those embodied in the semi-patriarchal family of the past.

The Reformation in one aspect, at least, represented an impetus to individualization, that is, to the emancipation of the individual from the control of the group. An immediate expression of this emancipation was the secularization of marriage—the recognition of marriage as a contract instead of as a sacrament—and the substitution of the civil for the religious ceremony. The Romantic movement was also a manifestation of individualism, a revolt of youth against the domination of parents in the arrangement of marriage, and against the regulation of the small family by the large family group. Furthermore, with the recognition of the principle of individualism came the ideal of the democratic organization of the family. [For patriarchal dominance was substituted the equality of husband and wife.

The achievement of this ideal has been directly fostered by the Industrial Revolution through the growing actual or potential economic independence of women. Then, too, city life as a natural consequence of the Industrial Revolution, with its mobility, its secondary contacts, and its impersonal relations, frees the individual from the continuous and close control of the neighborhood and the local community—a control which for centuries had made for the stability of the family.\

Indeed, the family in the past has been the most influential of institutions in imposing upon the new generation the ideals and forms of the old. Under the changing conditions of city life, however, the individual lives more in the community than in the family, and there he finds divergent views. The result is an attitude of experimentation on the part of the individual—a rebellion against the old ideals of family life and a tendency to enter into marriage relations along more individualistic lines than would have been tolerated under less mobile conditions.

Experimental arrangements, however, mean also tentative alliances. The fact that such relations are looked upon as tentative is not only symptomatic of the rebellion of the individual against the forms of the past but tends to increase the restlessness of the person. Thus the possibility of experimentation leads to a demand for continual variation.

This rebellion of the individual against the old forms of

family life indicates the lingering pressure of old social patterns, adapted to previous conditions and continuing into a changed social situation in spite of their inadequacy to function there. This condition, which Professor Ogburn has called a "cultural lag,"[1] leads directly to restlessness in the individual who finds poor provision for the complete realization of his wishes. Communicated to other persons, this restlessness represents a breaking down of the old order and a preparation for the new. As a group phenomenon it is ordinarily called "social unrest."[2] But before new behavior patterns can be substituted for those of the old order they must be worked out experimentally. This need for experimentation, whether consciously or unconsciously realized, tends always to place the emphasis upon individual efforts. The result, while it represents confusion in ideals, is to bring about profound changes in social institutions. The family, in modern life, has undoubtedly felt this changing influence of individualism as much as any social institution.

If, then, the modern family is an expression of individualism, so also is modern family disorganization. Indeed, family disorganization may be defined fundamentally as a way of thinking about the relations between the sexes in marriage where individual wishes are recognized in contrast to the older view entailing subordination of individual wishes to family attitudes. The possibility of family disintegration is thus accepted as an essential element of modern family life.

So long as the wishes of the group were paramount, as in the large or the small patriarchal families, conflict between husband and wife either did not occur or was of no

[1] Ogburn, *Social Change*, pp. 200–201.

[2] Park and Burgess, *Introduction to the Science of Sociology*, p. 866.

significance so far as the permanence of their relations was concerned. When, however, the wishes of individuals in marriage come to receive recognition as in the modern family, conflict between husband and wife tends not only to increase, but begins to threaten the continuance of marriage as a preliminary to sex relationship. When this stage is reached the family as an unchanging and indissoluble institution is no longer taken for granted, but becomes a subject for speculation and reflection.

At this point, programs of reform are formulated, the first of which tend to be rationalizations[1] of the reformer's individual experiences either as a member of a traditional family or as an experimenter in a new form of sex relationship. Reform programs represent, in this sense, experiments in family relations. But they show at the same time the current discontent in the family mores, and the degree to which the old ideals of the family have broken down. The result is a tendency for such experimenters to attempt either to revive the old family forms or to abandon them altogether for new types of family relations. One may speak, accordingly, of conservative programs of reform and of radical programs.

CONSERVATIVE REFORM PROGRAMS

The most obvious evidences of family disorganization, such as the increase in the divorce rate, or the sensational

[1] A school of modern psychologists asserts that human beings ordinarily act first and subsequently arrive at reasons for their actions; that is, the actions of the individual are determined by emotions, feelings, prejudices, unconscious urges, rather than by a logical consideration of the probable results of a particular mode of behavior. Then having acted, to excuse himself, to justify his choice of action, to satisfy the censor—his conscience—the individual builds up a pseudo-logical reason for his behavior. This explanation this school of psychologists calls a "rationalization."

publicity which dramatizes a single case of domestic infelicity, lead naturally to suggestions of reform. The first programs of reform tend to be conservative, or even reactionary, because they attempt to revive, under conditions of modern life, patterns of family organization of the past. These programs generally hark back to the family under rural conditions where contacts were primary and control was a matter of tradition and custom.[1] They vary from the most common-sense proposals to comprehensive recommendations based upon a more or less systematic analysis of the problem.

The favorite method relied upon by reformers of the common-sense sort is what Thomas and Znaniecki term the "ordering and forbidding technique."[2] This type of program may be illustrated in its most naïve form by a "recipe" for family discord proposed by Mr. McGee, an attorney for the Legal Aid Society of New York.[3]

[1] The distinction between primary and secondary contacts, to which is also related the distinction between primary and secondary groups both in their control and organization aspects, may be made as follows:

"Primary contacts are those of 'intimate face-to-face association'; secondary contacts are those of externality and greater distance. . . . . The neighborhood or the village is the natural area of primary contacts and the city the social environment of secondary contacts. In primary association individuals are in contact with each other at practically all points of their lives. In the village "everyone knows everything about everyone else." Canons of conduct are absolute, social control is omnipotent, the status of the family and the individual is fixed. In secondary association individuals are in contact with each other at only one or two points in their lives. In the city, the individual becomes anonymous; at best he is generally known in only one or two aspects of his life. Standards of behavior are relative. . . . . "—Park and Burgess, *op. cit.*, pp. 284–86.

[2] *The Polish Peasant in Europe and America*, I, 3.

[3] Doris Blake, *Chicago Tribune*, December 7 and 12, 1923.

His ten suggestions for women are:

1. Do not be extravagant.
2. Keep your home clean.
3. Do not permit your person to become unattractive.
4. Do not receive attentions from other men.
5. Do not resent reasonable discipline of children by their father.
6. Do not spend too much time with your mother.
7. Do not accept advice from the neighbors or stress too greatly even that of your own family concerning the management of your domestic affairs.
8. Do not disparage your husband.
9. Smile. Be attentive to little things.
10. Be tactful. Be feminine.

There are also ten suggestions for men:

1. Be generous according to your means.
2. Do not interfere with a woman in the management of purely domestic affairs.
3. Be cheerful, even though sometimes it may tax you to the utmost.
4. Be considerate.
5. Make love to your wife; continue to be her sweetheart.
6. Do not scold.
7. Establish your own home; if possible, remote from your wife's and your own immediate family.
8. Do not keep a lodger.
9. Cultivate neatness and personal cleanliness.
10. Be kind and just to your children.

Other remedies of this "Pollyanna" type may be briefly enumerated. A county in West Virginia issues a cookbook with each marriage license. The United States Department of Commerce has recently published a pamphlet, "How to Own Your Home: a Handbook for Prospective Home Owners," which proposes home ownership as the basis of happy family life. Clergymen have often asserted that church weddings would tend to prevent unhappy marriages.

Publication of the banns has also been advocated many times.[1] Other reformers have pointed out the need of co-operation between husband and wife; still others have asserted that domestic science in the schools, moral training, greater emphasis upon religious training, and the withdrawal of the "Bringing Up Father" type of comics from the newspapers will prevent many unhappy marriages. Social workers have often emphasized the importance of a wife dressing attractively as a technique for holding her husband's interest.[2]

[1] Charles F. and Carrie F. B. Thwing, *The Family: An Historical and Social Study*, p. 216.

[2] This confusion in popular methods of reforming family life may be further illustrated by the comments reported in a Chicago newspaper upon the merits of a housekeeping love test worked out by a couple in Los Angeles:

"The young folks who are conducting this unique experiment are Imogene Hadley and Albert Davis. They are living under the same roof, with Miss Hadley's mother as a chaperon. Imogene is doing all the cooking and housework, while Albert helps with the dishes. Their object is to determine under actual working conditions whether their marriage would be happy.

" 'That might be a good way to test out a housekeeper or a handy man about the house,' said Miss Irene Inderrieden, head of the Complaint Department of the Domestic Relations Court, 'but it's no way to test out love.

" 'A couple under these conditions would be on their good behavior. Albert would always be clean shaved in the morning before Imogene saw him, while Imogene would have time to doll up before breakfast, and would never, during the probationary period, reach the mop cap and kimono stage.'

" 'It looks to me like a rather dangerous tryout,' commented Lenora Z. Meder, attorney-at-law. 'If this were a case of true love, the young couple wouldn't need to experiment. If they were deeply in love with each other, the little problems incident to married life would gradually work themselves out.

" 'A man ought to marry a girl for companionship—not to get a good housekeeper. A competent cook and housekeeper can be hired for $25 a week.'

" 'It might give the girl an opportunity,' said Cyrena Van Gordon of the Civic Opera Company, 'of seeing her future husband asleep. No girl

A variation in the primary-group method of adjustment is represented by the religious or ethical program. Lofthouse, after surveying the institutional foundations of ethics in which the family plays a dominant part, casts aside political action and evangelistic activity as inadequate techniques for reform. The task of the reformer, he says, is to seek to restore and to preserve "that attitude of mind which unites a man first with those who are nearest to him," and to perfect in a small circle "those virtues which can then expand over a larger area." He can do this by reviving certain Christian conceptions, namely, that (1) the real wealth of any community consists in its men and women, healthy, happy, and loving one another; (2) love means service; (3) life consists in the conquest of the world. These conceptions, he believes, should be embodied in corporate and organized activity.[1]

---

ought to marry until she has seen her husband asleep and finds out whether he snores and sleeps with his mouth open.'

" 'While I believe young people ought to know something about each other before they rush headlong into matrimony,' said Mrs. Cathèrine Waugh McCulloch, attorney, 'I regard an experiment of this kind as positively dangerous. It leaves the door open for too many temptations. The mother might not be any too watchful as a chaperon.'

"A different view, however, was taken by Dr. Emma H. Salisbury, who thought such an experiment would be a wonderful thing.

" 'That is, it would be,' she qualified, 'if the mother would play fair and allow her daughter to go ahead as if she were mistress of her own house. She could caution the girl about such little pitfalls as forgetting to replace the cap on the toothpaste tube, leaving her hair in the comb and boiling the breakfast eggs so hard that they explode.

" 'Also she could warn the husband-to-be against such mistakes as burying his nose in the newspaper during breakfast, leaving his clothes around the floor and scattering cigaret ashes about the house. If she could refrain from showing her mother-in-law side, the experiment ought to work out beautifully.' "—*Chicago Evening Post*, July 31, 1923.

[1] W. F. Lofthouse, *Ethics and the Family*, pp. 362–74.

Besides these common-sense programs for reforming family life, based upon the mores of the group, there are others which, although still reflecting the mores, take into account more objective analyses of the problem. While the conclusions reached in these studies imply an emotional or sentimental attitude and a traditional approach to the problem akin to those of common sense, certain facts are cited in support of a program essaying to preserve the family in its traditional form.

Dr. Densmore[1] accepts the mental disability of woman, which is often cited as proof that she cannot play an equal rôle with man. He regards this inequality, however, as the result of heredity and environment, rather than as exclusively innate, but as a heredity and an environment which can be changed in such a way that the disability will disappear. Sex equality is therefore the solution of the woman's problem and the foundation of the family as a co-operative venture.[2]

The basic idea of this book is the fundamental and ultimate equality of the human ego, whether embodied in the one or the other sex; and the aim of these pages is to explain the nature of this equality and to promote its practical realization. When woman, through environment and heredity, has developed in similar degree the powers of generalization, initiative, invention, and logical deduction which characterize man, and when man has evolved those powers of intuition, refinement, patience and unselfishness which distinguish woman, then will men and women truly companion each other and then mutually uplifting influences will be at its culmination.[3]

Three methods for rectifying the divorce situation are proposed by Gillette: (1) passage of better laws which would

[1] *Sex Equality: A Solution of the Woman Problem.*

[2] Marriage as "co-operation in equality" is also the thesis of Louis F. Post (*Ethical Principles of Marriage and Divorce*, pp. 121–27).

[3] Emmet Densmore, *op. cit.*, pp. 370–71.

minimize and remove the present abuses in divorce; (2) establishment of special courts to hear domestic complaints; (3) reform of marriage, through education, the school, the church, and the home—education which would teach the young people the function of marriage and the duties of parenthood.[1]

"The real solution" of domestic problems, Dealey says, awaits the spread of scientific knowledge which aims to better economic conditions and general intelligence of the whole population. Removal of the taboo upon sex will bring about an appreciation on the part of women of the necessity for a single standard and thus add to the moral foundation of the family.[2]

The Thwings emphasize the necessity of a "higher standard of belief and practice" in the restoration of the family and marriage to their proper place in society. Sex should be hidden in family life, while the emotional, intellectual, and social elements should be made prominent. Emphasis upon the sexual aspect of family life is largely responsible for divorce, while its minimizing makes for permanence of the marriage bond. Such a goal, they believe, is commended both by the conscience of the individual and by the teachings of Christ.[3]

The assumptions underlying the various methods of reform presented above are far from being consistent, except in so far as they all tend to imply a rationalistic psychology. In Mr. McGee's suggestions it is assumed that in each marriage there is potential happiness which can be had by attention to a few general rules of conduct. It is also assumed that

[1] John M. Gillette, *The Family and Society*, pp. 113–14.

[2] James Q. Dealey, *The Family in Its Sociological Aspects*, pp. 132–33.

[3] Charles F. and Carrie F. B. Thwing, *op. cit.*, p. 213.

each person not only knows how to conform specifically to these general rules but that each person is equally capable of conforming. In certain proposals it is assumed that house-keeping is the basis of the family; in others, that the key-note is romantic love; in still others, that the family is a sacred institution. The result is a confusion rather than a consensus.

The significance of these reform programs lies in the fact that they represent attempts to reorganize the family upon the basis of the past, and that they also show at the same time a confusion in ideals of family life. Little recognition is given in these reform programs to the fact that the con-ditions of life have changed in such a way as to call for a new set of family mores and the abandonment of the old concep-tions of family life. Yet the recognition of the need for re-form itself implies an appreciation of the fact that there have been changes in family life and in family mores—that the old ideals of the family have broken down. Such reform programs represent, as has been said, attempts to recon-struct family life in conformity with the ideals of the past. As such they reveal the confusion which accompanies all social experiments attempting to revive old forms under changed social conditions.

RADICAL PROGRAMS

In contrast to the idealization of the past in conserva-tive programs of reform of family life, radical programs idealize the future. Social political writers indict the present family, both as an outlived social heritage and as an enemy of individualism. At best, they contend, it represents an institution in transition toward a future type of family.

Two movements, one popular and the other academic,

have been the chief sources of radical programs. Feminism and eugenics, while contradictory in many respects in their formulations of programs, have much in common in their assumptions as to the fundamental basis of family life. Comparison of these two points of view will bring out this relationship.

Feminism is concerned mainly with the demand for (1) equal political and legal status for the sexes, including the right to vote and hold office; (2) the same educational and industrial opportunities for women as are enjoyed by men; and (3) as much freedom in sexual relations for women as for men.[1] Through the woman's movement women demand the opportunity to develop their personalities in every direction that is open to men. They deny that woman's place is in the home any more than man's place is there. The only difference which they recognize between the sexes is that of sexual functions.[2]

Some feminists look upon the demand for sex freedom as the chief aim of the woman's movement. Meisel-Hess takes this point of view:

Of all varieties of bond-slavery, sexual bond-slavery is by far the worst. The demand for economic freedom is not the prime motive force of the women's movement. In its orbit, indeed, that movement centers in its idea of economic freedom, as a planet in its orbit revolves around a star; but this latter star itself pursues an orbit around a still greater star. The greater central sun of the whole movement, of the whole system, is the emancipation of sex. Around this center, the entire

[1] Mr. and Mrs. John Martin, *Feminism: Its Fallacies and Follies*, p. 9.

[2] Emphasis in America has been chiefly upon the first two demands. If any mention is made of the third, the plea is for making the morals of men those of women, rather than the other way about. See Gilman, *The Man-made World;* Coolidge, *Why Women Are So;* Scott Nearing, *Woman and Social Progress.*

movement is directed, and the stars of economic freedom, of political emancipation, and all the rest, are no more than subsidiary aims, no more than satellite suns.[1]

This emphasis upon sexual emancipation is taken by the opponents of feminism to mean that the goal of the movement is free love. But even Meisel-Hess recognizes that the ideal form of the family is a permanent monogamous relationship.[2] Practically, however, she sees difficulty in the attainment of that ideal. The only recourse is, then, to unions easily dissolved, so that by trial and error each person can find that marriage wherein there may be obtained "complete satisfaction of all desire for sexual relationships." For, she says:

It is false to assert that by the institution of marriage the sexual and amatory life is regulated to the general satisfaction. The truth is, that of those who marry the majority fail to find happiness, whilst a very large proportion never attain to marriage at all. It is a lying contention that the actual sexual conduct of men and women corresponds to the pretenses that are socially enforced; that people in reality behave as if the sexual life were a quite subordinate feature of existence; that the conduct which in these respects is regarded as "proper," corresponds in any way to our truly vital needs. The truth is that the sexual life is the focal point of every healthy being whose instincts have not undergone partial or complete atrophy; that upon the full satisfaction of sexual needs depends the true equilibrium of the mental no less than the physical personality; that the life which society, formed in the respect into a trust for the diffusion of lies, agrees to regard as consonant with its standards of propriety, is altogether unsatisfying to the average human being; and that people do not live as they pretend, or if they do so live, it is under compulsion.

Let us admit the truth: let us recognize that there is full justification for the desire of every human being to love and be loved; let us make it socially possible for everyone to satisfy his desire as may best

[1] Grete Meisel-Hess, *The Sexual Crisis*, p. 214.   [2] *Ibid.*, p. 60.

commend itself to the individual judgment—so long as no other person is harmed, and so long as nothing is done injurious to racial welfare.[1]

The attitude of the feminists upon the nature of family relations may be characterized, then, as one demanding the fullest development of individualism.

When every life is regarded as an end in itself from the point of view that it can never be lived again; that it must, therefore, be lived as completely and greatly as possible; when every personality is valued as an asset in life that has never existed before and will never occur again, then also the erotic happiness or unhappiness of a human being will be treated as of greater importance, and not to himself alone. No, it will be so also to the whole community—through the life and the work his happiness may give the race or his unhappiness deprive it of.[2]

⌐The argument follows therefore that love—erotic attraction and impulse—should be the only motive in marriage, and marriages should be continued only so long as love remains⌐ It does not follow, at least theoretically, that this emphasis upon the love relation will involve greater changeability in sex attraction and fixation. In fact, in some of the writings of feminists, the assumption seems to be made that the common entrance of woman with man into all phases of life will tend to prevent changes in affection. One feminist writes:

We have called the woman's movement of our age an endeavor on the part of women among civilized races to find new fields of labor as the old slip from them, as an attempt to escape from parasitism and an inactive dependence upon sex function alone; but, viewed from another side, the woman's movement might not less justly be called a part of the great movement towards common occupations, common interests, common ideals, and an emotional tenderness and sympathy between the sexes deeply founded and more indestructible than any the world has yet seen.[3]

[1] Meisel-Hess, *op. cit.*, p. 117.   [2] Ellen Key, *Love and Marriage*, p. 396.
[3] Olive Schreiner, *Woman and Labor*, p. 272.

⌈Feminism thus recognizes few obligations to society as a basis for family life, but rather stresses the amatory and sexual needs of the individual. These needs for the woman include not only sexual relations but also the experience of child-bearing. Whether or not she cares for the child after it is born is purely a personal matter. Family life is thus of secondary importance to the feminist while the primary interest is in the love relationship.[1]⌋

Eugenics, because it has received its impetus from academic circles, has had more scientific data at its command than has feminism. The eugenist bases his assumptions regarding the importance of heredity upon studies in biology, family histories of certain degenerate families, and the differences in the mental development of fraternal twins as compared to identical twins. He assumes that progress has been the result of incidental improvement in the human stock through the mechanism of heredity. The family to him is an institution primarily for breeding better human stock.[2]

Pure love between the sexes should be proclaimed as the noblest thing on earth, and the bearing and rearing of children as amongst the highest of all human duties. Some risks ought to be run in order to secure these joys and to fulfill these duties; and Cupid may well remain a little blind to all minor defects. To promote these ways of re-

[1] This does not mean, however, that all feminists are agreed upon the relative emphasis to be given each motive for marriage. Some of them take a more conservative view than that expressed above. Mrs. Coolidge says, "Until quite recently marriage had only two aims: offspring and the regulation of the sex instinct. It has now come to have another profound import: the comradeship of congenial temperaments."—*Op. cit.*, pp. 340–41.

[2] Even progress in resolving the conflict between the individual and the group is said to depend upon this eugenic principle. See M. M. Knight, Iva L. Peters, and Phyllis Blanchard, *Taboo and Genetics: A Study of the Biological, Sociological and Psychological Foundation of the Family.*

garding sexual problems and to show how often the moralist unknown to himself is in effect striving to better the racial qualities of future generations come well within the scope of our endeavors.[1]

The interests of the eugenists have been directed toward the family as a child-bearing institution, with little attention to the adjustment between husband and wife in marriage relations. The implication follows, perhaps, that emphasis upon the child-bearing and child-rearing functions of family life instead of upon the satisfaction of selfish interests will bring more happiness in family unions. On the whole, however, the eugenists approach the problem of the family from the standpoint of society as a whole rather than from that of the personal interests of its individual members. In so doing they are, of course, attempting to stem the tide of individualism—itself a large factor in the causation of family disorganization.

To both the feminists and the eugenists the fundamental basis of family life is thus seen to be physiological. For the former, it is primarily love relations adequate for the satisfaction of individual desires; for the latter, reproduction which will improve the racial stock. The feminists look to a future order of society where family life if it exists at all will be the expression of perfect freedom. The eugenists, however, demand control of marriage in the interests of biological progress. Both leave out of account human nature as a product of group life. Both represent, nevertheless, experiments in adjusting family mores and family ideals to modern conditions. In this sense they have much in common with the conservative programs of reform.

[1] Leonard Darwin, "The Aims and Methods of Eugenical Societies," *Eugenics, Genetics and the Family* ("Scientific Papers of the Second International Congress of Eugenics," I, 12).

URBAN NEEDS AND FAMILY MORES

Looking upon all these programs of reform as experiments one can scarcely avoid at least three conclusions with reference to family life of the present: (1) There is a great deal of confusion in family mores. (2) This confusion is both the result and the cause of the general discontent with present family mores. (3) But there is also a lack of consensus in ideals of family life as well as in conception of its fundamental basis.

The confusion in family mores is largely because of the mobility of urban life which, as the result of its multiplicity of contacts, brings into close proximity groups having divergent family mores. The child and the youth are no longer in contact with but one family pattern—that of their own group. Each learns to pass freely from one group to another, accepting for a time the mores of the group with which he is most intimately associated, but failing to work out for himself, or accept from any group, a definite and consistent system of family mores and ideals. Or, if he does idealize the family relations as represented by that group under which he was reared, he finds them of little use to him when he enters into a marriage relationship, because of the changed conditions of life, especially in the city.[1]

Two means of communication, both products of modern

---

[1] Under the old forms of family life everything was taken care of by the traditions and customs of the group. There was no discussion of sexual relations and of children prior to marriage—"instinct" was left to take care of that! Now, in some circles at least, sex and birth control are freely discussed. In spite of this more or less rationalistic attitude toward the marriage relation, there are no customs to exert control. Each couple venturing upon the road of matrimony is confronted with working out its own adjustment to the situation. In crises individuals act in diverse ways, blindly groping for some solution to their matrimonial tangles.

industrial development, the newspaper and the motion picture, probably more than any others have multiplied the opportunities of the individual to escape from the contacts and control of the primary group. Both present to the individual a confusion of behavior patterns, each implying divergent ideals of family life. In contrast to the traditional family of one's own experiences, one sees portrayed, in the news columns and on the screen, other pictures of family life in which marriage is not held to be indissoluble and even in which marriage relations are begun prior to a marriage ceremony.[1] And all this without the accompanying defense reaction of censure and criticism which characterizes such infractions of the mores in primary groups. The inevitable

---

[1] The following newspaper story represents a not unusual situation, and shows as well how individuals rationalize their behavior in conformity to traditional standards:

"LOS ANGELES, CAL. Feb. 18.—Baby Rex Tellegen, almost a year old, son of Lou Tellegen, 'the perfect lover,' and the former Isabel Dilworth of Philadelphia society, today made his presence known to a hitherto unknowing world in his mother's arms in their Hollywood garden.

"The marriage of the parents became known only yesterday. Mrs. Tellegen, known in film here as Nina Romano, held up curly headed Rex with pardonable pride.

" 'They say women can't keep secrets,' she said with sparkling eyes, while Master Rex smiled, kicked, and gurgled.

" 'But how did you keep from letting girl friends know about having this wonderful baby?' she was asked.

" 'He is our baby. He does not belong to the public. It is bad enough to share your husband with the public, but not one's baby,' she replied.

" 'We were afraid that knowledge of our domestic life would be detrimental to our careers so when we came out here eight months ago we moved into two separate establishments. We did not live together. That's how we managed that secret. It was just yesterday we moved into this new home.'

"The Tellegens were married in Rutherford, N.J., on December 17, 1923. The baby was born in Los Angeles May 12, 1924."—*Chicago Tribune*, February 19, 1925.

result upon the attitudes of the individual is the substitution of a relative code for the absolutism of rural life.[1]

This confusion represents, first, the result of discontent with present family mores, in so far as the accepted patterns are those developed under rural conditions. Life in the country was not without its compensations, no doubt, but it was communal in its direction rather than individualistic. The rapid changes going on in the city break down attachments to the soil and to one's kin, and tend to "atomize" the individual by throwing him completely upon his own resources and rewarding him for developing whatever peculiar inherent abilities he may have. The result is that one is encouraged to develop his own wishes and ideals in art and science, so why should he not also, he asks himself, in family relations? The traditional "rural" family mores, however, gave little encouragement to such development in family relations. The changed conditions of urban life, on the other hand, demand it.

The failure of rural family forms to function in urban life thus leads to experimentation with new forms of family relations. But the presentation of these experiments to others through the press and the motion picture leads to the formation of the experimental attitude on the part of others, without, however, any guidance as to the relative adequacy of any of these experiments.

[1] This does not mean, of course, that such things as literature and art have not in the past produced much the same results. The licentiousness of court life and of the aristocracy in all ages reveals the prevalence of relative standards wherever divergent behavior patterns have been accessible. This conception of life among the leisurely classes, however, has always met with the positive checks imposed by the overwhelming majority to whom all standards were absolute. But the spread of modern material culture practically exposes all classes to this "presentation of divergent behavior patterns" where in the past few other than those in the upper class were thus exposed.

⌐One of the factors making for the permanence of family relations in rural life was the accord, or apparent accord, between father and mother. Children grew up to idealize the relations between their own parents. This experience defined for them the goal of their own marital ventures. Children reared in a discordant family, however, no longer participate in the ideals of the past, but are prone to be skeptical of traditional family patterns. The ideal one has of family life, after all, is extremely important in the success of the family. But it is not a matter of choice of the family as to what form is to be preserved. It is only by adapting family life to modern urban conditions that any form can become satisfactory and survive.⌐

The lack of consensus in ideals of family life is largely due, therefore, to the fact that as yet there has been no satisfactory adjustment of the family to urban life. There have been many experiments, but all haphazard in their approach. No satisfactory technique of social experimentation has been developed. Neither is there any adequate method of studying social experiments. Why some marriages are successful and others not is still an unsolved problem and a matter of opinion.

Programs of reforms, however different they are in many respects, have at least two things in common: First, all assume that problems of the family can be solved by some rational program. If only the right solution can be found then family relations will at once take that ideal form which is in the heart of everyone. One group of reformers looks to the past for this ideal pattern while the other looks to the future, but both hope by some magical formula to reach the golden age in family relations.

The second assumption common to all reform programs

is that statistical facts are all that are needed for the formulation of the ideal program. If one can but get the right statistics then the problem of formulating the right solution to marital discord will be solved. This is the faith which has stimulated the collection of vast amounts of statistical data in the United States, not only upon divorce but also upon desertion. Both the conservative and the radical relies upon the statistical method to resolve the chaos into order.

Statistical materials upon the family and particularly upon family disintegration have, accordingly, been accumulating. Statistics of divorce and marriage are now available, not only for the United States, but for the leading countries of the world. Desertion statistics are also available for different cities in the United States. Do these data contribute any insight into the problem and so suggest a solution? And if not, may they not be manipulated in such a way as to furnish a real solution to the problem of family disorganization? This has been the hope of those who have laboriously compiled these data. Only a careful examination can reveal whether or not this faith arises from blind desire or hopeful insight.

PART II

STATISTICS AND STATISTICAL METHODS

CHAPTER II

THE WORLD-WIDE INCREASE OF DIVORCE

Caution is the rule which should be observed in the interpretation of comparative statistics on family disintegration. Especially is this true if these statistics are of divorce, which are often interpreted as absolute proof that family disorganization is more prevalent in one society than in another. The first form which caution assumes has to do with the relation of family disintegration to the local mores; the second, the difficulties in the collecting and handling of such statistics.

The need for an understanding of the relation of family disintegration to the local mores is apparent, though often unappreciated. Custom and tradition, whether contained in oral precepts or in formal legal statutes, determine, not only whether family disintegration shall exist, but the kind and degree which becomes known to the public. Statistics of family disintegration concern only those forms which become matters of public record. A decree for divorce and petitions for aid in desertion cases become a part of the court documents for the political area in which the plaintiff lives. These publicly documented cases can be counted, and hence become a part of the statistical record of family disintegration. But such statistics take no account of the concealed tensions and subdued quarrels of husband and wife in cases where these do not eventuate in separation, desertion, or divorce.

The number of cases of family tension which reach the public records, furthermore, is dependent in part upon differences in laws controlling legal separation and divorce. In the United States, Nevada with its adaptable divorce laws and South Carolina with its total lack of provision for divorce are at opposite poles in this respect. But even in localities in which one law holds, there are many seeming differences in the amount of family disintegration because of local attitudes toward public and legal forms of separation. It is altogether conceivable that one community may have more disruption of the family as a corporate body than another, but on a statistical table appear lower in the scale, because of aversion to divorce.

The second caution concerns the way in which the statistics themselves are handled and the difficulty in obtaining a comparable base upon which to compute rates, a difficulty caused in part by the propensity people have for moving around. The number of children or of old people living in the community as compared with the number of young married people, the ratio of the sexes to each other, and similar factors materially affect the rates, but are not always taken into account by those who prepare statistics on family disintegration, and must therefore be considered by the reader in interpreting those statistics.

Although there are several forms of family disintegration which may be studied statistically, most of the studies hitherto made have been concerned solely with divorce.

DIVORCE THE CENTER OF PUBLIC INTEREST

Statistical studies of divorce have been both result and cause of an almost exclusive public interest in this one type of family disorganization. The publicity which the filing of a petition for divorce receives both in spoken gossip and in the newspapers throws the searchlight of public attention upon family conflicts. Domestic infelicity, temperamental and sexual incompatibility, even desertion, are normally concealed as a part of the private life of husband and wife. Divorce, as a legal proceeding, cannot be concealed. Added to this unavoidable publicity is the curious or serious interest felt in the affairs of those whose lives do not conform to conventional standards. Except perhaps in the apartment and rooming-house areas of large cities, where undisciplined individual impulses tend to take precedence over social codes of conduct, divorce has not been accepted into the mores of the American people. Hence each case of family disintegration tends to be considered by the public individually in an effort to fix the responsibility and to determine whether or not the divorce was necessary.

Public attention has been further focused upon divorce by the greater availability of information upon it than upon other kinds of family disintegration, in the form of statistical data which could be compared, country by country, or state by state. Periodical publications, both in the United States and foreign countries, have devoted considerable space to the problem of divorce. Several studies, chiefly of the statistical sort, have been made of marriage and divorce in the United States. In addition, a great mass of data upon divorce has accumulated in the statistical reports of governmental bodies. While on the continent these data have been obtained incidentally, along with other social data collected for administrative purposes, in the United States their gathering has been largely the result of popular demand.

The first collection of statistics for the United States was made by the commissioner of labor, Carroll D. Wright, covering the period from January 1, 1867, to December 31, 1886. Prior to this investigation there has been considerable public interest shown in "better divorce legislation." This interest led in 1881 to the organization of the New England Divorce Reform League, which later became known as the National League for the Protection of the Family, and as such was instrumental in securing the legislation authorizing the investigation made in 1887–88.

During the years 1902 to 1905, petitions were sent to Congress asking for a second study of divorce. In the early part of 1905 a conference of representatives of various religious denominations meeting in Washington considered, among other questions, the subject of marriage and divorce. A committee called upon the President urging that statistics upon divorce be brought up to date. In response to this request President Roosevelt sent a special message to Congress upon the subject. On February 9, 1905, Congress authorized the Bureau of the Census to make the second investigation, which, when completed, covered the period from January 1, 1887, to December 31, 1906.[1]

In 1914 the International Committee on Marriage and Divorce requested that a third investigation be undertaken. A year later several petitions followed urging the passage of a joint resolution then pending in Congress providing for the collection of statistics of marriage and divorce from 1907 to 1915. No action was taken, but in 1917 money was appropriated for the collection of such statistics. Because of war conditions it was decided to limit the study to the calendar year 1916, and to make the collection annual thereafter;[2] a plan which was not put into effect, however, until 1922.

Thus it is seen that the collection of divorce statistics in the United States has been largely in response to a popular

[1] *Marriage and Divorce, 1867–1906*, Part I, pp. 3–4.

[2] *Marriage and Divorce, 1916*, pp. 5–6.

demand in the hope that some solution of the divorce problem might be found. It is largely to this popular interest, also, that we owe our comparative statistics of divorce collected by the United States government and published in the report of the Bureau of the Census.[1]

DIVORCE IN THE UNITED STATES AND FOREIGN COUNTRIES

The assertion is often made that the divorce rate is higher in the United States than anywhere else in the world. While not easy to confirm statistically, the assertion seems

TABLE I

COUNTRY	DIVORCES PER 100,000 POPULATION									
	1924	1923	1922	1921	1916	1913	1911	1907	1906	1901
United States	151	149	136	....	112	....	....	....	84	79
Japan	....	88	92	94	109	....	113	....	136	140
France	....	60	71	83	11	....	37	....	27	23
Germany	....	....	58	63	15	....	24	....	20	14
Switzerland	....	....	54	51	40	....	43	....	38	30
Belgium	....	....	49	49	....	16	14	....	9	12
Denmark	....	....	39	42	31	....	27	....	23	15
Netherlands	....	....	28	29	20	....	16	....	13	11
Sweden	....	....	24	21	13	....	11	....	10	7
Australia	....	....	22	26	13	....	12	....	8	10
Norway	....	....	21	23	20	....	17	....	9	6
Uruguay	....	....	....	17	13	....	7	0.1	....	....
Scotland	....	....	....	11	6	....	....	....	4	4

justified from the figures which can be obtained. Table I and Chart I show the divorce trend in the United States and in twelve foreign countries for two decades.

The current interpretation of this difference in divorce rates between the United States and other countries is that here there is disorganization of the family to a higher degree

[1] *Marriage and Divorce, 1867-1906*, Part I.

than elsewhere. Such a generalization, however, indicates a confusion in thinking. Family disorganization is the loss of common aims and of harmonious organization of effort in

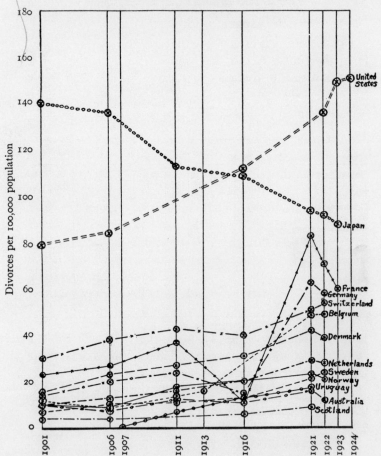

CHART I

THE INTERNATIONAL DIVORCE TREND, 1901–22

the family; divorce is merely legal recognition that the family has disintegrated. Hence, although the generalization may be true that the United States predominates in the degree of family disorganization, these statistics do not show it. All that these or any other figures can show is that there is in the United States a larger number of cases in which legal sanction is given to the discontinuance of marriage relations. Obviously, the mores of these countries concerning the relation of husband and wife and the permanence of the marriage relation are so different as to make of doubtful value any conclusions, based upon divorce rates, concerning the relative stability of family relations.

These data also indicate that except for Japan there has been a decided increase in the divorce rates in all these countries. These increases in rate may indicate an accelerated tendency on the part of families to disintegrate; or it may mean that a previously adverse attitude toward divorce has changed to a receptive attitude and that, given the same number of unadjusted families, more solve their problems by divorce than formerly. Although one explanation is as valid as the other so far as these data are concerned, casual observation would seem to confirm the first interpretation, but not to the exclusion of the second as a contributing factor.

THE UPWARD DIVORCE TREND IN THE UNITED STATES[1]

[1] Besides the three governmental reports upon divorce in the United States, two formal analytical studies have been made by Willcox (*The Divorce Problem: A Study in Statistics*) and Lichtenberger (*Divorce: A Study in Social Causation*), based, respectively, upon the first two governmental reports, which are mere compilations of statistics rather than analyses of the divorce problem.

The factors associated with divorce have been substantially the same in the studies of both Willcox and Lichtenberger, so far as their statistical

Divorce as a form of family disintegration is common to the whole of the United States except for South Carolina, where the law does not provide for it. This absence of a divorce law does not mean that family disintegration does not exist in South Carolina, but that it must take some other form then divorce.

For the rest of the United States, divorce seems to be

---

materials go. There is considerable divergence, however, in their interpretations. Statistically, Willcox shows the following: comparison of divorce rates in the United States with those in other countries; increase of divorce with reference to courts granting same; increase with reference to the population; increase with reference to married couples; increase with reference to possible outcome; increase among the Negroes; increase in the several states; duration of marriage before divorce; remarriage after divorce; distribution of divorce between Catholics and non-Catholics; distribution between Negroes and whites; distribution between city and country; distribution between couples with children and without; distribution as granted to husband or wife; distribution among the several states; comparison of number of causes with divorce rate; comparison of changes in law or court procedure with divorce rate; relation of marriage law to divorce.

The causal factors found by Willcox are the two conceptions of marriage law, religious and secular; the popularization of law; laxity in changing and administering the law; age at marriage; the emancipation of woman; growth of cities; increase of industrialism; the spread of discontent; two ideals of the family, the Roman and the Teutonic.

Lichtenberger shows, statistically, the following: increase with reference to population; relation of divorce to marriage; increase with reference to geographical division; variation among states; city and country rates; rates in white and colored populations; variations in regard to libellant; variations in regard to causes; conditions as to children; conditions as to occupation; relation of changes in the divorce and marriage laws to divorce rates.

The causal factors given by Lichtenberger are the stress of modern economic life; modern standards of living; pressure of modern economic life upon the home; passing of the economic function of the family; economic emancipation of women; individualism; popularization of law; increase in popular learning; improved social status of women; equal standard of morals; higher ideals of domestic happiness; a new basis of marriage, mutual attraction and preference.

CHART II

Divorces per 100,000 Population in the United States, 1870–1924

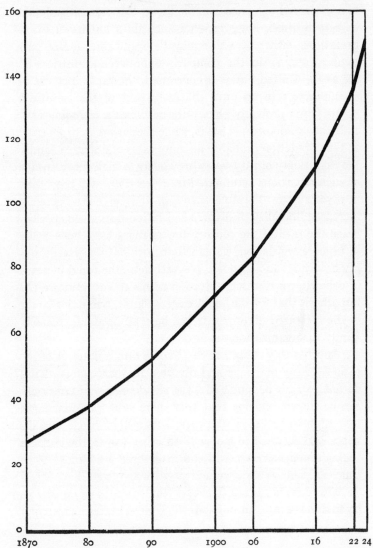

steadily increasing. In 1870, there was an average of 28 divorces granted for each 100,000 persons; in 1924, this ratio had increased to 151. Chart II shows this trend. It should be remembered, however, that such data have two interpretations, either of which may be applicable to this particular case, as in the comparison between countries. So far as the United States is concerned, the rapid increase in the divorce rate up until the early part of the twentieth century was probably chiefly the result of a changing attitude toward divorce. That is, while there were in proportion to the population probably no more cases of unhappy family life than thirty or fifty years previously, a higher percentage of such situations terminated in divorce in, say, 1900 than in 1870 or 1850. This tolerance toward divorce is reflected in increased liberality of divorce legislation during this period. Since the turn of the century few changes have been made in divorce legislation, though that does not necessarily imply no change in attitudes. Nevertheless, the rapid increase in other forms of disorganization seems to substantiate the hypothesis that for the last decade, at least, the major factor in the increased divorce rate has been an actual increase in family disorganization.

Another way of stating the divorce rate is in terms of the ratio between marriage and divorce. As marriage statistics do not go back beyond 1887, the trend since that time only can be shown. During that year there were 17.3 marriages to 1 divorce. In 1924, the ratio between marriage and divorce had declined to 6.9 to 1. In other words, the chances that a given marriage will end in divorce are almost three times as great as they were fifty years ago (see Chart III).

This does not mean, however, that there is any uniformity in divorce rates throughout the United States. The oppo-

CHART III

NUMBER OF MARRIAGES TO ONE DIVORCE IN THE
UNITED STATES, 1887–1924

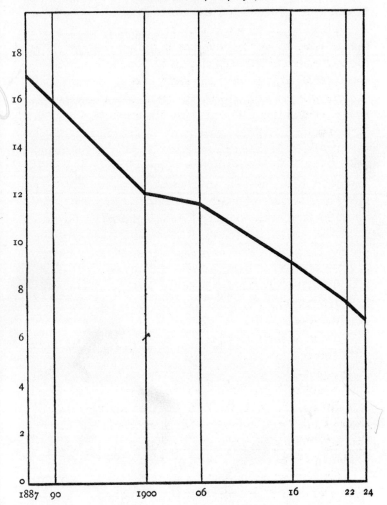

site is true. There is within the United States a wider range
in divorce rates than between the countries of the world.
At the foot of the scale stands the District of Columbia with
a rate of 25 per 100,000, while Nevada is far in the lead with
a rate of 1,296 per 100,000 persons.[1] Table II shows the divorce rates for the five states having the highest and the
five having the lowest rates in 1924.

The comparison of ratios between divorce and population, however, is not without its fallacies. Even with a rela-

TABLE II

States Having Highest Rates	Divorces per 100,000 Population	States Having Lowest Rates	Divorces per 100,000 Population
Nevada...............	1,296	District of Columbia...	25
Oregon...............	368	New York............	42
Texas................	307	North Carolina........	54
Wyoming.............	295	North Dakota........	54
Oklahoma............	292	New Jersey..........	59

tively low ratio one state might actually present a more
serious divorce situation than another state where the ratio
was higher. In a state where a relatively larger number of
persons in the population were either below the marriageable age or were single the number of divorces per 100,000
persons would be small in comparison to a state in which
there were fewer persons in the age groups below marriageable age and where few of marriageable age were single. But
in the latter case, the divorce situation would not be nearly
so serious if it did not involve so large a group of the married
population. It is to correct this error that the ratio between
marriage and divorce has been used as a measure of the divorce rate.

[1] These figures leave out of account South Carolina, where no divorces
are granted.

Comparison of states upon the basis of the ratio between marriage and divorce does not, as anticipated, produce the same results as found in the ratio between divorce and population. Table III shows the five highest and the five lowest divorce rates for states according to this ratio.

It is obvious that if the divorce rate in Nevada—if it were a true picture of the situation—were to continue for long, there would soon be no married persons in the state, the loss each year by divorce and death being greater than

TABLE III

States Having Highest Rates	Number of Marriages to One Divorce	States Having Lowest Rates	Number of Marriages to One Divorce
Nevada................	1.0	District of Columbia...	42.7
Nebraska..............	2.2	New York............	23.0
Oregon................	2.4	Georgia..............	17.1
Wyoming..............	3.7	North Carolina........	16.0
Oklahoma.............	4.2	Maryland............	15.2
Ohio.................	4.2		

the gain in marriages. But the ratio of marriage to divorce does not give one a reliable measure in this case. The majority of those who marry in Nevada may never obtain divorces. Most of the divorces are granted to persons who come in from states where legal restrictions are more severe. There is little relationship between marriages and divorces in Nevada, for the larger part of these divorces should be added to the rates in those states from which the persons came. The ratio between marriage and divorce may thus become a fallacious measure of the divorce rate.

Another method of measuring the divorce rate is the use of the ratio of divorce to the marriageable population. This is probably more adequate than where the entire population is used but not so useful as the ratio between marriage

and divorce, for the proportion of the marriageable population who are actually married may be quite different in two
states. If such were the case, the state having apparently
the lowest divorce rate might, upon comparison with the
married population, have the highest.

The difficulty in finding a suitable unit of measure is
only one difficulty arising in the comparison of states. Not
only is there a tacit assumption of relative permanence of
population in the use of the units of measurement, but there
is also the assumption that the same thing is measured in
each case. The situation is somewhat comparable to that
between countries. Divorce is one thing in Nevada, where
residence can be established in six months and divorce obtained upon several grounds, but quite another in New York
where adultery is practically the only cause.[1] The difference in the legal situations between states and the mores
which support the legislation is often so great as to invali-
date any comparisons. If comparisons are to be made, it
would seem, they had better be confined to comparable situ-
tions, such as areas within a state, or at least to states where
the legal situations have been found to be substantially the
same.

URBAN AND RURAL AREAS

It has been shown that biological factors, such as the
predominance of certain age and sex groups, and social
factors, such as attitudes and mores, have much to do with
divorce rates, and that a high divorce rate is not necessarily
indicative of a high degree of family disorganization. Urban
and rural areas offer another opportunity to study the effect
of these same factors in influencing the divorce rate.

It has been said that the increase of divorce has been

[1] Cf. Bureau of the Census, *Marriage and Divorce, 1916*, pp. 13–14.

more rapid in urban areas than in rural communities. Data upon this point were presented in the report of the Bureau of the Census for the period 1870–1900.[1] The method in general consisted in selecting for a given state the county or counties containing large cities in 1900, providing the city embraced considerably more than one-half of the population of the county. Conditions in such counties were then compared with the conditions existing in the remainder of the state with the results shown in Table IV.

TABLE IV

AREA	AVERAGE ANNUAL NO. OF DIVORCES PER 100,000 POPULATION							
	1900		1890		1880		1870	
	City Counties	Other Counties	City Counties	Other Counties	City Counties	Other Counties	City Counties	Other Counties
Total.........	72	68	53	51	44	38	34	31

These data seem to indicate a higher divorce rate for the city counties than for the "other" counties. The rate of increase since 1870, however, seems to have been substantially the same. But such data can hardly be said either to gainsay or to substantiate the current impression. The city counties, though predominately urban, are not necessarily so. Neither are the other counties exclusively rural, though undoubtedly they tend to be more rural than the city counties.

For the purpose of testing out the current impression, statistics of marriage and divorce were compiled for the counties in which were located the ten largest cities in 1920 as representative of urban areas, and for ten of the most

[1] *Marriage and Divorce, 1867–1906*, p. 17.

rural counties in each of the states in which the cities are located. The ten most rural counties selected were those in which were located minor divisions (townships, villages, etc.) the largest of which were smaller than the largest in any of the excluded counties. In Massachusetts, however, it was possible to find only four minor divisions, "towns," which could be thought of as rural (see Appendix A for tables). The results of this tabulation are somewhat inconclusive. For the period 1887-1916 the divorce rates for both urban and rural areas remained substantially the same, both showing, however, a decided increase. Since 1916 the urban rate has made a pronounced gain over the rate for the rural areas. Chart IV shows both trends calculated in terms of the number of divorces per hundred marriages.

The problem immediately arises: Is the statistical distinction based upon aggregates of population a significant one? No one would argue, of course, that a city of 2,400 is necessarily more rural than one of 2,500 population, though statistically it is customary to include one in the rural class and the other in the urban group. But no such fine distinction has been made in the data presented in Chart IV. Instead, so far as aggregates of population are concerned, only extremes have been compared. If the distinction is a real one, such data as have been presented in Chart IV should indicate the trend with reference to both urban and rural areas. Furthermore, if the current impression is true, then this comparison should substantiate it, unless the statistical distinction is not the same as the sociological. These data do not, on the whole, substantiate the conclusion that divorce is increasing more rapidly in urban than in rural areas, differentiating these terms statistically. What, then, does the sociologist mean by "rural" and "urban"?

When the sociologist uses the term "rural" as contrasted with "urban," he is attempting to define social life, not in

CHART IV

NUMBER OF DIVORCES PER 100 MARRIAGES FOR RURAL AND
URBAN AREAS IN THE UNITED STATES, 1887–1924

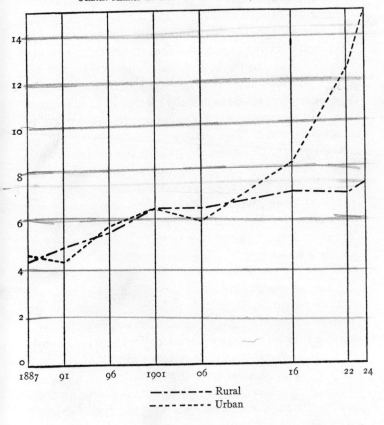

terms of mere aggregates of population, but in terms of characteristic types of social relations. He may use the terms loosely, it is true, but by "rural" he is likely to mean the emotionalized and uncritical attitudes which Cooley has called the "primary-group attitudes," since they are characteristic of the first groups (family, play group, and neighborhood) into which the individual enters and in which his personality is developed. In these groups the person comes to embody in himself all the aims and purposes of the group, and hence cannot conceive of himself as independent of it. He is controlled by the current mores through such personal means as scorn, praise, and ridicule, and to disregard the group attitudes is not only to be ostracized by the group but to become disorganized personally. Hence if, as in many of the rural communities, the life of the person is circumscribed by contacts within the primary groups, the person will live according to the dictates of the group, even though at times he has contrary impulses. Under this method of control and with relatively unchanging social conditions, ideals of the past tend to be preserved, among them the ideal of life-long monogamy historically developed in this country. In the urban areas, however, contacts and attitudes may be described as secondary. The circle of intimates to whom one's conduct matters is very limited, and in addition divergences of conduct are easily concealed. Nor is there the unanimity of attitudes found in the rural community; one group believes this, another that. It becomes a relatively simple matter for the person to rationalize his impulses without reference to any particular group and to lead an organized life independent of strict group control. It is this detachment and individualization, together with the new content of attitudes, which differentiates the typically urban community from the rural community.

The fallacy in the statistical method lies in taking as a basis of distinction the aggregate population of a prescribed area, and assuming that such a measure is an adequate criterion of whether or not the area is characterized by one type of attitudes or the other. It is well known that many areas of our large cities, such as "Little Italy" and the "Ghetto," are more "rural minded" than rural hamlets in the open country. Indeed, only a few regions of the city, such as rooming- and apartment-house districts, are distinctly "urban" in social relationships. In this sense, then, the statistical definition is of no value in comparing the divorce trends for these two types of areas, and it leads only to fallacious conclusions.

This treatment of data also assumes that the population elements are the same for both types of areas—an assumption which may be entirely unjustified under certain conditions. Let us go back to the material presented for the period 1887–1924. Here it was found that the divorce rate was substantially the same for both rural and urban areas until 1916, though both showed considerable increase in rate. It is generally known that in most of the cities chosen, there was during this period a considerable influx of immigrants whose cultural and religious background was different from that of the native population. This introduction into city life of large numbers of persons, who, for religious and traditional reasons, are opposed to divorce would tend to keep down the divorce rate for the urban areas. In 1920, 28.4 per cent of the population in the selected urban areas was foreign born as compared to 6.5 per cent for the selected rural areas. Unless these religious and cultural differences were offset by other factors, it might be expected that the difference between the divorce rates in urban and rural areas would be less than a comparison between urban and rural conditions might lead one to anticipate.

Also where there is a drift, as there has been, from the country to the city, the rural *emigrés* are those in the early years of maturity. This, combined with a lower birth-rate tends to produce in the city a larger number of persons in the adult-age groups. Comparison of rural areas with urban areas under these circumstances readily leads to error if the measure of divorce is the ratio to population. This can be corrected to some degree if the ratio of divorce to marriage is taken as the measure. Even here, however, because of the tendency for persons to marry in rural areas and then emigrate to the city, the ratio may be misleading. This may be illustrated in the case of the apparent increase of divorce in urban areas since 1916, though little change is shown for rural areas.

It is difficult, of course, to show statistically that the low divorce rate in rural areas is partly attributable to the emigration of newly married couples to the city, except in so far as it may be inferred from the decrease in population of those areas. The population of the rural areas studied reached its height in 1900, at which time there were 1,312,-725 persons in the selected counties. The average decrease per year for the next decade was 4,060; while for the decade 1910–20 it had reached 7,488. The probabilities are that this rate has continued until 1924, the last year for which divorce statistics are available.

NEGLECT OF MULTIPLE FACTORS

This analysis of the methods used in comparing divorce rates for different areas shows some of the difficulties in making statistical comparisons, and also throws light on factors affecting divorce rates. One is confronted first with the variance in the unit measured. Divorce gets its meaning from the mores of the people concerned, as expressed both in law and in popular sentiment. Allowing for or disregarding the differences in social definitions of the phenomenon, the next problem is that of measuring the rate adequately. The ratio of divorce to population puts a premium upon those areas in which there are large numbers of persons either below marriageable age or still single. The ratio of divorce to marriage, while superior in many respects to the ratio of divorce to population because it corrects the difficulty just pointed out, fails to take into consideration the fact that one group in the population may contribute many marriages and few divorces. Neither does it serve so well in an area where the population is decreasing as in one where it is relatively stationary. Where population is decreasing, the divorce rate tends to be lowered by the predominance of persons who have been married long enough to decrease the probability of divorce. In areas where population is increasing, however, the predominance is in favor of the newly married couples. A more adequate ratio would be that between divorce and the total married population. But even this measure would be adequate only where the persons divorced actually were a part of the married population of the area, and where in the comparison of areas the distribution of married couples for each year-period of married life was approximately the same.

This leads to the general conclusion that comparisons between countries, between states, between rural and urban areas, and even between cities are not fair. Not only are they not fair, but they are without point, because they assume a homogeneity in the legal situation and in the population which does not exist. What seems to be desirable, then, are monographic studies of communities where, at any rate, the legal situation is constant, and where, perhaps, differences in the population by nationality, religion, occupation, and social class may be taken into account.

CHAPTER III

DIVORCE IN AN URBAN COMMUNITY: CHICAGO

The distinction between divorce (the legal dissolution of marriage) and family disorganization (the process by which the family group becomes disintegrated) has already been suggested. Divorce is but the legal recognition of the group that the family no longer has any existence in the attitudes of husband and wife—that the interests and aims of each have become completely differentiated. Studies which attempt to give causes or factors of family disorganization from an investigation of legal causes upon which divorces have been granted tell little. They ignore the human-nature aspect of the problem, and regard divorce as the breach of a legal contract. It is necessary to go beyond the formality of the legal process of obtaining a divorce to discover what may be called the "natural" causes of family disintegration and factors which effect them.

Statistics may seem a very formal method to use in discovering the factors affecting human relationships, yet through the proper manipulation of divorce records significant light may be thrown on the real causes of divorce. For such a statistical study it is advisable to select one community for intensive investigation. The chief advantage of this limitation is that the grounds upon which divorce may be obtained are uniform, not only for the community, but for the state in which it is located. This makes possible statistical comparisons of the local divorce rate with that of the larger political area of which it is a part. Also, a study of one community makes possible a more versatile massing and presentation of extant data available for statistical manipulation.

The urban community of Chicago was chosen for an investigation of divorce which is at once an exposition of the variance between legal and natural causes and of the limitations of a statistical study in penetrating behind the externals of a given case. The writer has made two separate inquiries into the court records of Cook County, the first covering 1,000 cases of divorce in the Circuit Court and the second including all the cases of divorce (6,094) for the year 1919 in both the Circuit and Superior courts. It is to be noted that these are records for Cook County, which includes—besides the city of Chicago, with a population in 1920 of 2,701,705—cities and villages with a population of 280,963 and unincorporated places with a population of 70,349. The metropolitan area of Chicago, however, takes in all of Cook County, as well as territory beyond its frontiers. Accordingly, statistics for Cook County may be taken as fairly representative of a heterogeneous urban area.

CHICAGO, THE DIVORCE CENTER OF ILLINOIS

Local newspapers have played up the fact that there are more divorces granted in Cook County than in any other county in the United States. The inference is that the divorce rate is higher in this locality than elsewhere in the Union. This conclusion illustrates the fallacy into which one is often led when the measure of a phenomenon is in absolute rather than in relative terms. While it is true that the total number of divorces is greater in Cook County than in any other county, so also is the population. If the ratio of divorce to population is taken as the measure of the divorce rate, then the rate for Cook County per 100,000 population is found to be 245 for 1924. This rate is exceeded by eight whole states, the highest of which is Nevada, where the rate is 1,296 per 100,000 persons. If the measure taken is that of the ratio of divorce to marriage, the rate in Cook County (1 to 4.9) is exceeded by eleven states, Nevada leading again with a ratio of 1 to 1.0.[1]

There are, as has been shown, certain fallacies which creep into statistical work as the result of the impression made upon the mind by sheer magnitude. The elimination of these errors is dependent upon the use of some ratio; in this particular case, the ratio of divorce either to marriage or to population. But even with this precaution it has been shown that, in the comparison of geographical areas divergence in the mores as reflected in divorce legislation may vitiate any conclusion regarding the relative stability of the family in the areas compared. This difficulty can be eliminated to the highest degree where comparisons are between areas within the same states, i.e., areas wherein divorce is granted upon the same basis. In this way the legislative factor may be held constant where otherwise it varies. This does not, of course, imply a constant administrative factor, since the policy of courts may vary according to local public opinion or the personal equation of the judge.

While divorce in Chicago cannot be compared with fair-

[1] The other states in which the divorce rates exceed those of Cook County are, ratio of divorce to 100,000 population: Oregon, 368; Texas, 307; Wyoming, 295; Oklahoma, 292; California, 288; Missouri, 260; Arkansas, 251; ratio of divorce to marriage: Nebraska, 1:2.2; Oregon, 1:2.4; Wyoming, 1:3.7; Ohio, 1:4.2; Oklahoma, 1:4.2; Missouri, 1:4.4; Washington, 1:4.5; Arizona, 1:4.7; Montana, 1:4.7; Texas, 1:4.7.

ness with divorce in other states than its own, a legitimate comparison can be made with Illinois, or any of its parts, in which the legal status of divorce cases is the same. In 1887 the ratio in Illinois of divorce to marriage was 1 to 13.3. By 1924 this ratio had declined to 1 to 6.0. In view of the fact that there have been in that period no substantial changes in the divorce law, this increase in rate indicates a growth, apparently, in the occurrence of a type of behavior —the legal dissolution of marriage. The ratios for Cook County and for the rest of Illinois in 1887 were substantially the same, viz., 1 to 13.1 and 1 to 13.4, respectively. By 1924, however, the divorce rate for Chicago had gained over that for the rest of the state, the ratios being 1 to 4.9 and 1 to 8.6.[1] That this is a measure of the difference in urban and rural attitudes between the several parts of Illinois may be somewhat offset by the tendency for persons married down state to become divorced in Chicago while many Chicago couples go into adjoining counties, or at any rate to those outside the state, to be married. Yet there is no direct evidence that this tendency has increased in the period from 1887 to 1924.

Comparison of the divorce rate in Chicago with that in the ten most rural counties in Illinois shows a greater divergence in the two trends. For Chicago the rate has almost tripled since 1887, while for the ten selected rural counties it has scarcely doubled. Chart VI shows the trends for these

[1] Chart V shows the divorce rates for Illinois, Cook Co., and the remainder of the state in terms of the number of divorces per 100 marriages, rather than in terms of the ratio of marriages to one divorce, which is used in the text. This change shows the trend as an ascending curve, which is more associated with increase in the average mind. This form of presentation will be used in all charts showing the divorce rate, though the ratio of marriages to divorce will be retained in the text, it being the more familiar.

CHART V

NUMBER OF DIVORCES PER 100 MARRIAGES IN ILLINOIS, 1887-1924

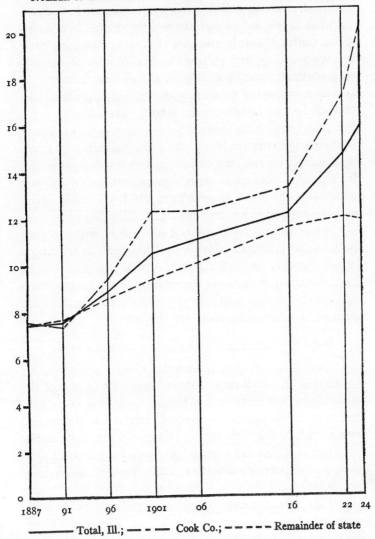

——— Total, Ill.; — — — Cook Co.; - - - - Remainder of state

two areas. In spite of the limitations of the unit of measurement, this undoubtedly indicates a difference in attitude toward divorce, as well as a more rapid change in Chicago. To what degree is this indicative of the decline in primary-group control? This is probably the chief sociological problem suggested by the difference in divorce rate. Its solution by statistics cannot be attempted at this time, however, for lack of a method of measuring the decline of primary contacts to be correlated with the divorce rate.

Chicago, with its thousands of divorce cases each year, offers excellent material for probing the possibilities of statistical studies for reaching significant aspects of divorce. One limitation to this type of study is predetermined by the data entered on the court records, from which the crude figures must be compiled. For instance, occupation and nationality of the husband and wife are not entered. Of great interest is the inquiry into the relation of legal grounds to natural causes for divorce. Other factors whose study is possible from the court records are the relation of the presence, sex and number of children to divorce, and the relation between number of years of marriage and divorce.

VARIANCE BETWEEN LEGAL AND NATURAL CAUSES

The family has already been described as a cultural organization, in which disintegration appears as a loss of the consciousness of unity and of the appearance of conflicting interests which cannot be merged. Divorce is the formal recognition by the state that family consciousness has broken down and that the husband and wife have lost the attitude of intimate identification and consensus which they presumably had when the state gave sanction, through marriage, to their entrance into the family relationship. As justi-

CHART VI

NUMBER OF DIVORCES TO 100 MARRIAGES IN COOK COUNTY AND
TEN MOST RURAL COUNTIES, ILLINOIS, 1887–1924

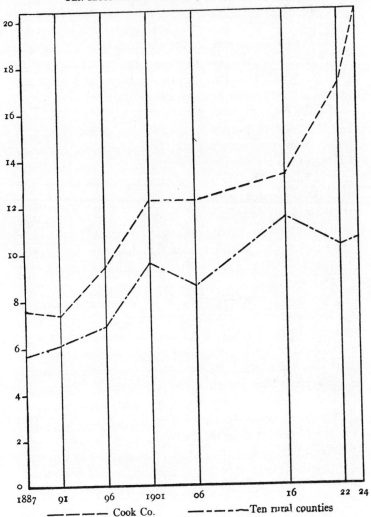

—————— Cook Co.   — — — —Ten rural counties

fication for this dissolution of the family, each state has provided certain causes, such as infidelity, desertion, cruelty, and in terms of these defections all divorce cases are legally stated. But an investigation of the divorce records clearly indicates that these so-called causes prescribed by law are not in reality the causes for the cleavage between husband and wife which results in divorce. Legal causes appear as the *externalia* which for reasons of appropriateness or expediency were chosen to cloak the ruptured relationship.

Of the 6,094 divorces granted in Cook County in 1919, 73 per cent were granted to the wife (cf. Chart VII). This preponderance of women plaintiffs is 4 per cent higher in Chicago than for the United States in 1916, but the difference is slight. The excess of divorces granted to the wife over those granted to the husband is probably not highly attributable to the chivalry of the male, as is sometimes suggested, but rather to the facility with which a man may break home ties. Neither does this difference necessarily indicate that the wife is less often responsible for the discord in the family.

The most frequent legal cause for divorce in Chicago in 1919 was desertion, for which 50 per cent of all decrees were granted. In the United States in 1916 the rate was not so high (36.8 per cent), though this is probably due to nothing more than the absence of desertion as a cause for divorce in a few states. The next three leading causes in Chicago, in the order of their importance, were cruelty, 27.5 per cent; adultery, 12.7 per cent; drunkenness, 6.1 per cent (see Table V). It will be seen from this table that there is considerable difference in the proportion of divorces granted to husband and to wife for each of the four major causes. The difference in each case is significant and could not have occurred as

CHART VII

PROPORTION OF TOTAL NUMBER DECREES GRANTED TO EACH PARTY BY
FIVE-YEAR PERIODS OF MARRIED LIFE, CHICAGO, 1919

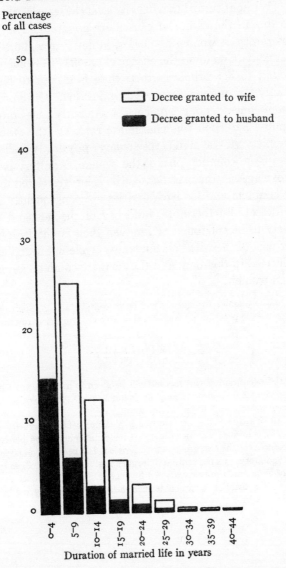

Duration of married life in years

an error of sampling.[1] The husband most frequently charged desertion and adultery against his wife, while the wife found cruelty and drunkenness the most serviceable charges.

Without regard to what the legal causes indicate, certain factors in the choice of causes are apparent. The physical inferiority of women precludes, in most cases, possibility of her conviction upon the charge of cruelty. A woman is more bound to her primary group than is a man to his, hence adultery is more easily proved against her. The mores forbid drunkenness among women, consequently cases prosecuted against her upon this charge are rare. On the other hand, the fact that the man is the stronger physically makes cruelty a more common plea of the woman. Adultery is hard to prove against the man because he is less restricted to primary contacts and his irregularities are consequently difficult to detect. Furthermore, infidelity of the husband is more likely to be condoned or forgiven than is unfaithfulness on the part of the wife. Drunkenness, while not in the mores, is tolerated in the man, and thus is more common among men than women.

[1] The practice throughout will be to consider as significant only those differences in percentage which equal or exceed 2.576 standard errors, where

$$\epsilon = \sqrt{pq\left(\frac{1}{n_1} + \frac{1}{n_2}\right)}$$

A brief exposition of this method will be given in a footnote on p. 75. A more complete exposition may be found in Yule, *An Introduction to the Theory of Statistics*, chaps. xiii and xiv.

In this case 2.58ϵ for desertion is 3.72 per cent; for cruelty, 3.36 per cent; for adultery, 2.48 per cent; and for drunkenness, 1.76 per cent. The differences for the two groups are: desertion, 22.2 per cent; cruelty, 28.9 per cent; adultery, 15.4 per cent; and drunkenness, 6.2 per cent. Even the smallest of these could not be exceeded by chance oftener than once in a billion trials. It is therefore improbable that these differences occurred by chance.

This difference in proportionate weight given the several legal causes by the husband and the wife is often interpreted as indicating differences in the situations culminating in

TABLE V

DIVORCES CLASSIFIED BY CAUSES AND BY PARTY TO WHOM GRANTED, CHICAGO, 1919

CAUSES	ALL CASES		PARTY TO WHOM DECREE WAS GRANTED				
			Husband		Wife		Not Report-ing
	Number	Percent-age	Number	Percent-age	Number	Percent-age	Number
Total............	6,094	100.0	1,615	100.0	4,467	100.0	12
Desertion............	3,044	50.0	1,073	66.3	1,967	44.1	4
Cruelty..............	1,672	27.5	101	6.3	1,570	35.2	1
Adultery.............	783	12.7	391	24.2	392	8.8	......
Drunkenness.........	371	6.1	24	1.5	346	7.7	1
Conviction of felony...	54	0.9	......	......	54	1.2	......
Cruelty and drunkenness............	57	0.9	2	0.1	55	1.2	......
Desertion and cruelty..	24	0.4	3	0.2	21	0.5	......
Cruelty and adultery..	13	0.2	2	0.1	11	0.2	......
Desertion and drunkenness..............	11	0.2	......	......	11	0.2	......
Impotency...........	17	0.3	3	0.2	14	0.3	......
Bigamy..............	12	0.2	3	0.2	9	0.2	......
Adultery and drunkenness..............	5	0.1	1	0.1	4	0.1	......
Desertion and adultery.	17	0.3	9	0.6	8	0.2	......
Attempt to take life....	5	0.1	2	0.1	3	0.1	......
Desertion and bigamy.	1	*	......	......	1	*	......
Cruelty and attempt to take life............	2	*	1	0.1	1	*	......
Not reporting cause...	6	0.1	......	......	......	......	6

* Less than 0.1 per cent.

break-up of family life according to whether husband or wife is cited as the offender. That there is no constant relationship between the legal causes for divorce and the factors in the situation bringing about family discord may be demonstrated by the results obtained from a study of 1,000 certificates of evidence in cases tried in the Circuit Court of Cook County, Illinois. Two hundred were cases in which suit was brought in 1920, while the remaining 800 were filed in 1917. All records were taken from the files in chronological order, no selection of any sort being made. Divorces were granted for the legal causes shown in Table VI.

TABLE VI

LEGAL CAUSES FOR WHICH DIVORCE WAS GRANTED	DIVORCES	
	Number	Percentage of Distribution
All causes...........................	1,000	100.0
Desertion..............................	497	49.7
Cruelty................................	265	26.5
Adultery..............................	96	9.6
Drunkenness..........................	87	8.7
Bigamy...............................	30	3.0
Conviction of felony..................	13	1.3
Infancy...............................	8	0.8
Insanity or intoxication...............	2	0.2
Impotency............................	1	0.1
First cousins..........................	1	0.1

Suits brought on the charges of desertion, cruelty, and adultery, constituting as they do about 86 per cent of the total, present the most complete data upon the variance between legal and "natural" causes. However, in 311 of these it was impossible, from the records, to find out anything more about the situations than the legal causes indicate. This leaves 542 cases for an analysis of what appears to be the natural causes so far as could be ascertained from the court records. The percental distribution of these cases follows: (1) desertion, 54; (2) cruelty, 29; (3) adultery, 17.

DESERTION THE CLIMAX OF FAMILY TENSIONS

The certificates of evidence in 295 cases in which divorce was granted for desertion reveal nine types of situations. These types of situations will be referred to hereafter as the "natural" causes of family disintegration. The distribution is shown in Table VII.

Forty per cent of the 295 divorces granted for desertion culminated out of the financial or economic tension in family

TABLE VII

Apparent Natural Causes	Number	Percentage
Total..................................	295	100.0
Financial tension.........................	119	40.2
Desertion for another.....................	39	13.2
Dissatisfaction with home or married life.....	32	10.9
Infidelity................................	31	10.5
Drink and cruelty........................	29	9.9
Refusal to leave old home..................	23	7.8
Irregular habits..........................	13	4.4
Irregular work, and drink..................	7	2.4
Forced marriage..........................	2	0.7

relations, that is, breakdown in the family relationship between husband and wife arose out of refusal of the husband to support his wife, refusal of the wife to support herself or to give her husband money, indebtedness or business failure, or any other situations in which the tension centered about questions of finance, which did not lead, however, to acts of cruelty, but to desertion.

Wherever it was clear in the evidence that one party left the other to live with a third party, whether the charge of adultery may or may not have been included in the bill along with desertion, but in which there was no evidence brought to prove illicit relations, the cases have been included under "desertion for another." There were thirty-nine of these instances.

"Dissatisfaction with home or married. life" includes those cases where the dissatisfaction arose over the community in which the home was located, over the presence of kin in the home, or because the husband was not able to furnish the sort of home the wife was accustomed to. Here were included, also, those cases where one party became tired of married life for reasons not revealed by the evidence, and those cases where the desire to follow a vocation separated the couple, as not infrequently the desire on the part of the wife to become an actress or chorus girl. These cases numbered thirty-two.

Cases of desertion in which the tension between husband and wife centered about the suspicion by one party, whether founded upon fact or not, that the other was untrue to the marriage contract, but where there was no proof of immoral conduct, have been classed as "infidelity." All cases of jealousy, as long as there was no abusive treatment resulting therefrom, have been included under this characterization, bringing the number to thirty-one.

Under the class, "drink and cruelty," are those cases, twenty-nine in number, in which the couple quarreled about drinking intoxicating liquors. In some instances this disagreement over drink resulted in cruelty prior to desertion.

Certain cases are noted where the husband went to some distant place and his wife refused to accompany him; or where he came to the United States without his wife, sending for her later, and she refused to join him; or where, after leaving her old-home community with her husband, the wife became dissatisfied with the new home in a short time and returned to the old. Twenty-three are of such a nature, and may be characterized as "refusal to leave old home."

Desertion resulting from "irregular habits" are those cases in which the tension centered around staying out late at night, gambling, and carousing. Late hours, in some instances, probably led to suspicion that the offender was untrue; in other cases, simply to lonesomeness. Gambling and carousing mean, not only neglect of the wife, but often financial loss as well. There were thirteen of these cases.

"Irregular work, and drink" indicates those cases where desertion was the result of discouragement from unemployment, irregular employment, or tension created by the refusal of the defendant to work regularly and refrain from drinking. There were seven of these instances.

The last class under desertion is "forced marriage," and includes only two cases where the husband married the wife through fear of proceedings under the "bastardy" law, and after marriage deserted her.

CRUELTY THE RESULT OF DISCORD

The 156 cases of cruelty fall into six types of situations, the distribution being as shown in Table VIII.

TABLE VIII

Apparent Natural Causes	Number	Percentage
Total	156	100.0
Financial tension	68	45.0
Drink	43	28.6
Jealousy, infidelity, etc	22	14.6
Excessive and unnatural sexual intercourse	12	7.9
Irregular habits	6	3.9

Cruelty resulting from the "financial tension," sixty-eight cases, epitomizes those in which tension centered about the financial situation in the family as described under "desertion," except that cruel acts were the direct result rather than desertion.

From the evidence, it appears that in forty-three of the cruelty cases the inhuman acts were committed while the offender was in an intoxicated condition. The term "drink" is used to characterize this situation.

Under "jealousy, infidelity, etc.," have been included twenty-two cases where cruelty was the result of tension centered about jealousy, and infidelity as defined under "desertion." Whether or not adultery might have been made the ground for divorce in these cases one cannot be sure, but the presumption is that it might have been.

"Irregular habits" covers six cases in which the tension centered around irregular habits as described under "desertion," i.e., quarrels about one person staying out late at night, gambling, and carousing. These irregular habits probably were indicative of infidelity in some instances.

"ADULTERY," AN UNDIFFERENTIATED TERM

Three types of situations are revealed in the ninety-six cases of adultery as shown in Table IX.

TABLE IX

Apparent Natural Causes	Number	Percentage
Total..................................	96	100.0
Illicit intercourse.........................	55	57.3
Living with another as spouse...............	33	34.4
Venereal infection.........................	8	8.3

More than half of the adultery cases fall under the natural cause, "illicit intercourse." In these fifty-five cases the irregularity in the sex life of the individuals occurred while the couple were, for all intents and purposes, still living together, though one party may have been absent from home at the time. There had been infidelity, but not abandonment of the marital relation.

The eight cases classed as caused by "venereal infection" represent practically the same situation as described for "illicit intercourse." The detection of infection by the other made the innocent party think that his spouse had been untrue, though he may have contracted the disease before marriage. In both situations, however, the attitude of the innocent person would be little different.

In the thirty-three cases epitomized "living with another as spouse," while from the legal point of view the act is just as serious as for the type "illicit intercourse," from the point of view of personal behavior there is an important difference. There has been abandonment of the marriage relation and entrance into a second family relationship without, however, the sanction of the law.

LEGAL CAUSES ARE BLANKET TERMS

That legal causes of divorce, in so far as the three major causes are concerned, are blanket terms, has been demonstrated, but a classification which simplifies a mass of concrete material is not objectionable in itself. However, not only are "desertion," "cruelty," and "adultery" blanket terms, but they overlap, that is, the same type of situation may in certain instances lead to suit for divorce upon the ground of either desertion, cruelty, or adultery.

Four hundred and sixty-six of the 542 cases just analyzed may be classified into types which overlap two or more legal causes, as shown by Table X.

In 40 per cent of these 466 cases the tension centered

about questions of finance, which were distributed between the two legal causes "desertion" and "cruelty." In 15 per cent there had been "desertion for another" or "living with another as spouse"—substantially the same situation in each instance—these represented by the legal causes "desertion" and "adultery."

While the evidence in the cases classed as "infidelity" is quite different, from the legal point of view, from the

TABLE X

APPARENT NATURAL CAUSES	NUMBER	PERCENT-AGE OF ALL CASES	LEGAL CAUSES		
			Desertion	Cruelty	Adultery
Total................	466	100.0	231	139	96
Financial tension.........	187	40.1	119	68	....
Infidelity, jealousy, illicit intercourse, venereal infection...............	116	25.0	31	22	63
Desertion for and living with another...........	72	15.5	39	....	33
Drink and cruelty........	72	15.5	29	43	....
Irregular habits..........	19	4.0	13	6	....

evidence in the cases classed as "illicit intercourse," the first being circumstantial and the second testimonial, the situations in both classes were identical in so far as attitudes were concerned. "Venereal infection" suggests a similar situation. By combining these three groups, one has ninety-four cases falling under the legal causes of "desertion," "cruelty," and "adultery."

Nineteen cases have been classed as having culminated from a situation where tension centered about certain irregular habits of either husband or wife. While these habits were usually expressed as "gambling" and "carousing," they were in some cases reported in the evidence as "staying out all night," or "late at night," which probably in many instances represent infidelity. These situations culminated in divorces granted for both desertion and cruelty.

In the last class, amounting to over 15 per cent of all the cases upon which this summary analysis is based, and which have been classed under the head of "drink and cruelty," the situation was substantially the same for both of the legal causes "desertion" and "cruelty."

This analysis of the situations culminating in divorce reveals that several types of situations are common for suits brought upon two or more legal grounds. That being the case, any reliance upon the legal causes for explaining the situations resulting in the disruption of family relations is misleading. In other words, the same type of situation may be indicated by two or more legal causes. This variance may be illustrated in the following cases where the legal ground for divorce given was "desertion" but the testimony indicates quite clearly other causes, which by contrast may be termed "natural causes" of marital discord:

CASE I: DEATH AND POVERTY LEAD TO DESERTION

Case No. B-33282 was filed by the husband, who charged desertion. The wife filed a cross-bill, but failed to appear in court on the day of the trial. They had lived together seven years, and had been separated four years when the case was tried. There were two children in the family, a girl twelve years old, and a boy six. The tension in the family arose as the result of the death of a little boy, whose sickness threw the father out of work because of quarantine, with all the discouragement which follows death and economic loss. The desire of the wife's parents to have her come home perhaps caused the despondent mother to idealize her parents' home as compared to her own, with the inevitable result, desertion. The husband had failed in business not long before; times were hard and work scarce, and he was forced to become a solicitor, a loss in status from that of an independent business man.

Excerpts from testimony of complainant (B-33282):

THE COURT: *Q.* What was the cause of your separation?—*A.*
Well, we had a death in our family; we lost a little boy; he died from
diphtheria. Then after his death her folks wanted her to come home,
so she went home to her folks, and I never could get her to come
back. . . . .

Q. How long had you been out of work when your wife left?—*A.*
From the 15th of December, 1914, until the 12th of February, 1915.

Q. What had you been doing before the 15th of December?—*A.*
I had been working for the Peoples Gas, Light and Coke Company,
as a solicitor.

Q. How much were you making?—*A.* About fifteen dollars a
week.

Q. Well, your wife states in her cross-bill that you forced her to
leave, by reason of the fact that she was not provided with clothes
nor coal, and that to save the lives of herself and children she had to
leave and go to her parents' home—*A.* At the time my wife left me,
we had taken a house; we were paying on the installment of $40 a
month, and we had a room on the second floor, and in 1912 I had failed
in business, lost everything I had, and from that time on I had been
in the hole all the time. It was the time of the year when it was hard
—1912, 1913, and 1914 were pretty hard years in Chicago, hard to get
work. So in order to get work I had to work in the Peoples Gas Company as solicitor, and admit fifteen dollars was not a whole lot to get
along on, but was doing the best we could under the circumstances;
and her folks being fairly well fixed, they imagined they could keep
her better than I could keep her, if they got her to their house.

Q. Well, were the conditions as bad as what she says they were
when she left?—*A.* Well, we did owe—we had to buy a lot of coal in
a week to get the house warm, and it might have been we were back
in our gas bill, but we never were without anything to eat; always
had something to eat in the house; we never went hungry. . . . .

Q. She don't make any charges against you, except she says that
at the time she left you conditions were bad in the home, and she had
to leave so herself and the children could have food and be properly
clothed, but she don't really account for her continuing to remain
away from you?—*A.* Well, she probably feels that she is getting more

money from me and from her employment than she would have if we were living together—I look at it in that light.

[Wife working at the C.E. for $75 a month, and receiving upon order of the court as temporary alimony $40. Permanent alimony granted, $20 a month. Defendant did not appear in court and apparently filed cross-bill only to prevent complainant from getting the children.]

While the divorce in the foregoing case was granted on the ground of desertion, the testimony indicates clearly the relation of the crisis of illness and death in the family, as well as unemployment and lowered economic status.

CASE II: WIFE'S AMUSEMENTS CAUSE CONFLICT

Desertion is the ground for the suit in Case B-34283, though the situation is widely different from that of the preceding one. This couple had lived together a little over a year, and had been separated over two years when the divorce was granted. Suit was brought by the husband. There was one child, a little girl three years old.

Excerpts from testimony of complainant (B-34283):

Q. What was the cause of the separation?—A. She started an argument with me that morning [the morning she left] on account of her being out that evening to a party. She got in about 3 o'clock in the morning and she said I ought to have been with her at this party. . . . .

THE COURT: Well, you ought to have been.—A. I had some business to attend to.

Q. Then you should have kept her home.—A. But she was not the kind that would stay home; she wanted to go to different parties and affairs which I could not afford to take her to, and she told me about how the different fellows spoke to her at the party and what a fuss they made over her, and so on, and she said that she did not care for me after she had been to this party, and she said I was not like the fellows because she thought I should be more of a husband and give her more money and things she wanted, and silk dresses and things of that kind. . . . .

THE COURT: You should have taken her to parties—husbands should take their wives with them to parties.—A. But these were not proper; she went with people I did not approve of. There was one woman in the party that she went about with who was a married woman, and I had no use for her and I did not like to have my wife associate with people of that kind that went to those parties—women who flew around without their husbands, and so forth.

As in the preceding case, the wife left her husband, but there is little in common in the two situations. The testimony indicates, as a cause of family discord, the relation of the behavior of the wife in the absence of her husband to his wishes concerning her behavior. Brief as is the testimony in this case, it shows the variance between the legal cause for divorce, i.e., desertion, and the natural cause, i.e., disagreement regarding the behavior of the wife.

Legal causes thus represent the standards to which family discord must be made to conform before the state will grant divorce and sanction the discontinuance of the marriage relationship; but those standards are not at all in conformity with the personal standards of great numbers of our population. Neither do they represent causes of family disintegration, but rather results of family discord. This distinction has been confused in too many of the studies of divorce, and has resulted in many abortive attempts to deal with the divorce problem. It represents, furthermore, an all too common error in statistical analysis; an error which arises, however, not as a fallacy in the statistical method per se, but instead as a misinterpretation of statistical data. No refinement of statistical method can be substituted for objective logical analysis of concepts.

CHILDREN AND DIVORCE

In the developing discord between husband and wife, certain factors are widely assumed to act as deterrents or as accelerators of the process. There is an impression, for example, that children prevent divorce. This impression is based upon the fact that for a given year there may be more divorces granted to couples who do not have children than to those who have. Just because there were no children, however, does not necessarily mean that had there been offspring there would have been no divorce. It might be claimed, for instance, that if a group of families of similar duration of marriage as the divorced group were taken at random one would find a similar proportion having no children. The absence of a control group with which to compare the group studied makes generalizations upon this point indefinite, if not misleading. The difficulty in solving this problem lies in the absence of statistics showing the number of families having children for each year-period of married life.

If, however, as probable, it were found that there was a difference in the presence of children in the divorced group as compared with a normal group, that would not necessarily indicate that children prevent divorce. It may be that to a large degree the persons who get divorces are those who do not want children, and for much the same reason, i.e., because they wish to retain their personal freedom. This brings up again the problem of whether or not the factor which is being measured is fundamental for the understanding of the behavior of the individuals. In Table XI is the distribution of cases in Chicago for 1919, with respect to children. There are children, as this table shows, in only 37 per cent of the divorce cases under consideration. It is reasonably safe to assume that where there was no report of children there was none to be reported. In the divorces reported to the Bureau of the Census in 1916 there were children in 37.7 per cent of the cases.[1]

TABLE XI

Class with Respect to Children	Number	Percentage
All cases..............................	6,094	100.0
'Reporting children........................	2,265	37.1
Reporting no children.....................	3,383	55.5
Not reporting as to children...............	446	7.4

Not only does one find a difference in the legal causes for the two groups of cases, i.e., those where the decree was granted upon the plea of the wife and those where it was the husband's plea which won the divorce, but they are not alike

TABLE XII

CLASS WITH RESPECT TO CHILDREN	TOTAL		DIVORCE GRANTED TO				
			Husband		Wife		Not Reported
	Number	Percent-age	Number	Percent-age	Number	Percent-age	Number
All cases..	6,094	100.0	1,615	100.0	4,467	100.0	12
No children....	3,829	62.8	1,120	69.3	2,703	60.5	6
Children......	2,265	37.2	495	30.7	1,764	39.5	6

in regard to the presence of children. Table XII shows that there were no children in 69.3 per cent of the divorces granted to the husband as against 60.5 per cent to the wife.

Is this difference of 8.8 per cent of any significance? If it is, then it can be assumed that it indicates some factor

[1] Bureau of Census, *Marriage and Divorce, 1916*, p. 22.

in the divorce situation which is not equally common to both sexes. The common test as to whether a difference in the attributes of two groups is of significance is to compare it with what might easily occur by chance. The customary rule is that if the probabilities are at least 100 to 1 that a difference could not have occurred by chance, then it is significant.[1] Here the probability is about 1,000,000,000 to 1 that the result is not due to chance (2.58 ϵ = only 3.6 per cent). The probability that the wife rather than the husband will receive the divorce is greater, therefore, if there are children in the family than if there are no children. But this may indicate nothing more than a reluctance on the part of courts to grant divorces to husbands in cases where there are children.

RELATION OF CHILDREN TO CAUSES

It has been seen that there is some variance between the proportion of families having children where the divorce was

[1] This procedure is based upon the theory of sampling for attributes. Theoretically, if two samples are drawn from an infinite universe the proportion of cases having a particular attribute in each sample will be the same as that for the universe as a whole, unless there is some factor in the selection of cases which prejudices the results. In practice, however, samples are not ordinarily large enough to give the precise proportions expected. The degree to which two samples may vary and still not indicate some selective factor in operation depends upon the size of the samples. This is customarily indicated by what is known as the "probable error," which measures the range within which the chances are equal that the true proportion falls. The probability that a given proportion, falling outside the range so indicated, could have occurred by chance declines rapidly, becoming about a 100:1 when this range has been multiplied by about 4. Proportions falling beyond the range indicated by about four times the probable error (2.576 standard errors to be exact) are ordinarily considered significant, i.e., not to have occurred solely as the result of chance. This measure assumes, of course, that the distribution of cases is normal and that the number is large. For the mathematical justification of this procedure the reader will find Yule, *loc. cit.*, as readable as any of the systematic treatments.

granted to the husband and where it was granted to the wife. There is also some variance between the distribution of cases by legal causes for these two groups. May not these two factors be related? Classifying all cases first according to the four major causes and with respect to children, one obtains Table XIII. Here the largest difference is that for desertion where the group having no children leads in its proportion of divorces for this cause. The difference in favor

TABLE XIII

LEGAL CAUSES	TOTAL		STATUS AS TO CHILDREN			
			No Children		Children	
	Number	Percentage	Number	Percentage	Number	Percentage
Total......	6,094	100.0	3,829	100.0	2,265	100.0
Desertion.......	3,044	50.0	1,956	51.1	1,088	48.0
Cruelty.........	1,672	27.5	1,016	26.6	656	29.0
Adultery.......	783	12.7	522	13.6	261	11.5
Drunkenness....	371	6.1	195	5.1	176	7.8
Others.........	224	3.7	140	3.6	84	3.7

of those families in which there were no children is 3.1 per cent, which slightly exceeds 2.8 times the standard error and therefore would not have occurred by chance oftener than once in a hundred trials. Desertion is therefore more characteristic of divorces granted to families having no children. Cruelty, on the other hand, is characteristic of families having children, though here the difference for the two groups is not generally considered significant, as it might have occurred by chance once in fifty pairs of samples.[1] Adultery is more common where there were no children as indicated by the difference for the two groups of 2.1 per cent. The chances are 100 to 1 that this difference could not

[1] For cruelty, 2.58 e = 2.7 per cent.

have occurred except for the operation of some causal factor.[1] It may indicate that in some cases at least the absence of children is symptomatic of lack of sexual satisfaction in the marriage relationship.

The relationship which has been shown makes no differentiation between those divorces granted to the husband and those granted to the wife. In Table XIV this factor has

TABLE XIV

PARTY GRANTED DECREE AND STATUS AS TO CHILDREN	DESERTION		CRUELTY		ADULTERY		DRUNKENNESS	
	Number	Percent-age	Number	Percent-age	Number	Percent-age	Number	Percent-age
All cases...	3,044	100.0	1,672	100.0	783	100.0	371	100.0
No children....	1,956	64.3	1,016	60.5	522	66.6	195	52.7
Children.......	1,088	35.7	656	39.5	261	33.4	176	47.3
Husband......	1,073	100.0	101	100.0	391	100.0	24	100.0
No children..	752	70.0	71	70.3	262	67.0	15	62.5
Children.....	321	30.0	30	29.7	129	33.0	9	37.5
Wife..........	1,967	100.0	1,570	100.0	392	100.0	346	100.0
No children..	1,201	61.0	944	60.0	260	66.4	179	51.7
Children.....	766	39.0	626	40.0	132	33.6	167	48.3

been taken into account. It may be seen in this table that the absence of children is a larger factor in desertion cases in which the decree was granted to the husband than to the wife, confirming the results obtained from an earlier table where the same result was found without any distinction as to legal causes. Here the difference between the proportion granted to the husband and that to the wife amounts to 9 per cent, and could not have occurred by chance once in several billions of trials.[2] Cruelty, also, is more commonly the legal cause for divorce granted to the husband where

[1] In the case of adultery, 2.58 ϵ = 2 per cent.

[2] The standard error multiplied by 2.58 for desertion is 2.6 per cent.

there were no children. This difference, however, is not so great, and might have occurred by chance once in about fifty trials.[1] Or, to state it in another way, in cases where there were children desertion and cruelty were more commonly the legal causes for divorces granted to the wife than to the husband.

This analysis suggests that for the two groups of cases, i.e., those in which the decree was granted to the husband and those where it was granted to the wife, there may be certain differences in the distribution between the four major causes according to whether or not there were children. In the analysis of the divorces granted to the husband, drunkenness has been included with all other causes, because the number of cases is not large enough to be of any significance.

TABLE XV

LEGAL CAUSES	ALL CASES		STATUS AS TO CHILDREN			
			No Children		Children	
	Number	Percentage	Number	Percentage	Number	Percentage
Total......	1,615	100.0	1,120	100.0	495	100.0
Desertion.......	1,073	66.3	752	67.0	321	64.7
Adultery.......	391	24.2	262	23.4	129	26.1
Cruelty.........	101	6.3	71	6.3	30	6.1
All others.......	50	3.2	35	3.3	15	3.1

In the group of cases where divorce was granted to the husband, the differences in the distribution between the three major legal causes with respect to children are not large enough to be of significance, and might have occurred as errors in sampling. The largest difference is for adultery and that could have occurred by chance once in about five trials (see Table XV).[2]

[1] For cruelty, 2.58 standard errors = 12.8 per cent.

[2] 2.58 e for desertion is 6 per cent; for adultery, 5.9 per cent.

The relation of children to the cause for divorce is somewhat different for those cases in which the divorce was granted to the wife. The most outstanding difference for the two groups with respect to children, is that where the cause was drunkenness, as shown in Table XVI. This difference in the occurrence of drunkenness for the two groups with

TABLE XVI

LEGAL CAUSES	ALL CASES		STATUS AS TO CHILDREN			
			No Children		Children	
	Number	Percentage	Number	Percentage	Number	Percentage
Total......	4,467	100.0	2,703	100.0	1,764	100.0
Desertion.......	1,967	44.1	1,201	44.5	766	43.6
Cruelty.........	1,570	35.2	944	34.8	626	35.6
Adultery.......	392	8.8	260	9.2	132	7.5
Drunkenness....	346	7.7	179	6.6	167	9.5
All others.......	192	4.2	119	4.9	73	3.8

respect to children is significant,[1] and shows the association between drunkenness of the husband and the presence of children. As for the remainder of the causes, there seems to be no significant relationship. For adultery, in contrast to those cases where divorce was granted to the husband, the difference favors those where there were no children, but it could have occurred by chance once in twenty trials, and so cannot be given much weight.[2]

It has been shown that certain relationships exist between legal causes and whether or not there were children in the family. May it not be expected, likewise, that the

[1] The standard error multiplied by 2.58 equals 2.1 per cent for drunkenness, and the difference between those cases in which there were children and those in which there were none exceeds this by 0.8 per cent. This difference could not have occurred by chance oftener than once in some twenty-five hundred trials.

[2] 2.58 ϵ = 2.3 per cent.

sex of the children was a significant factor? This has been tested by compiling data concerning families in which only one sex was represented by children (Table XVII). It is quite apparent that the proportion between boys and girls in families in which the children were of one sex only is approximately that of the ratio between the sexes in the birth-rate, namely, 104 males to 100 females. This represents an excess of about 3 per cent of boys in those cases granted to the husband over those granted to the wife.

TABLE XVII

SEX OF CHILDREN	TOTAL		DECREE TO			
	Number	Percentage	Husband		Wife	
			Number	Percentage	Number	Percentage
Total......	1,691	100.0	360	100.0	1,331	100.0
Boys only......	871	51.5	195	54.2	676	50 8
Girls only.......	820	48.5	165	45.8	655	49.2

However, this could have occurred by chance three times in ten trials, and cannot therefore be considered of any significance but would probably disappear in a larger number of cases.[1] For cases in general, the sex of the children seems to be of no significance.

The next step in this analysis is to find out whether or not this absence of relationship between sex of children in families having children of one sex only and the party to whom the decree was granted was characteristic of each of the major legal causes. If the contention of the psychoanalysts is true that parents of one sex prefer children of the other, it would be expected that in the families having children of one sex only girls would predominate in those in which the husband

[1] Standard error $\times 2.58 = 8.5$ per cent.

was granted the divorce. For desertion, however, the situation is just the opposite. There were in this selected group 9.3 per cent more boys in the cases where the husband received the decree than in those cases in which the wife was granted the divorce. This difference is approximately equal to 2.58 standard errors, and the probabilities are about 100 to 1 that it did not occur as an error in sampling.[1] For the

TABLE XVIII

PARTY TO WHOM DIVORCE WAS GRANTED, AND SEX OF CHILDREN	LEGAL CAUSES FOR DIVORCE					
	Desertion		Cruelty		Adultery	
	Number	Percentage	Number	Percentage	Number	Percentage
Both...........	835	100.0	478	100.0	195	100.0
Boys only....	431	51.5	237	49.4	103	52.8
Girls only.....	404	48.5	241	50.6	92	47.2
Husband.......	241	100.0	22	100.0	88	100.0
Boys only....	138	58.5	13	59.0	39	44.7
Girls only.....	103	41.5	9	41.0	49	55.3
Wife...........	594	100.0	456	100.0	107	100.0
Boys only....	293	49.2	224	49.2	64	60.0
Girls only.....	301	50.8	232	50.8	43	40.0

other legal causes there were no significant differences (see Table XVIII).

Table XIX shows the number of divorces granted for each of the major causes classified by the number of children in the family and by the party to whom the divorce was granted. In Table XX this distinction between husband and wife has been dropped and the percentage distribution for each size of family calculated for families where there were children. Comparison of cases for different legal causes immediately reveals a predominance of large families for some

[1] Standard errors × 2.58 for each of the three causes in the following table are desertion, 9.7 per cent; adultery, 25 per cent; and cruelty, 27.7 per cent.

TABLE XIX

DIVORCES CLASSIFIED BY NUMBER OF CHILDREN IN FAMILY, BY MAJOR CAUSES, AND BY PARTY TO WHOM GRANTED, CHICAGO, 1919

No. of Children	Total No.	Desertion Div. To			Cruelty Div. To			Adultery Div. To			Drunkenness Div. To			Others Div. To		
		Husband	Wife	N.R.*	Husband	Wife	N.R.*	Husband	Wife	N.R.*	Husband	Wife	N.R.*	Husband	Wife	N.R.*
Total..	6,094	1,073	1,967	4	101	1,570	1	391	392	0	24	346	1	26	192	6
0	3,829	752	1,201	3	71	944	....	262	260	....	15	179	....	20	119	3
1	1,373	202	494	1	17	358	1	70	87	....	2	94	1	4	39	3
2	503	76	179	....	9	168	....	31	32	....	1	39	....	2	26	....
3	207	28	66	....	....	60	....	17	8	....	3	21	....	....	4	....
4	72	9	18	....	2	24	....	5	4	....	1	7	....	....	2	....
5	36	5	7	....	....	13	....	5	1	....	1	3	....	....	1	....
6	9	1	....	....	1	3	....	1	....	....	....	2	....	....	1	....
7	5	....	2	....	1	....	....	....	....	....	1	1	....	....	....	....

* N.R. = No record.

TABLE XX

DIVORCES IN FAMILIES HAVING CHILDREN CLASSIFIED BY NUMBER, AND BY MAJOR CAUSES, CHICAGO, 1919

No. Children	Total Percentage	Percentage Desertion	Percentage Cruelty	Percentage Adultery	Percentage Drunkenness	Percentage of Others
Total......	100.0	100.0	100.0	100.0	100.0	100.0
1	60.6	64.0	57.3	60.2	54.9	56.1
2	24.8	23.4	26.8	24.2	22.6	34.2
3	9.1	8.7	9.2	9.6	13.6	4.9
4	3.2	2.5	4.0	3.4	4.5	2.4
5	1.7	1.1	2.0	2.3	2.3	1.2
6	0.4	0.1	0.6	0.4	1.1	1.2
7	0.2	0.2	0.1	....	1.1	....

causes and small families for others. If a large family is defined as one in which there are three or more children, Table

XXI is obtained. The greatest differences here are those for desertion and drunkenness. When the desertion cases are compared with all other cases, there are 3.4 per cent more small families where the charge was desertion. Where the comparison is made between cases in which drunkenness was the charge with all others, 9 per cent more large families appear. The difference for desertion is slightly less than 2.58 standard errors, and so might have occurred as an error in sampling once out of some thirty trials.[1] The difference,

TABLE XXI

No. Children	Total Percentage	Legal Causes for Divorce				
		Percentage Desertion	Percentage Cruelty	Percentage Adultery	Percentage Drunkenness	Percentage of Others
Total......	100.0	100.0	100.0	100.0	100.0	100.0
Less than three..	85.4	87.4	84.1	84.4	77.5	90.3
Three or more...	14.6	12.6	15.9	15.6	22.5	9.7

however, in the case of drunkenness so far exceeds 2.58 standard errors as not to have occurred by chance oftener than once in some twenty-five hundred trials.[2]

If, however, a large family is considered as one having more than one child, one gets slightly different results which confirm the predominance of small families where the legal cause was desertion. The distribution in percentages is shown in Table XXII. According to this classification, adultery was no more characteristic of small families than of large families. Significant results, however, may be obtained for the remainder of the causes. In the case of desertion, as has been said, the predominance of small families still ob-

[1] For desertion, 2.58 standard errors = 3.9 per cent.

[2] Standard error × 2.58 = 6.4 per cent.

tains as it did where less than three children were counted a small family. For cruelty and drunkenness large families seem more characteristic though the differences here could have occurred as errors of sampling once in thirty to fifty trials. When comparison is made, however, between the divorces granted for cruelty and drunkenness combined in comparison to all other causes, the difference is significant.[1]

TABLE XXII

| No. Children | Total Percentage | Legal Causes for Divorce | | | | |
		Perecntage Desertion	Percentage Cruelty	Percentage Adultery	Percentage Drunkenness	Percentage of Others
Total......	100.0	100.0	100.0	100.0	100.0	100.0
One...........	60.6	64.0	57.3	60.2	54.9	56.1
More than one..	39.4	36.0	42.7	39.8	45.1	43.9

Cruelty and drunkenness were more characteristic, then, of those cases in which there was more than one child. But it does not follow that children add an economic burden to the father and cause him to get drunk and beat his wife. It may mean only that the same persons who are either temperamentally or habitually inclined toward drink and cruelty are also likely to have more children.

YEARS OF MARRIED LIFE AND DIVORCE

Fifty per cent of the divorces granted in Cook County for the year 1919 were to couples who had lived together less than five years (see Chart VIII and Table XXIII). As it

[1] Standard errors×2.58 used in these calculations are as follows: desertion, 5.2 per cent; cruelty, 5.7 per cent; drunkenness, 9.1 per cent; cruelty and drunkenness, 5.2 per cent. The differences in each case are desertion, 7.3 per cent; cruelty, 4.7 per cent; drunkenness, 8.1 per cent.; cruelty and drunkenness, 6.4 per cent.

CHART VIII

PERCENTAGE DISTRIBUTION OF CASES BY FIVE-YEAR PERIODS WITH RE-
SPECT TO CHILDREN FOR: I. DIVORCES TO HUSBAND
AND II. DIVORCES TO WIFE; CHICAGO, 1919

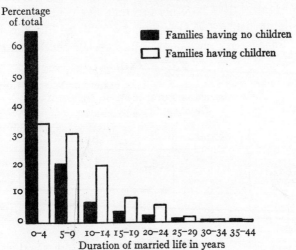

I. Decree to Husband

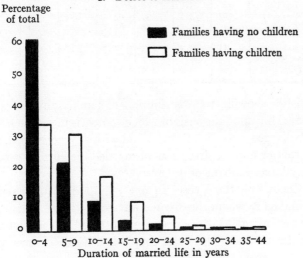

II. Decree to Wife

stands this is a striking fact. But if one remembers that there were, undoubtedly, many more families in Chicago in 1919 who had lived together less than five years than there were in any other five-year period of married life, this fact loses some of its sensational qualities. In the absence of

TABLE XXIII

DISTRIBUTION OF CASES BY FIVE-YEAR PERIODS OF MARRIED LIFE
AND CLASSIFIED BY PARTY TO WHOM DECREE WAS
GRANTED, CHICAGO, 1919

MARRIED LIFE BY FIVE-YEAR PERIODS	ALL CASES		DECREE TO				
	Number	Percentage	Husband		Wife		Not Reporting
			Number	Percentage	Number	Percentage	Number
Total.....	6,094	100.0	1,615	100.0	4,467	100.0	12
0–4..........	3,164	51.9	887	55.0	2,273	50.8	4
5–9..........	1,515	24.8	367	22.7	1,141	25.5	7
10–14.........	743	12.3	176	10.9	566	12.6	1
15–19.........	348	5.7	86	5.3	262	6.0	....
20–24.........	191	3.1	57	3.5	134	3.0	....
25–29.........	70	1.2	23	1.4	47	1.1	....
30–34.........	25	0.4	11	0.7	14	0.3	....
35–39.........	15	0.2	3	0.2	12	0.3	....
40–44.........	4	0.1	1	0.1	3	0.1	....
Not reporting..	19	0.3	4	0.2	15	0.3	....

statistics showing the distribution of families by years of married life upon the basis of which comparison can be made with divorce cases, little can be said with any accuracy as to whether or not the first years of married life furnish a relatively larger amount of divorce cases.

Classifying these cases in five-year periods of married life and as to whom the divorce was granted, one finds that a larger proportion of divorces were obtained by the husband than by the wife where the couple had lived together less than five years. That this indicates a tendency on the part of the wife to give up the experiment more quickly than the husband one cannot say upon the basis of this evidence alone. At any rate, the chances are about two hundred and fifty to one that this difference was not the result of an error in sampling.[1] For the other periods there are no significant differences, as may be seen in Table XXIII.

In this connection there arises another problem: Was there any difference in the distribution of cases by years of married life in relation to whether or not there were children? This relationship is shown in Chart VIII. There was little difference in the distribution of the divorces granted to the husband as compared with those granted to the wife. There was in both instances, however, a proportionate absence of children in the early years of married life. Whether or not that is of significance, however, cannot be determined so long as there is no normal group available with which to compare it.

In summary, a statistical study of divorce in Chicago as representative of an urban community indicates:

1. *Ratios more significant than numbers.*—While the absolute number of divorces in Cook County is larger than that for any other county in the United States, the divorce rate (the number of divorces per 100,000 population) of this county is exceeded by eight states.

2. *Natural causes often differ widely from legal causes.*—A study of court records indicates, for example, that desertion, although a legal ground for divorce, was itself invariably the result of one or more natural causes of family disintegration.

---

[1] The standard error for the first five-year group is about 1.4 per cent; multiplied by 2.58, this gives approximately 3.7 per cent.

3. *Factors associated with divorce may themselves be results of more fundamental causes.*—Absence of children, for instance, was reported in only three-eighths of divorce records. Is childlessness a cause, therefore, of family disintegration or an effect of a more fundamental factor which results both in divorce and childlessness?

4. *Correlations between legal grounds for divorce and certain types of family relations significant.*—While further research into the meaning of the following correlations is needed, there can be no doubt about their significance: (*a*) desertion and adultery as legal causes more frequent where there were no children, (*b*) drunkenness of husband associated with presence of children in the family, (*c*) desertion of wife more frequent where the children were all boys, (*d*) correlation of desertion and adultery with small families, and (*e*) the predominance of large families in cases where the legal causes were drunkenness and cruelty.

5. *Certain limitations of the available statistical material.*—Under this head should be noted: (*a*) lack of an adequate ratio by which to measure the amount of divorce, (*b*) inadequacy of legal causes as indicative of attitudes, (*c*) absence of a normal or control group, and (*d*) failure to eliminate chance where conclusions are based upon differences in the relative weight of attributes in two groups of cases.

Divorce is not the only index of family disorganization, however. It may be, and is, characteristic of certain classes in the population. For the poor, the expense of a divorce may be prohibitive. To those of certain religious faiths, divorce may be impossible. Certain groups have therefore another way of ending family relations, i.e., by desertion. An adequate monographic study of family disorganization in a community such as Chicago, therefore, must include an inquiry into the extent and causes of desertion.

CHAPTER IV

DESERTION IN AN URBAN COMMUNITY: CHICAGO

"Desertion is the poor man's divorce" is not an uncommon expression among those who have to deal with the problem. Such a characterization of desertion expresses a recognition that there is no fundamental difference between these two forms of family disintegration, except the differences between the two population groups from which the cases come. Desertion characterizes the poverty group, i.e., that group in the population which in an economic crisis must fall back upon the social agency for assistance. Divorce, on the other hand, is confined largely to the middle and upper classes. That the motives are essentially the same in both types of cases is implied in this expression. Unfortunately, no attempt has been made to study the two types together, though common sense would tend to confirm the assumption that fundamentally the causes of family disintegration differ little in the two groups, except in so far as poverty is a greater factor in desertion than in divorce.

A comparison of desertion rates in various countries or in different areas within the same country has not been feasible, because of the lack of statistics. There is an impression, probably correct, among social workers that desertion is a phenomenon of city life; moreover, there is no "desertion" in any legal sense in the country, because there are no social agencies to report the cases, and no special courts to prosecute the offenders. At any rate, desertion is at present characteristically a problem of the city.

To repeat, desertion statistics may come from the courts or from social agencies. Where the record of court cases is depended upon to give one a measure of desertion, the statistics are technically either of non-support or abandonment. In non-support cases the law provides a penalty in case the husband fails to support his family, whether or not he ceases to live at home. Because it is more generally understood, the word "desertion" will be used instead of "non-support" or "abandonment" throughout for the cases considered in this chapter. These cases were taken from the records of the Chicago Court of Domestic Relations for the year 1921.

DESERTIONS ON THE INCREASE

According to a story appearing in the *Chicago Tribune*, desertion has decreased phenomenally within the last seven years in Chicago.[1] This conclusion is based upon figures given out by the United Charities showing that less than 9 per cent of the families receiving major help for 1922 had been deserted as compared with 13 per cent in 1916. While it may be true that so far as charity cases are concerned desertion is becoming less a factor than previously, there is no indication that desertion cases in the Court of Domestic Relations are declining in numbers. Chart IX seems to indicate that desertion has increased more rapidly since 1907 than has the population of the city.

The difference in trend shown by figures from these two sources may or may not be a real difference. If it is a real difference, it might be accounted for by changes in the policy of either the United Charities or the Court of Domestic Rela-

[1] Louise Bargelt, "Husbands Who Desert Going Out of Style," August 23, 1923. In 1916–17 desertion cases numbered 987 out of 7,507; in 1921–22, 530 out of 5,416. See *Sixty-six Years of Service: An Account of the Activities of the United Charities of Chicago*, p. 35.

CHART IX

DESERTION CASES IN COURT OF DOMESTIC RELATIONS BY
YEARLY TOTALS AND BY MOVING AVERAGES (FIVE
YEAR PERIODS): POPULATION BY DECADES

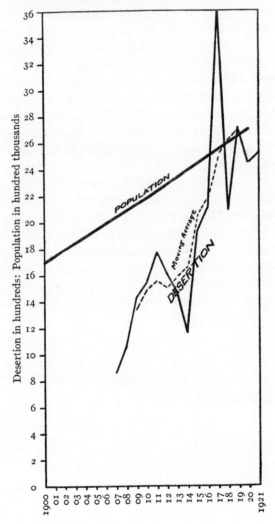

tions. If it is not a real difference, it arises as the result of comparing a trend covering fifteen years with another trend of only six years. If the figures from the Court of Domestic Relations are taken for the same period as that for the United Charities, it is found that the number of desertions declined from 2,591 in 1917 to 2,525 in 1921 for the former and from 987 to 530 for the latter. That is, the decline for the Court of Domestic Relations has been 29 per cent compared to 42 per cent for the United Charities. However, the total number of cases for the United Charities declined 29 per cent within the same period, and this may account for the difference between these two rates.

This illustrates three errors which often creep into statistical studies of desertion. First, the series of figures upon which conclusions are based may be too short to give a reliable index of the trend. Second, it is difficult to be sure that desertion is a constant unit of measurement. It is what may be called an "administrative concept," and so changes with fluctuations in the policies of both legal and charitable institutions. Third, no adequate ratio has been substituted for the absolute figures.

NATIONALITY AN INDEX TO CULTURE

In every major study of desertion there has been an attempt to determine the part which nationality played. The procedure has been to compare the distribution of desertion cases by nationality with either the distribution of population or with all cases coming to the social agency. Two studies[1] conclude that nationality is a factor; two others arrive at somewhat different conclusions. Eubank,[2] inter-

[1] Brandt, *Five Hundred and Seventy-four Deserters and Their Families*, pp. 18–19; Colcord, *Broken Homes*, pp. 44–45.

[2] *A Study of Family Desertion*, pp. 15–16.

preting his statistics in conformity with his preconceptions regarding the disintegrating effects of city life, concludes that "desertion is not a racial or a national characteristic, but an effect of the social situation." He fails to take into account the differences in desertion rates by nationalities shown by his own statistics. Patterson,[1] however, is more cautious. He concludes that, while certain nationalities seem to be represented disproportionately by desertion cases in comparison to their numbers in the population, his material does not prove nationality to be a causal factor.

Table XXIV shows the distribution by nationality of cases which came to the Court of Domestic Relations in 1921. In each case the nativity of the father of each person was taken as the index of nationality. Comparing this distribution with that for the population in 1920,[2] it is found that there were proportionately more Negro husbands and fewer Russian, Swedish, Bohemian, Canadian, Hungarian, Norwegian, and Danish husbands than persons of those nationalities in the total population. Comparing the number of wives by nationality with the total persons in the population for the same national groups, there was an excess of Polish, German, and Negro, and too few Americans, Russians, Swedes, Italians, Bohemians, Canadians, Hungarians, Norwegians, Danes, Greeks, and Dutch. As in the chapter on "Divorce," only those differences which exceed 2.58 standard errors are considered significant.

It will be seen that there are in addition some differences

[1] "Family Desertion and Non-Support," *Journal of Delinquency*, VII, 270–72.

[2] An estimate of population by the Chicago Chamber of Commerce has been used because the Census classifies persons who are native born of foreign parentage upon the pre-war basis, which is not comparable to the classification used by the Court of Domestic Relations in 1921.

in the distribution of husbands by nationality as compared
with that of wives. These differences, however, prove of

TABLE XXIV

DISTRIBUTION OF DESERTION CASES BY NATIONALITY OF BOTH
HUSBAND AND WIFE IN COMPARISON WITH POPULATION,
CHICAGO COURT OF DOMESTIC RELATIONS, 1921

	POPULATION		PARTIES TO DESERTION CASES					
			Total		Husband		Wife	
NATIONALITY	Number	Percent-age	Number	Percent-age	Number	Percent-age	Number	Percent-age
Total...	2,701,705	100.0	5,322	100.0	2,661	100.0	2,661	100.0
American...	642,871	23.8	1,184	22.2	618	23.2	566	21.2
Polish......	319,644	11.8	715	13.4	343	12.9	372	14.0
German....	285,216	10.6	676	12.7	319	12.0	357	13.8
Russian....	230,668	8.5	320	6.1	170	6.4	150	5.6
Swedish....	154,919	5.7	121	2.3	63	2.4	58	2.2
Irish........	154,051	5.7	319	6.0	148	5.6	171	6.4
Italian.....	129,815	4.8	199	3.7	113	4.2	86	3.2
Bohemian...	116,115	4.3	156	2.9	69	2.6	87	3.2
Negro......	109,458	4.0	828	15.6	414	15.6	414	15.6
Austrian....	72,531	2.7	129	2.4	54	2.1	75	2.8
Canadian...	68,045	2.5	67	1.3	34	1.2	33	1.2
English.....	67,907	2.5	113	2.1	51	1.9	62	2.3
Hungarian..	61,847	2.3	76	1.4	36	1.3	40	1.5
Norwegian..	53,891	2.0	58	1.1	29	1.1	29	1.1
Lithuanian..	43,274	1.6	79	1.5	41	1.5	38	1.4
Danish.....	29,450	1.1	33	0.6	16	0.6	17	0.6
Greek......	27,017	1.0	28	0.5	24	0.9	4	0.1
Scotch.....	25,173	0.9	43	0.8	24	0.9	19	0.7
Jugo-Slav...	22,211	0.8	19	0.4	9	0.3	10	0.4
Dutch......	22,165	0.8	19	0.4	10	0.4	9	0.3
Roumanian.	11,644	0.4	17	0.3	7	0.3	10	0.4
French.....	11,379	0.4	29	0.5	16	0.6	13	0.5
Swiss......	8,662	0.3	9	0.2	7	0.3	2	0.1
Belgian.....	7,900	0.3	13	0.2	8	0.3	5	0.2
All others...	33,933	1.3	72	1.4	38	1.4	34	1.3

significance in one nationality only, that of the Greek. This
disparity between the proportion of husbands to wives probably does nothing more than reflect the disparity between

men and women in the Greek portion of the population. It is a well-recognized fact that in any immigrant group there tends to be a disproportionate number of men.[1] This raises

TABLE XXV

DISTRIBUTION OF DESERTION CASES BY NATIVITY OF HUSBAND IN COMPARISON WITH POPULATION, CHICAGO, 1921

NATIVITY	POPULATION		DESERTION	
	Number	Percentage	Number	Percentage
Total....................	2,701,705	100.0	2,661	100.0
United States—white.........	1,787,765	66.3	1,224	46.0
United States—Negro.........	109,458	4.0	414	15.6
Poland......................	136,611	5.0	259	9.7
Germany....................	112,288	4.2	101	3.8
Russia......................	102,095	3.8	143	5.4
Italy.......................	59,215	2.2	94	3.5
Sweden.....................	58,563	2.1	35	1.3
Ireland.....................	56,786	2.1	54	2.0
Czecho-Slovakia.............	50,392	1.9	39	1.5
England including Scotland....	36,330	1.3	35	1.3
Hungary....................	26,106	1.0	34	1.3
Canada.....................	26,054	1.0	20	0.8
Norway.....................	20,481	0.7	17	0.6
Lithuania...................	18,923	0.7	39	1.5
Greece.....................	11,546	0.4	24	0.9
Austria.....................	30,491	1.1	46	1.7
Other countries..............	58,601	2.1	83	0.7

the question as to whether or not the total population is an adequate control group with which to compare such a phenomenon as desertion. May not there actually be little difference in the distribution of desertion cases by nationality and that for the social group from which they come?

So far the criterion of nationality has been the nativity of the fathers of the two persons concerned. It may be ob-

[1] Patterson recognized this difficulty and so used as his base the number of persons fifteen years of age and over in the population, though he is skeptical even about its adequacy.

jected that the nativity of the parents is not an adequate
index of the cultural background of the persons themselves.
That, after all, is what one hopes to take into account by
nationality. Would, then, the same results be obtained if
the criterion of cultural differences be made the nativity of
the persons themselves?

When the criterion of cultural differences is made the
nativity of the husband, somewhat different results are obtained. This is shown in Table XXV. According to this
classification, the numbers of Americans and Swedes were
proportionately small in comparison to the total population
of those groups. There were still many more Negroes than
can be explained by chance. This was also true for the following nationalities: Polish, Russian, Italian, Austrian, and
Greek. But these nationalities are characteristically of low
economic status, and one may contend that this factor is
fundamental rather than that of nationality.

"MIXED MARRIAGES"

Thirty-five per cent of the cases coming to the Chicago
Court of Domestic Relations showed a difference in nationality between husband and wife, where the criterion of nationality was the nativity of the fathers of the couple. Obviously, this fact means little unless it can be shown that this
proportion is much higher than for the group from which
these cases come. Unfortunately, no such statistics are available. Social workers, however, recognize difference in nationality as a causative factor in desertion, according to Miss
Colcord.[1] The basis for this assertion seems to be about five
hundred cases in Miss Brandt's study,[2] in which it was found
that in 28 per cent there was a difference as compared to the

[1] *Op. cit.*, pp. 26.   [2] *Op. cit.*, pp. 18-19.

population of New York City where less than 13 per cent were of mixed parentage in 1900.

It would seem to be quite obvious that the proportion of the population of mixed parentage would not be an adequate base with which to compare desertion cases.[1] The only satisfactory base would be the proportion of mixed marriages in the social class from which desertion cases come. Nevertheless, it is possible by a more elaborate analysis to get some conception of the importance of this factor in spite of the absence of such a control group as has been indicated.

In the analysis which follows, the procedure will be to compare cases of marriages within the same nationality, "like marriages," with marriages where the nationality of the persons is different, "mixed marriages." The nationality in each case will be determined by the nativity of the fathers of the two persons. It should be remembered, however, that such a comparison can reveal only the characteristics of desertion cases and does not necessarily disclose anything about the population as a whole, nor about the social class from which desertion cases come.

These two groups of cases differ, in the first place, with regard to the distribution by nationality as shown by Table XXVI. For mixed marriages the distribution by nationality

[1] The use of the population of mixed parentage as a base assumes that the proportion of marriages between different nationalities had remained constant for a generation, which may or may not be true. It also assumes that desertion is equally common of all classes in the population, which is generally conceded not to be true. In addition, there is another implication for which there is little justification, namely, that each person of mixed parentage is equally representative of a mixed marriage. For the social group from which desertion cases come this is is more justified than for the total population.

is based upon the nationality of the husband.[1] The proportion of mixed marriages was significantly larger for Ameri-

TABLE XXVI

DISTRIBUTION OF CASES BY NATIONALITY FOR LIKE MARRIAGES AND FOR MIXED MARRIAGES

NATIONALITY	TOTAL CASES		TYPE OF MARRIAGE			
			Like		Mixed	
	Number	Percentage	Number	Percentage	Number	Percentage
Total......	2,661	100.0	1,725	100.0	936	100.0
American.......	607	22.8	321	18.6	286	30.6
Polish..........	325	12.2	280	16.2	45	4.8
German........	314	11.8	135	7.8	179	19.1
Jewish.........	199	7.5	180	10.4	19	2.0
Swedish........	63	2.4	26	1.5	37	4.0
Irish..........	147	5.5	67	3.9	80	8.5
Italian.........	110	4.1	79	4.6	31	3.3
Bohemian.....,	69	2.6	45	2.6	24	2.6
Negro..........	414	15.6	414	24.1	0	....
Austrian........	47	1.7	32	1.9	15	1.6
Canadian.......	34	1.3	4	0.2	30	3.2
English.........	49	1.8	7	0.4	42	4.5
Hungarian......	33	1.2	27	1.6	6	0.6
Norwegian......	29	1.1	11	0.6	18	1.9
Lithuanian......	39	1.5	35	2.3	4	0.4
Danish.........	16	0.6	5	0.3	11	1.2
Greek..........	24	0.9	4	0.2	20	2.1
Scotch.........	24	0.9	3	0.2	21	2.2
Jugo-Slav.......	9	0.3	7	0.4	2	0.2
Dutch..........	10	0.4	2	0.1	8	0.9
Roumanian.....	4	0.1	3	0.2	1	0.1
French.........	16	0.6	0	....	16	1.7
Swiss...........	7	0.3	1	0.1	6	0.6
Belgian.........	8	0.3	2	0.1	6	0.6
Russian........	38	1.4	19	1.1	19	2.0
All others.......	26	1.0	16	0.9	10	1.1

cans, Germans, Swedes, Irish, Canadians, English, Norwegians, Danes, Greeks, Scotch, and French than that of
like marriages. The same thing was probably true for Dutch,

[1] See Appendix A for nationality of the wife.

Roumanians, Belgians, and Swiss, though the number of cases was so small as to be less certain. For the Polish, Jewish, Negro, and Lithuanian groups, however, the proportion of mixed marriages was smaller than that for like marriages. This result is significant because it demonstrates that the national composition of these two groups was not constant for both mixed and like marriages. Conclusions from further comparisons must, then, take into account this variance in national composition.

CHILDREN AND DESERTION

It is often asserted upon the basis of divorce statistics, which show a large proportion of families without children, that children tend to hold the family together. Unfortunately, desertion statistics may show the opposite. Miss Brandt[1] found that in only 3.48 per cent of the families she studied there were no children. She concludes that in the first years the birth of a child may increase the economic burden to such an extent as to cause the husband to desert.

In both the interpretations referred to above, the difficulty is the same. A ratio is found between cases with children and those without. In the absence of a control group with which to compare results, one concludes after a process of reasoning from assumptions conforming largely to one's own experience that children tend to cause desertion or tend to prevent divorce. The social worker, being impressed with the economic burden of the poor, sees the added burden which a child brings and concludes accordingly. The reformer, considering the family as primarily an institution for the reproduction of the race, draws his own conclusions.

There were no children in 29 per cent of the cases ap-

[1] *Op. cit.*, p. 16.

pearing in the Chicago Court of Domestic Relations, as compared to 62 per cent for divorce cases analyzed in chapter iii and 3.48 per cent in Miss Brandt's study. Upon the basis of these data, little can be said except to conclude that the presence of more children in desertion cases than in divorce cases only reaffirms the statement that these two types of family disintegration characterize different social groups. Further than this the presence or absence of children may or may not be of any significance.

TABLE XXVII

STATUS AS TO CHIL-DREN AND SEX OF CHILDREN	TOTAL		TYPES OF MARRIAGES			
			Like		Mixed	
	Number	Percentage	Number	Percentage	Number	Percentage
Total......	2,661	100.0	1,725	100.0	936	100.0
No children.....	774	29.1	495	28.7	279	29.8
Boys only......	562	21.1	352	20.4	210	22.4
Girls only.......	565	21.2	363	21.0	202	21.6
Both sexes......	751	28.2	510	29.6	241	25.8
Not reporting sex	9	0.3	5	0.3	4	0.4

There was also no significant difference with regard to children for the two groups of desertion cases as shown by Table XXVII. There was, however, one difference which may have been something more than a chance occurrence. The proportion of families having children of both sexes in the like-marriage group was higher than that in the mixed-marriage group. This difference of almost 4 per cent could not have occurred by chance oftener than once in about fifty trials. It suggests, therefore, that large families may characterize like marriages rather than mixed marriages. But this, again, may have been the result of a preponderance of certain national groups among the mixed marriages.

PERILOUS FIRST FIVE YEARS

Forty-eight per cent of the couples had lived together less than five years. There was, however, considerable difference in the proportion of couples living together less than five years for the two groups, like marriages and mixed marriages, as shown by Table XXVIII. There was also a significant difference in the proportion of cases in the two groups falling within the first nine years, the larger number of cases being mixed marriages. If Table XXVIII is com-

TABLE XXVIII

YEARS OF MARRIED LIFE	TOTAL		TYPE OF MARRIAGE			
			Like		Mixed	
	Number	Percentage	Number	Percentage	Number	Percentage
Total......	2,661	100.0	1,725	100.0	936	100.0
0–4..........	1,268	47.7	769	44.6	499	53.5
5–9..........	627	23.6	295	21.9	332	25.2
10–14.........	371	13.9	180	13.4	191	14.5
15–19.........	206	7.7	101	7.5	105	8.0
20–24.........	96	3.6	60	4.5	36	2.7
25–29.........	45	1.7	27	2.0	18	1.4
30–44.........	31	1.1	18	1.3	13	1.0
Not reporting...	17	0.6	8	0.6	9	0.7

pared with that on page 86 for divorce it will be seen how close a resemblance there is between the two, and especially between the distributions of total divorces and of desertions in cases of mixed marriages.

The difficulty in drawing any very definite conclusions upon the basis of the distribution of desertions by years of married life is due to the absence of an adequate control group just as it is with divorce cases. One can, however, re-affirm more vigorously the parallel between desertion and divorce so far as the stability of the family is concerned. As for the difference in duration of married life for like marriages as compared with mixed marriages, little can be said conclusively because the nationality of the cases has not been kept constant for the two groups.

SIZE OF FAMILY

In spite of the general impression that children tend to keep the family together, there are few data to substantiate

TABLE XXIX

| NUMBER OF CHILDREN | TOTAL | | TYPE OF MARRIAGE | | | |
| | | | Like | | Mixed | |
	Number	Percentage	Number	Percentage	Number	Percentage
Total......	2,661	100.0	1,725	100.0	936	100.0
0..............	774	29.1	495	28.7	279	29.8
1..............	793	29.8	505	29.3	288	30.8
2..............	513	19.4	322	18.7	191	20.1
3..............	287	10.8	180	10.4	107	11.4
4..............	161	6.1	118	6.8	43	4.6
5..............	71	2.6	57	3.3	14	1.5
6..............	40	1.5	32	1.9	8	0.9
7..............	13	0.5	9	0.5	4	0.4
8..............	6	0.2	5	0.3	1	0.1
9 and 10........	3	0.1	2	0.1	1	0.1

such an impression in desertion statistics. In Table XXIX is shown the distribution of cases by the number of children in the family for both types of marriages. As in the case of divorce, it is difficult without statistics showing the number of children in normal families for each year-period of married life to prove or disprove that children tend to prevent family disintegration. On the face of the material as it stands, if the duration of married life is taken into account, it would seem that the number of children in desertion cases is about what would be found in normal families, and not therefore a significant factor in the situation. This conclusion is confirmed if desertion cases are compared with divorce cases (see p. 82). There was more than one child in only 14.7 per cent of the divorce cases as compared to 41.1 per cent of all desertion cases and to 39.4 per cent of the mixed-marriage group, in spite of the fact that the distribution by years of married life was substantially the same for both. The size of the family seems to characterize the social class from which the cases of family disintegration come rather than being a significant factor in the situation.

There was substantially no difference in the distribution of cases by the number of children for like marriages and for mixed marriages. However, if a large family is defined as one in which there are four or more children and a small family is defined as all others, then in the like-marriage group 12.9 per cent were large families while in the mixed-marriage group only 7.9 per cent. The difference here is significant, revealing again apparently the difference in the national composition of the two groups.

RELIGION

Differences in religion are recognized as having a causative relation to desertion, according to Miss Colcord.[1] Again her data were taken from the study by Miss Brandt,[2] in which it was found that there was a difference in religion in 19 per cent of the cases. The statistical procedure is of course fallacious, because of the lack of comparison with a control group. In reality, however, this conclusion has been based upon contact with and analysis of cases, and may be true nevertheless.

One method of testing out the hypothesis that differ-

[1] *Op. cit.*, p. 26.   [2] *Op. cit.*

ences in religion tend to cause discord would be to classify cases by years of married life for that group in which the religion is the same and that where it is different. Ordinarily, only extreme religious differences are considered, as between Catholic, Protestant, and Jewish. Defining as "like religion" those cases in which both persons were Protestant, Catholic, or Jewish, and as "mixed religions" those in which there was

TABLE XXX

DURATION OF MARRIED LIFE	TOTAL		RELIGIOUS STATUS				
			Like-Religion		Mixed-Religion		Not Reported
	Number	Percent-age	Number	Percent-age	Number	Percent-age	
Total.....	2,661	100.0	2,205	100.0	416	100.0	40
0–4..........	1,268	47.7	1,012	46.0	234	56.4	22
5–9..........	627	23.6	537	24.4	81	19.5	9
10–14........	371	13.9	316	14.4	49	11.8	6
15–19........	206	7.7	179	8.1	25	6.1	2
20–24........	96	3.6	84	3.8	12	2.9	......
25–29........	45	1.7	36	1.6	9	2.2	......
30–44........	31	1.2	27	1.2	3	0.7	1
Not reporting..	17	0.6	14	0.6	3	0.7	......

any combination of the three, Table XXX is obtained. In this table there is a significant difference in the proportion of cases in the two groups for the first five-year period, there being proportionately more where there was a difference in religion. From this it would seem that difference in religion hastens discord for the group which comes to the Court of Domestic Relations. One cannot be sure, however, that other factors were constant, so that these may have been fundamental and religion only incidental.

One can, however, go back to the distinction between like marriages and mixed marriages and compare the differ-

ence in thé duration of married life in the two groups for
Catholics or for Protestants with intermarriages between
Catholics and Protestants. For the mixed marriages the
distribution was substantially the same for the three religious groups (see Table XXXI). At least where there was a

TABLE XXXI

DISTRIBUTION OF DESERTIONS BY FIVE-YEAR PERIODS OF MARRIED
LIFE AND BY RELIGIONS: MIXED MARRIAGES

YEARS OF MARRIED LIFE	TOTAL		RELIGION							
	Num-ber	Per-cent-age	Cath.		Prot.		Cath.-Prot.		Jew.-Prot. or Cath.		N.R.*
			Num-ber	Per-cent-age	Num-ber	Per-cent-age	Num-ber	Per-cent-age	Num-ber	Per-cent-age	Num-ber
Total...	936	100.0	344	100.0	303	100.0	244	100.0	31	100.0	14
0–4........	499	53.5	188	54.7	150	49.5	131	53.7	22	72.0	8
5–9........	230	24.6	85	24.9	79	26.0	54	22.1	7	22.6	5
10–14.......	104	11.1	41	11.9	35	11.5	25	10.2	2	6.4	1
15–19.......	55	5.9	15	4.3	23	7.6	17	7.0	....	.....	....
20–24.......	24	2.6	10	2.9	7	2.3	7	2.8	....	.....	....
25–29.......	12	1.3	3	0.9	4	1.3	5	2.0	....	.....	....
30–44.......	9	0.9	1	0.3	5	1.6	3	1.2	....	.....	....
Not reporting	3	0.3	1	0.3	....	.....	2	0.8	....	.....	....

* Not reported.

difference in nationality the added difference between religions seems to have been of little or no significance. The
situation was, however, somewhat different for the like-
marriage group. Here the proportion of desertions within
the first four years of married life was significantly higher
for the Protestants as compared to the Catholics, and higher
than either of these for the intermarriages between Catholics
and Protestants (see Table XXXII).[1] This seems to indicate

[1] If comparison is made between the proportion of desertions within the
first four years of married life for intermarriages between Catholics and
Protestants with the combined proportion of Catholics and Protestants,

that the probability of desertion is increased where there are religious differences but no differences in nationality. The difference between the Catholics and Protestants is probably to be accounted for as the result of difference in the national composition of the two groups.

TABLE XXXII

DISTRIBUTION OF DESERTIONS BY FIVE-YEAR PERIODS OF MARRIED LIFE AND BY RELIGIONS: LIKE MARRIAGES

YEARS OF MARRIED LIFE	TOTAL		RELIGION								
			Cath.		Prot.		Cath.-Prot.		Jewish		N.R.*
	Number	Percentage	Number	Percentage	Number	Percentage	Number	Percentage	Number	Percentage	Number
Total..	1,725	100.0	667	100.0	711	100.0	141	100.0	180	100.0	26
0–4.......	769	44.6	236	35.2	350	49.4	81	57.5	88	49.0	14
5–9.......	397	23.0	157	23.6	169	23.8	20	14.2	47	26.1	4
10–14......	267	15.5	143	21.4	78	11.0	22	15.6	19	10.6	5
15–19......	151	8.7	68	10.2	60	8.4	8	5.7	13	7.2	2
30–24......	72	4.2	41	6.2	23	3.2	5	3.5	3	1.7	....
25–29......	33	1.9	10	1.5	14	2.0	4	2.8	5	2.8	....
30–44......	22	1.3	8	1.2	10	1.4	....	.....	3	1.7	1
Not reporting..	14	0.8	4	0.6	7	1.0	1	0.7	2	1.1	....

* Not reported.

On the other hand, if comparison is made between like marriages and mixed marriages for each religious group, it is found that there was no substantial differences in the distributions by years of married life except in the case of the Catholics. Here, apparently, the difference in nationality was the significant factor, assuming that the national composition of both Catholic groups was constant. The con-

which seems to be a reasonable base, the difference could not have occurred by chance oftener than once in a thousand trials. It can hardly be therefore the result of chance alone.

clusion seems to be, then, that differences in nationality are more significant than differences in religion as factors in family desertion. This does not, however, solve the problem as to whether or not there are just as great religious differences within the Protestant group itself, nor the related problem regarding the negligibility of certain differences in nationality as compared to others.

The problem here seems to resolve itself into whether or not the causes used in desertion statistics are fundamental or only indicative of more elemental factors. The statistics presented here seem to indicate the latter. This problem will be discussed at length in a later chapter. Here it is sufficient to show what are the errors arising in the use of the statistical method in studying the problem of desertion.

SHORTCOMINGS OF STATISTICS

The following fallacies in the application of the statistical method have been pointed out: (1) prediction of trend upon too short a series of years; (2) failure to take into account the changes in the definition of desertion as an administrative concept in interpreting trends; (3) failure to substitute a ratio for the absolute number of cases per year; (4) inadequacy of base with which to compare distributions by such factors as nationality, number of children, religion, etc.; (5) failure to eliminate chance results by comparison with the standard error of sampling; and (6) assumption that the factors measured are significant without further analysis.

In addition to the limitations pointed out in the application of the statistical method, the monographic method for a city as large as Chicago is also dubious. The use of this method assumes that the population of the community is homogeneous. Actually, there are many communities in

Chicago, each having its own distinct characteristics. In fact, these communities may exhibit the widest differences, as between a suburban neighborhood and a rooming-house district. To give full meaning to statistics of divorce and desertion, then, they should be collected upon the basis of these homogeneous parts rather than for the heterogeneous whole. Or, if collected for the whole city, the cases may be redistributed by the use of a spot map and considered with reference to the local areas to which they belong.

CHAPTER V

THE ECOLOGY OF FAMILY DISORGANIZATION

Statistics of family disintegration, such as of divorce and desertion, collected upon the basis of political areas are misleading whenever such areas do not possess the cultural homogeneity assumed for them. A city like Chicago is made up of not one area but of many areas—resident neighborhoods, industrial communities, immigrant colonies, rooming-house districts—all tending to have certain distinctive cultural characteristics. Instead of a homogeneous population there is a heterogeneity of population by racial and national origin, by economic status, by marital conditions, and by cultural type. Certainly, statistics of divorce and desertion compiled and tabulated for the entire city of Chicago will mean little or nothing for any one of these areas.

This inadequacy of statistics for the whole of Chicago to be significant for localities may be suggested by a comparison of an immigrant colony with a cosmopolitan community. "Back of the Yards," where the population is almost exclusively Catholic and largely foreign born, the divorce rate is low. On the Lower North Side, with its rooming-house population tending toward the Bohemian type, the divorce rate is comparatively high. Moreover, the ratio of divorces in either of these areas varies considerably from that for the whole of Chicago. Even the layman recognizes the difficulties involved in assuming that the divorce rate for all of Chicago is an adequate expression of that in any particular area, just as he recognizes that any interpretation of the rate for the city would not apply adequately to either of the two areas mentioned. He would say, "But the people in these two areas are so different. How can the explanation you give for all apply to one area as well as to the other when they have so little in common?" By this question he recognizes in his own way the need for considering statistical data with reference to local areas.

There are cultural differences in the various areas of the city which need to be taken into account. These find expression not only in the formal but in the informal life of the communities. They are reflected in the activities and interests of the people. Standards vary from neighborhood to neighborhood. What is considered moral in one community may be judged immoral in another. Even the institutions are not the same in all. Family life, for example, is quite a different thing in Washington Heights from what it is in the Ghetto.[1] This difference is reflected in the way in which the family becomes disorganized.

ECOLOGY OF FAMILY LIFE

Areas of the city may be classified with reference to the type of family life found in each community. Chicago, from this point of view, may be divided into five types of areas: (1) non-family areas, (2) emancipated family areas, (3) paternal family areas, (4) equalitarian family areas, and (5) maternal family areas.

The non-family areas tend also to be one-sex areas, i.e., predominately male. These may be represented by the Loop, Greektown, Chinatown, Hobohemia, Bohemia, and

[1] Washington Heights is a high-class residential area of the restricted type; the Ghetto is a slum area into which the poor immigrant Jew drifted before the current restrictions were placed upon immigration.

the areas of hotels which cater to transients. In the growth of the city these areas tend to find a place in or near the center.

The areas of the emancipated family are the rooming-house areas, the kitchenette-apartment areas, and the residential-hotel areas. Garfield Park is such an area, as are also Oakland and Wilson Avenue. The so-called "emancipated" family feels itself freed from the conventions which have been the anathema of feminism. There are no children; relations with the neighborhood are casual or of the "touch-and-go" sort; the interests of both husband and wife lie outside the home; both are employed for the most part, though not necessarily.

Paternal family areas are those of the proletariat and the immigrant. Here the husband is superior and superordinate in the home. The size of families is large. The interests of the wife are confined to the affairs of the home and the care of the children. This type of family is characteristic of the tenement areas and the immigrant colonies, as, for example, the Ghetto and Little Sicily.

The equalitarian family areas are those of the middle and professional classes. Here there are children, though families tend to be small. There is the minimum of superordination and subordination in the relationship between husband and wife in these areas. The wife has interests outside the home, delegating the care of the children largely to a nurse-maid. Representative communities of this type are residential districts like Edgewater, Windsor Park, Hyde Park, Kenwood, and Ravenswood.

The maternal family areas are those of the commuter. These are outlying districts characterized by single dwellings, typically bungalows, and by large yards. There are children here also. These areas are those, primarily, of the upper bourgeoisie. Here the wife tends naturally to become the head of the family, at least so far as neighborhood relations are concerned. For the husband is absent from home most of the time, since he is employed in the central business district (in Chicago, the Loop). Any interest taken in the affairs of the community falls to the wife. Representative areas with this type of family life are Edison Park, Washington Heights, and Beverly Hills.

In a city the size of Chicago these different areas just described tend to take an idealized form of concentric circles. This form is shown in Chart X. The first or innermost circle is that of the non-family areas. This includes the downtown business district and the areas immediately adjoining. The second circle represents the paternal family areas. In this area land values are high, but the buildings are not adapted to the uses to which the land will eventually be put by the invading commercial and industrial development. Until the invasion is complete, low rents make this area a favorable location for immigrant colonies, rooming-houses, and vice. The emancipated family is found here also, though it is hardly characteristic of it. In fact, the areas of the emancipated family tend to be interstitial, in the sense that they spread across other areas, following the lines of rapid transportation.

The third circle is that of the equalitarian family areas. This is the true apartment area where there is considerable movement, but movement which tends to keep the home of the family within the same community for a considerable length of time. Transportation is by surface cars, elevated railways, automobiles, motor coaches, and even steam railways. Beyond this is the outer circle of the maternal family areas. The homes in this area are single houses constructed largely in accordance with a code of building restrictions.

CHART X

FAMILY AREAS IN CHICAGO, 1920

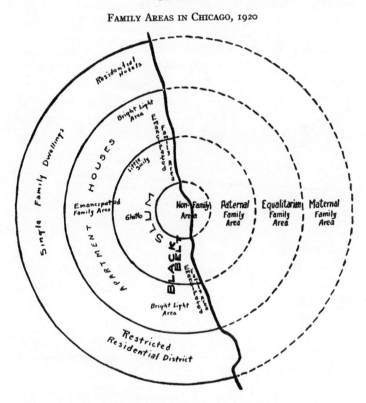

The automobile and the commuters' "Special" are the chief means of transportation.

But how do these areas become differentiated? What are the forces making for segregation? What determines the boundaries of communities? How does this process of differentiation affect the family? In what way is family disorganization related: first, to the variations in the cultural life of the city represented by these different communities; and, second, to the forces making for segregation?

GROWTH OF THE CITY

As the city grows, there is not merely an increase in the number of buildings, an expansion over a larger territory, or a multiplication of avenues of communication; a process of segregation and differentiation also takes place which gives character to the areas of the city. Institutions and residences spread out in centrifugal fashion from the center of the city tending always to find the most advantageous position. The population is drawn, likewise, by its interests to those parts of the city which are favorable for survival and success. This process of selection is not wholly conscious on the part of each individual, though it may be largely so.[1]

Transportation has not only accelerated the growth of the city, but it has also determined the direction of its growth. Extension of transportation lines not only draws the outer areas of the city toward the business center in time, but it draws business out of the central areas as well. As a result there grows up a series of subcenters which tend to break up further the community into areas bounded by thoroughfares, railways, street-car lines, bus lines, elevated lines, etc. The city becomes, thus, a network of intercrossing barriers differentiating areas which have their own peculiar selective and cultural characteristics. These characteristics act as a magnet in drawing to the area those social types which are appropriate and repelling those which are incon-

[1] A resident of Lawndale remarked that those families who want home life and children move from Lawndale to Albany Park; those who want to have "a good time" go to Wilson Avenue.

gruous. Thus there are family and non-family areas, class areas, racial areas, occupational areas, and cultural areas. Even the age and sex distributions vary for the different areas.

Systems of communication—the newspaper, the telephone, the telegraph, and the radio—also have a profound influence upon the growth of the city. They tend to counteract differentiation and segregation upon the basis of external characteristics such as race, and substitute for these or accentuate the more subtle interests such as aesthetic interests and philosophies of life.

Another factor in the growth of the city is that of industrial expansion. Industries tend to locate along the railways and waterways; light manufacturing just outside the area taken by business and heavy manufacturing at outlying points. The light-manufacturing zone constantly encroaches upon the area held for residential purposes, and thus lowers its value for residence. This causes a selection by this area of those elements in the population, who, either because of low financial status can find a foothold nowhere else, or because of low repute cannot remain securely elsewhere.

On the other hand, the location of heavy manufacturing at outlying points tends to build up colonies of workers about such industries, while the management lives outside these districts. Sub-business centers tend also to grow up in these areas producing, in so far as family life is concerned, the same differentiation of areas which characterizes the city as a whole.

Inventions and discoveries influence profoundly the growth of the city and its accompanying differentiation of areas. Both are, obviously, largely responsible for the extensions of transportation and communication as well as for industrial expansion. Fashions in the construction and furnishing of houses and the increasing size of motion-picture theaters are only two of the many illustrations of the effect of discoveries and inventions upon the differentiation of local communities within the city. But more than that, they introduce new forces which act either as attractive or.repellant drives upon the diverse elements in the population.

Inventions and discoveries produce specialization in industry which tends to create a specialization in the interests of the population elements. By a process of segregation these elements invade a community and make it their own, drawn by certain characteristics which repel discordant elements either within or without.

It is in the growth of the city, then, that communities become differentiated: first, in terms of structure which serves as a selective force in the distribution of population; second, in terms of institutions which come to serve the differentiated local groups. The result is to give to the city a wide variety of cultural areas which mold even the family life into a diversity of forms. Five types of areas with reference to family life have been described in this chapter revealling four types of families. These are, however, almost as wide variations within each type as between types of families. A more thorough study of family types in such a city as Chicago is likely to reveal a much more complex, but more exact, classification, which will take into account differences which have passed unobserved or have been ignored.

DISTRIBUTION OF FAMILY DISINTEGRATION

In 1919 6,094 divorces were granted by the Circuit and Superior courts of Cook County, Illinois. In 4,333 cases the addresses of the plaintiffs have been plotted on a map of the city of Chicago.[1] During the year 1921 there were 2,661 cases heard in the Chicago Court of Domestic Relations. The addresses of the plaintiffs in 2,311 cases were plotted also.[2] The distribution of these cases serves as an index of the distribution of family disintegration. It is assumed that within the two intervening years between the divorce and desertion (non-support) cases there had been no fundamental change in the distribution of family disintegration. Inasmuch as this is primarily a study in methodology such an assumption, obviously, varies from the truth so little as to be of little or no consequence.

Ecologically, Chicago may be divided into seventy communities. The rate of family disintegration for each can be calculated in terms of the population and correlated with the cultural factors in each area. In Table XXXIII the index of family disintegration has been computed for each of these seventy communities.

It is to be seen, thus, that family disintegration varies widely by communities, the range being from none at all to 68 per 10,000 population.[3] The average for the city is 25 per 10,000 persons, but this can have little meaning when the range is so great.

[1] About 2.6 per cent of the total number of cases are known to have fallen outside Chicago. In 27 per cent of the remainder either the address was not given, or if given was found to be incorrect or incomplete. In the comparison of these statistics by areas with those of another city it will be necessary, therefore, to multiply the figures given for Chicago communities by 1.375 in order to put them upon a comparable basis.

[2] In 14 per cent of these cases the address was either not given, or incompletely or inaccurately given. The figures for Chicago communities must therefore be multiplied by 1.155 before being compared with statistics for areas in any other city.

[3] This rate of 68 per 10,000 population for a high-class rooming-house and apartment-house area exceeds that of any state in the United States, with the exception of Nevada.

TABLE XXXIII

Family Disorganization in Chicago by Communities

Community	Pop. in 10,000's	Total		Divorce		Desertion	
		Number	Per 10,000 Pop.	Number	Per 10,000 Pop.	Number	Per 10,000 Pop.
Total............	270.1	6,644	25	4,333	16	2,311	9
Neither divorce nor desertion:							
Ardale Park........	0.2	0	0	0	0	0	0
Clearing-Glendale...	0.2	0	0	0	0	0	0
Galewood..........	0.1	0	0	0	0	0	0
Hegewisch..........	0.6	0	0	0	0	0	0
Irondale...........	0.1	0	0	0	0	0	0
Rosehill............	0.3	0	0	0	0	0	0
South Deering......	0.6	1	2	1	2	0	0
Norwood Park......	0.3	1	3	1	3	0	0
Cheltenham........	2.6	4	2	3	2	1	0
Avalon Park........	0.6	6	10	5	8	1	2
East Side..........	1.4	11	8	11	8	0	0
West Pullman......	1.5	15	10	12	8	3	2
Washington Heights.	2.4	15	6	13	5	2	1
Desertion:							
Kelvin Park........	1.6	17	11	9	6	8	5
California..........	7.6	91	12	34	4	57	8
Back of the Yards...	3.6	46	13	15	4	31	9
Cragin.............	1.3	17	13	10	8	7	5
Mt. Clare-Olive.....	0.7	9	13	5	7	4	6
Bowmanville.......	1.9	26	14	17	9	9	5
Lawndale..........	10.5	148	14	97	9	51	5
West Englewood....	4.6	74	16	40	9	34	7
McKinley Park.....	2.3	39	17	18	8	21	9
Sherman Park......	4.4	85	19	37	8	48	11
Bridgeport.........	6.5	155	24	58	9	97	15
Divorce:							
Edison Park........	0.1	1	10	1	10	0	0
Oakdale............	0.2	2	10	2	10	0	0
Northwest..........	2.1	23	11	20	10	3	1
South Chicago......	1.5	16	11	15	10	1	1
Roseland...........	3.8	47	12	40	10	7	2
Chicago Lawn......	0.4	5	13	4	10	1	3
Austin.............	7.2	103	14	76	11	27	3
Ravenswood........	1.4	20	14	16	11	4	3
Rogers Park........	3.0	43	14	39	13	4	1
Grand Crossing.....	2.5	38	15	28	11	10	4
Windsor Park.......	3.5	57	16	42	12	15	4

TABLE XXXIII—*Continued*

COMMUNITY	POP. IN 10,000's	TOTAL		DIVORCE		DESERTION	
		Number	Per 10,000 Pop.	Number	Per 10,000 Pop.	Number	Per 10,000 Pop
Divorce:—*Cont.*							
Burnside............	0.3	5	17	4	13	1	4
Gage Park.........	1.7	28	17	22	13	6	4
Montrose...........	6.2	106	17	78	13	28	4
Edgewater.........	5.2	97	19	84	16	13	3
Normal Park.......	1.2	26	22	21	18	5	4
South Park Manor..	0.6	14	23	12	20	2	3
Wilson Avenue......	2.3	157	68	146	64	11	4
Both divorce and desertion:							
Brighton Park......	3.3	52	16	32	10	20	6
Englefields.........	1.1	18	16	12	11	6	5
Auburn Park.......	2.0	33	17	20	10	13	7
Eureka.............	4.7	82	17	45	10	37	7
Portage Park.......	2.1	38	18	25	12	13	6
Logan Square.......	14.0	263	19	134	10	129	9
Dauphin Park......	0.3	6	20	3	10	3	10
Riverview..........	4.5	92	20	59	13	33	7
Humboldt Park.....	23.4	490	21	268	11	222	10
Englewood.........	9.5	206	22	141	15	65	7
Pilsen..............	8.3	186	22	82	10	104	12
Marquette Park.....	0.4	10	25	6	15	4	10
Ireland.............	1.4	36	26	14	10	22	16
Lakeview..........	13.9	356	26	254	18	102	8
Lincoln Park.......	5.8	159	27	109	19	50	8
Hyde Park.........	3.7	105	28	85	23	20	5
Garfield Park......	9.9	287	29	203	21	84	8
Kenwood...........	2.1	67	32	56	27	11	5
Near Westside......	19.7	660	34	409	21	251	13
Woodlawn..........	6.2	222	36	177	29	45	7
Corwith............	0.2	8	40	6	30	2	10
Lower North.......	8.4	337	40	235	28	102	12
Near South.........	2.5	106	42	67	27	39	15
Washington Park....	5.2	253	49	194	37	59	12
Loop..............	1.3	69	53	61	47	8	6
Black Belt.........	8.1	447	55	276	34	171	21
Oakland...........	3.5	194	55	153	44	41	11
Douglas...........	4.8	314	65	171	36	143	29

DIVORCE AND DESERTION

Chicago communities may further be classified with reference to the distribution of divorce and desertion: (1) areas without desertion and divorce, (2) areas of desertion, (3) areas of divorce, and (4) areas of desertion and divorce.[1] The distinction between each class is relative, rather than absolute, for there are few areas having only one form of family disintegration and still fewer having none.

The areas without desertion and divorce are Ardale Park, Clearing-Glendale, South Deering, Hegewisch, Irondale, Galewood, East Side, West Pullman, Washington Heights, Cheltenham, Avalon Park, Rosehill, and Norwood Park.

Areas having only desertion are West Englewood, Sherman Park, Back of the Yards, Bridgeport, McKinley Park, California, Lawndale, Kelvin Park, Cragin, Mount Clare-Olive, and Bowmanville.

Divorce areas are Edison Park, Rogers Park, Northwest, Montrose, Ravenswood, Wilson Avenue, Edgewater, Austin, Gage Park, Chicago Lawn, South Park Manor, Grand Crossing, Burnside, Normal Park, Windsor Park, Roseland, South Chicago, and Oakdale.

Areas having both divorce and desertion are Dauphin Park, Auburn Park, Englefields, Marquette Park, Woodlawn, Hyde Park, Kenwood, Washington Park, Ireland, Englewood, Corwith, Black Belt, Oakland, Douglas, Near South, Pilsen, Brighton Park, Loop, Lower North, Lincoln Park, Near Westside, Garfield Park, Humboldt Park, Eureka, Lakeview, Riverview, Logan Square, and Portage Park.

Comparison of this classification of areas with reference

[1] See chart XI for a graphic presentation of this classification.

CHART XI

AREAS OF FAMILY DISINTEGRATION IN CHICAGO, 1920

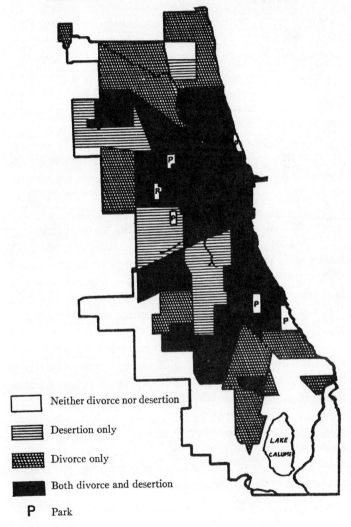

Neither divorce nor desertion

Desertion only

Divorce only

Both divorce and desertion

P Park

to family disintegration with the earlier classification of family areas reveals these correlations: (1) maternal family areas and the communities in which there is no family disintegration; (2) paternal family areas and communities having only desertion; (3) equalitarian family areas and both divorce and desertion, as well as those areas in which there is divorce only. The emancipated family, being an interstitial group, ecologically, cannot be said to be correlated with any particular group of communities classed with reference to family disintegration.

These results reveal, then, the great disparity between the rate of family disintegration in one part of the city and that of another. Interpretation would depend, therefore, upon having a complete knowledge of the cultural characteristics of each area or community. But such a procedure would be a distinct departure from the method ordinarily employed in the interpretation of statistical data. Such, however, is necessary unless one is willing to ignore such differences as that of the rate of family disintegration for Hegewisch, in which there was neither divorce nor desertion, and the rate for Wilson Avenue, where the combined rate was 68 per 10,000 persons.

This study of statistics of family disintegration with reference to the natural areas of the city definitely relates family disintegration to the cultural life of the area. In so doing it exhibits the wide differences in social life in a metropolitan area. It suggests that certain areas, like immigrant colonies, are more rural in outlook on life than districts in the so-called "open country." It calls attention to possible correlations of desertion and divorce rates with ratios of rooming-houses, apartments, mobility of population, etc.

Nevertheless, social statistics even when given this ecological setting retain the fundamental limitations of the statistical method when applied to the analysis of common-sense data. While trends may be determined and comparisons made, no description or explanation of the processes of family disorganization are possible so long as the data subjected to statistical treatment are those having to do with the events of common sense, e.g., divorce and desertion. For such statistics are always limited to external traits in the behavior of individuals which are susceptible to enumeration or measurement. As such they do not deal directly with the phenomenon of the interaction of personalities in marriage. And the description and explanation of this interplay of attitudes between husband and wife, and between parents and children, is the chief objective of sociological research upon the family. Another method, that of the case-study, has been introduced into social work and sociology which has already accumulated materials which may be examined for the light they throw upon the process, or processes, of family disorganization.

PART III
CASE-STUDY METHODS

CHAPTER VI

FAMILY DISORGANIZATION AS A PROCESS

Statistics of family disintegration, i.e., of divorce and of desertion, have been concerned primarily, as has been seen, with the measurement of this phenomenon in order to discover three things: (1) the extent of disintegration, (2) the historical trend, and (3) the causal factors. Counting the number of cases within an area for a particular year gave the extent in absolute numbers for that area. Ratios, if desired, could then be computed from these data with reference to whatever data were thought to show significant relationships. Measurement of the extent of family disintegration at regular historical intervals gave a picture of the trend for a particular area.[1] Here, again, the data were considered either in absolute numbers or in ratios. In the determination of the relative weight of causal factors, however, emphasis was directed almost exclusively to ratios, i.e., the proportion to the whole of the number of cases representing any one causal factor.[2]

[1] No attempt has been made in this study to take directly into account the method of correlating social phenomena with the business cycle developed in three recent studies: Thomas, *Social Aspects of the Business Cycle;* Hexter, *Social Consequences of Business Cycles;* Ogburn and Thomas, "The Influence of the Business Cycle on Certain Social Conditions," *Journal of the American Statistical Association*, XVIII (Sept., 1922), 340. Some attention has been given in each of these studies to divorce (see chap. iii in the book by Thomas and chap. vi in Hexter's monograph). The writer, in view of the recent publication of the two first-mentioned studies, has reserved discussion of them for a subsequent volume on family disorganization.

[2] It should be remembered, however, that the selection of the particular factors to be tested as to whether or not they represented "causal" factors

The measurements of extent and trend involved simply the counting of events defined in the legal codes of states or municipalities or in the administrative procedure of courts or social agencies. As has been pointed out, these definitions are functions of both the legislative and administrative processes and so vary within rather wide limits.[1] In so far, then, as the statistical data representing extent and trends are inadequate, one or both of the following factors are involved: (1) the addition of units which were not commensurable because of variance in either the legislative or administrative process, or (2) the failure to define sociologically the events counted.[2]

---

preceded the application of the statistical method. The error in the selection of such factors cannot, therefore, be laid to the statistical method, but rather to the logical assumptions with which the investigator started.

[1] Divorce, for example, is one thing in Nevada, where the business men of Reno capitalize the lax divorce laws of the state; another thing in New York, where adultery is practically the only cause; and still quite a different thing in South Carolina, where it occurs only by act of the legislature. Desertion, likewise, varies from place to place. If a man leaves his wife without support in a city where there is a charity organization to which she can appeal for financial aid, that may be called "desertion," though not in the legal sense. But if a husband fails to support his wife and there is a law which penalizes his failure to support her, that is "non-support," or "desertion" as it has been called in this study. If there is no charity organization nor any court-enforced law against non-support, then there will be no desertion in the legal sense in that area, just as there is no divorce in South Carolina.

[2] This may, of course, be stated the other way about. There is no necessity for defining events sociologically so long as one does not imply in his interpretation that he has done so. The fallacy in using divorce and desertion as events to be enumerated lies in the temptation to interpret one's statistics as though these events represented something other than that embodied in the definition implied in the legislative and administrative processes. One can, therefore, escape this difficulty by interpreting his statistical data strictly in conformity with the implied definition; the inadequacy of most analyses lying thus in the sociological interpretation of units not so

The analysis of causal factors in statistical studies has depended, on the other hand, upon the enumeration of isolated traits or attributes which, for some empirical reason, were thought to be significant. Even for these attributes the investigator has tried in some cases to shift the responsibility for his selection to the legislative and administrative processes, as, for example, in the selection of legal causes as the explanatory causes of divorce. In other cases he has depended largely upon common-sense definitions of causal relations which too often involved moral implications.[1]

It is thus in the analysis of causal factors that the statistical method becomes the most hopeless in its contribution to a fundamental explanation of family disorganization. But the fallacies arising out of such analysis are not so much the result of limitations in the statistical method as of the fallacious logic which accompanies its application. The fallacies in the logic arose from reasoning from a legalistic or common-sense definition of causes as defined by a legislature or administrative bureau to an interpretation in sociological terms.[2]

---

defined. The temptation, for example, is to assume that there is no family disintegration in a community where there is no record of divorce or desertion. But families break up, whether or not this is called "divorce" or "desertion." Husbands leave their wives and wives leave their husbands, whether or not the law forbids or recognizes it. Not only that, but where there is divorce and desertion there may be many more cases of separation than those which get into court. Furthermore, there are many cases of family discord in which there is no open break such as divorce or desertion, or even separation. Yet these marginal cases are, perhaps, the most significant for an understanding of the processes of family disorganization.

[1] See the classification of causes by Misses Brandt and Colcord in the following chapter.

[2] There can be, for example, no logical objection to the statement that desertion is the cause of more than half of the divorces in the United States

Such a treatment of factors as causal elements, currently involved in the application of statistical method, also raises the question as to whether or not human behavior can be treated as belonging to an atomic rather than to an organic system. That is, can human behavior be broken up into parts, each part being considered not in integral relationship to every other part in the same organism but rather in relationship to other parts in a group of organisms?[1]

Statistics of the causes of family disintegration assume the individual but nowhere do they take him into account as a functioning organism. Such data do not give, therefore, a description of family disorganization as a process in terms either of individual responses or of interaction. Neither do they take into account the fact that the family itself is a changing relationship. Rather they assume that there is only one form of family organization, definitely recognized and fixed. In this way such data imply a categorical conception

---

provided one interpret such a statement to mean only that in more than one-half the cases where a judge, acting in accordance with the procedure defined by the legislative process and upon the basis of evidence submitted in conformity with the legal requirements, decides that such evidence warrants legal sanction to the separation of husband and wife because one party has been guilty (though not if both are equally guilty) or committing an act, i.e., desertion, legally declared sufficient cause for a decree of divorce. There is nothing ambiguous nor illogical in such a statement so interpreted, though the word "cause" is used in something other than the "natural" sense, and divorce represents a legal act and not a sociological one.

[1] Ritchie has defined an atomic system as "one in which the laws of the parts composing the aggregate are not altered by the fact of their being parts of the aggregate so that laws of the aggregate as a whole are some simple function of the laws of the independent parts. An organic system on the other hand is such that the parts act differently when combined and in isolation, so that the law of the aggregate may not be a function of the laws of the separate parts at all, or, if it is, is a very complex function."—*Scientific Method: An Inquiry into the Character and Validity of Natural Laws*, p. 179.

of family disorganization, rather than recognizing the relative disorganization of all families.[1]

It is this tendency of the family to lose its unity which is, in fact, of primary importance in the control of family disintegration. Ordinarily, an understanding of the disintegration of the family is of no use because the process of disorganization has been completed and nothing can be done about it. But to understand the way in which families become disorganized, not as a group phenomenon but in terms of the interaction of the principals in the case, necessitates an appreciation of the changes in relations between husband and wife which are typical of disintegrating families.[2] This

[1] Family disintegration is likely to imply, and probably does in the minds of most persons, a static conception of family relations. A "disintegrated" family is one which has lost all unity, i.e., a marriage relationship which is only a family in terms of the past—its identity having been lost by the complete differentiation of attitudes of its members. Family "disorganization," on the other hand, implies a relative differentiation of interests and aims of its members in terms of another or other family groups. Disorganization may be partial or complete, varying over a wide range in the degree of disorganization. In this sense all cases of family disintegration represent family disorganization, but all the cases of family disorganization are in no wise included in those of family disintegration, the former being the more inclusive group.

[2] The chief difficulty with the statistical method of analysis based upon an atomic conception of social phenomena is that it furnishes, ordinarily, an understanding of the phenomenon studied only as a group experience. Control, therefore, depends upon manipulation of the group, which ordinarily is a difficult thing. The case-study method, however, based upon an organic conception of the individual, furnishes an understanding of a phenomenon in terms of the relationship between factors in the experience of the individual, who can be more easily manipulated for purposes of control. The situation in the study of family disintegration is comparable to that in medicine where the statistical study of typhoid fever, let us say, shows the relationship between a typhoid "epidemic" and the water supply of an area, but does not afford any basis for diagnosis and treatment of the individual cases making up the "epidemic." Family disintegration in the ordinary

conception of disorganization as a process implies, also, that the identification of interests, characteristic of highly organized families, results from interaction and involves changing attitudes. But such a change in relations from the beginning of courtship on into what is more strictly family life is also a process running counter to that of disorganization.

A review of the literature of family organization may be useful, accordingly, in defining the constructive process of family organization as a preliminary to a definition of family disorganization. It may be anticipated, of course, that family organization will be described in static terms in the earlier literature. But this will not detract from the usefulness of such a review because some conception of the form of family organization is a logical prerequisite to the discovery and description of the process whereby families become disorganized.

STUDIES IN FAMILY ORGANIZATION

While the literature upon the family is voluminous, it yields only a limited number of studies which have attempted to describe family organization objectively. Such studies may be classified by the point of view from which each writer approached the description or analysis of family organization as (1) historical, (2) anthropological, (3) philosophical,

---

sense with which statistical analysis has been concerned is accordingly an "epidemic" of family disorganization. But for purposes of control an understanding of family disintegration is much less effective than that of family disorganization, just as in the illustration given control depends upon understanding individual cases of typhoid rather than the epidemic. It must, of course, be acknowledged that in the case of family disintegration, as in typhoid epidemics, prevention proceeds by understanding the relationships between mass factors rather than those between various attributes within the organism. Nevertheless, prevention is a more difficult problem than treatment and therefore dependent upon the latter.

and (4) psychoanalytical. A fifth type of approach might be added, viz., the sociological, but since such an approach is only suggested in certain brief treatments, rather than actually achieved, little reference is made to this literature.[1]

THE FAMILY AS A SOCIAL INSTITUTION

One type of approach has made use of historical materials, another of anthropological data. Though in certain studies the approach has been exclusively from the historical standpoint,[2] it has more often been combined with descriptions of contemporary family organization among so-called "primitive" peoples.[3] In the latter case the method has been comparative rather than historical. In each case, however, the institutional character of family organization has been the point of approach except in one outstanding study.

Westermarck,[4] while by no means ignoring the institutional character of family organization, by comparing the animal family with that of man gives in effect the greater emphasis to biological factors in the evolution of family organization. He says:

Marriage, so far as I can see, is rooted in instincts which can only be explained by biological facts—either peculiar to mankind and its nearest relatives, or of a more general character—and so are many particular customs and rules relating to marriage. Such instincts have been formed in accordance with the need of the species, which again

[1] See, for example, James Michel Williams, "*Principles of Social Psychology*, chaps. xviii, xix, and xx; Park and Burgess, *An Introduction to the Science of Sociology*, pp. 213–16.

[2] For example, Howard, *History of Matrimonial Institutions;* Calhoun, *A Social History of the American Family.*

[3] A straightforward portrayal of the evolutionary development of the family is represented in Ch. Letourneau, *The Evolution of Marriage and of the Family.*

[4] *History of Human Marriage.*

depends upon anatomical and physiological factors of various kinds. This is true both of the sexual instinct with its peculiarities and of other instincts by which marriage is determined.[1]

Howard,[2] on the other hand, centers his attention upon the legal aspects of the institutional family. He is primarily concerned, accordingly, with the evolution of the legal status of the family institution to the partial though not complete, neglect of its social status.

The fundamental basis of family organization is, according to these studies, the satisfaction of the sex instinct and the care and maintenance of the offspring. By tracing the evolution of the forms of relationship between the sexes, the conclusion is generally stated or implied that monogamy, with relatively permanent relations, best serves in solving the problems presented by these two fundamental needs.[3]

This institutional approach to the study of family organization has been ably defined by Calhoun in the Preface to the first volume of his study:

The three volumes of which this is the first are an attempt to develop an understanding of the forces that have been operative in the evolution of family institutions in the United States. They set forth the nature of the influences that have shaped marriage, controlled fecundity, determined the respective status of father, mother, child, attached relative, and servant, influenced sexual morality, and governed the function of the family as an educational, economic, moral, and spiritual institution as also its relation to state, industry, and society in general in the matter of social control.[4]

[1] *Op. cit.* (5th ed.), I, 22.

[2] *A History of Matrimonial Institutions Chiefly in England and the United States.*

[3] See, for example, Goodsell, *The Family as a Social and Educational Institution*, p. 550; Parsons, *The Family: An Ethnological and Historical Outline*, p. 345.

[4] *Op. cit.*, I, 9.

Anthropological and historical studies of family organization show, thus, that the pattern of family organization has undergone a long evolutionary process—a process, however, continuous from the earliest times. Westermarck thought the process to be biological while in reality it is traditional. Howard and Calhoun appreciated this traditional aspect, though Howard conceived of family organization so strictly in legal terms that he overlooked many important characteristics.

This picture of changing forms of family organization serves as a wholesome corrective to the assumptions of reformers that the pattern of family organization is unchanging, and should be preserved in its traditional form. It does not furnish, however, a description of the process of adjustment in family relations. For anthropology and history have been concerned with descriptions of the evolution of concrete forms or patterns of family organization rather than with family organization as an abstract description of the process of adjustment and accommodation between husband and wife. This latter conception has grown out of the more abstract analyses of philosophers and psychoanalysts, who conceive of family organization as a unity of interacting members. These writers, accordingly, carry on the analysis, at least logically, started by the historians and anthropologists.

THE BASIS OF FAMILY UNITY

Although differing widely in method and in type of data, philosophy and psychoanalysis are not unlike in their conclusions as to the fundamental characteristics of family organization. Though interest and attention is directed toward the interaction of all members of the family, chief emphasis has been placed upon the interaction between child and parent rather than that between husband and wife.

The philosophical approach is best represented by Mrs. Bosanquet,[1] who recognizes the family as a co-operative institution based mainly upon economic interests,[2] but with another bond.

Finally, underlying all others, there is one fundamental bond which I have not yet dwelt upon—it is the primitive instinctive attachment which, with rare exceptions, binds parent to child throughout the whole range of the animal world. It is sometimes called the maternal instinct, as if it were confined to the mother; but though the father may occasionally be more reticent in his demonstrations, it is very doubtful whether his feeling is not just as real and compelling in the first instance. Though the physical tie is not so close as that between the mother and her infant, yet the protective instinct of the strong toward the weak is perhaps even more strongly developed in the man than in the woman.[3]

It is upon the basis of these instinctive tendencies that Mrs. Bosanquet builds her conception of interaction between members of the family out of which develops a psychic unity.

The family type is the theme, of which the individual members are the variations—variations sometimes so changed and complex that only the trained ear can grasp the fundamental theme, and sometimes so broadly simple that every passing listener is caught and smiles to hear the same old tune repeating itself. And however strange and subtle the variations, members of the Family themselves always recognize the theme running below: they are never wholly strange to one another; the chords respond, or echo, or clash, as the case may be.[4]

It is this subtle adjustment of interests between members of the family which gives to it unity and variation from

[1] *The Family.*
[2] *Ibid.*, chap. viii.
[3] *Ibid.*, p. 218.
[4] *Ibid.*, p. 249.

other families and becomes the fundamental bond between the members.

Within such a family intercourse is on a different basis, is of another quality from what it is between members of different families; the very language used takes on a shape of its own which may be hardly intelligible outside. Partly, no doubt, its mystery consists in allusions to experiences shared in common, and needing the merest hint to call them to mind, which are a sealed book to the outsider; but partly also it is the outcome of the fact that certain quaintnesses of expression and turns of thought appeal to, or represent, certain fundamental characteristics shared in by all members of the family.[1]

The psychoanalytic approach may be typified by Flügel's book, *The Psycho-Analytic Study of the Family*. His emphasis, however, is upon the individual product which results from interaction rather than upon the psychic unity of the family itself. In summarizing the descriptive portion of his book he says:

We have traced, with such degree of detail as the scope of this book has permitted, the growth within the individual mind of some of the more important of those feelings and tendencies which owe their origin and development to the relations of the individual to the other members of his family. We have seen how these feelings and tendencies are of fundamental importance in the formation of individual character and how they have also exercised a vast influence on social life and social institutions. We have seen also that, throughout their multitudinous transformations and ramifications, the tendencies originally connected with the family preserve some likeness to their primitive character, being ultimately reducible upon analysis to a series of displacements of a very few original trends and impulses. These original impulses fall naturally into two main groups:—those which bind the individual to the family (or to one or more of its members) through a relationship of love, esteem or dependence; and those which are based on a relationship of hate or fear; the trends falling within each of these groups being manifested whether in a direct and

[1] *Ibid.*, p. 254.

positive, or in a reactionary and negative form; the latter being assumed as the result of a conflict between one of the trends in question and some other trend of an opposite, or at any rate a different, character (very often one of the family trends belonging to the opposite group).[1]

The fundamental characteristic of family organization, according to this conception, is conflict between like sexes and accommodation between opposite sexes. The sex impulse not only binds husband and wife together, but also binds son to mother and daughter to father. The relationship between husband and wife, furthermore, represents a substitution for the earlier relationship between child and parent. The process of family organization is thus a process of adjustment in which one finds full satisfaction for his sexual tendencies—sexual tendencies pervading the whole life of the individual rather than intimately connected only with the reproduction of the species.

From both the philosophical and the psychoanalytic points of view the fundamental basis of family organization lies in the satisfaction of instinctive impulses. Both also emphasize the complementary rôles which various members of the family play, but from different points of view. To the psychoanalyst family unity is to be thought of in terms of repressed conflict, at least so far as the relationship between the child and the parent is concerned. To Mrs. Bosanquet all members tend toward a complete identity of interests in conformity either with the traditional aims of the family or with the objectives dominant at any time.

Unbiased studies of family organization, anthropological, historical, philosophical, and psychoanalytic, have thus

[1] *Op. cit.*, p. 175.

in a sort of progression described the process of family organization first as an evolution of changing patterns, now determined by biological evolution, again by cultural evolution, and finally as a process of interaction between the members of the family. This latter conception of the process paves the way for a more fundamental description of the process of conflict, as involved in family disorganization.

THE "FAMILY COMPLEX"

Studies in family organization may, accordingly, consider the family from three fundamental aspects: (1) as a natural organization for response, (2) as a cultural group, and (3) as a legal entity. Studies of divorce and desertion have treated the family largely as a legal entity alone, thus emphasizing the legal and institutional aspects of its organization. The cure for the problem of family disintegration appeared, therefore, to be a matter of legislation or of administration. The human nature aspects of the family were ignored.

As a natural organization, the family is the union of two human beings of opposite sex, with or without children, largely for the satisfaction which may be obtained by both in intimate relationship. In the human animal the desire for response ("a craving for the more intimate and preferential appreciation of others") is so strong that in every human society of which we know anything, the natural family has existed.

But a family is more than merely a natural organization. It develops within itself certain attitudes, sentiments, and ideals. That is, it develops a culture of its own beyond the culture of the larger community of which it is a part. The members of the family have a common feeling of oneness, a common consciousness of unity as over against other families and other cultural groups. Each family has its own universe of discourse wherein certain things have different meanings to the members of the family than to the outsider, due to a difference in past experiences. The family is, then, a cultural organization as well as a natural organization for response.[1]

Or the family may be defined in terms of attitudes. Thus in its final analysis the family is found to be an organization of attitudes that may be called the "family complex." These attitudes tend to assume the form of intimate identification and consensus between the members of the family, with a feeling of common purpose and of common interests, i.e., family consciousness. The process of family organization may be defined, accordingly, as that process of interaction through which this identification and consensus of interests and purposes is accomplished both in habitual and reflective behavior. It is the process through which attitudes become organized into a "family complex." A definition of the process of family disorganization must harmonize, therefore, with that of family organization.

LOSS OF FAMILY CONSCIOUSNESS

Preliminary to a definition of family disorganization, a clear understanding is essential of two, more general, conceptions: the processes of organization and disorganization. Sociology, like every other science, looks upon the field of experience as in a continual state of change, and attempts to describe this change in terms of processes. The situation with regard to social relations is conceived as closely analogous to the physiological conception of the relations within the individual organism. The physiologist explains the continual change in the substances of which the body is made up as the process of metabolism. He differentiates within

[1] Mowrer, "The Variance between Legal and Natural Causes for Divorce," *Journal of Social Forces* (March, 1924), pp. 388–89.

this process two antagonistic types of processes: anabolism —those processes by which the body is built up, chiefly digestion and assimilation; catabolism—those processes by which worn-out materials are discarded, such as expiration and excretion. Healthy life consists in maintaining an equilibrium between the effects of these two processes. But both operate at the same time and to the same degree so long as the organism remains healthy.

Social relations may be thought of in the same way. Here the two processes are organization and disorganization. The organization of society is made up of the ties between persons. The process of organization consists in the building up of these relations—the process of disorganization as in their breaking down. When these ties are of the most intimate sort between a man and a woman and between parents and children we have family organization.

It should be recalled that in the case of the living organism both the anabolic and the catabolic processes operate simultaneously, though not necessarily to the same degree— depending upon the state of health of the organism. So in human relations organization and disorganization are reciprocal, one being a function of the other. With this methodological approach in mind, the next step is the definition of family disorganization in more precise terms.

Thomas and Znaniecki describe the process of family disorganization by implication in the following excerpt:

The real cause of all phenomena of family disorganization is to be sought in the influence of certain new values—new for the subject— such as: new sources of hedonistic satisfaction, new vanity values, new (individualistic) types of economic organization, new forms of sexual appeal. This influence presupposes, of course, not only a contact between the individual and the outside world but also the existence in the individual's personality of certain attitudes which make

him respond to these new values—hedonistic aspirations, desire for
social recognition, desire for economic security and advance, sexual
instincts. The specific phenomenon of family disorganization consists
in a definite modification of those preëxisting attitudes under the influence of the new values, resulting in the appearance of new, more or
less different attitudes. The nature of this modification can be generally characterized in such a way that, while the attitudes which existed
under the family system were essentially "we"-attitudes (the individual did not dissociate his hedonistic tendencies, his desires for recognition or economic security, his sexual needs from the tendencies and
aspirations of his family group), the new attitudes, produced by the
new values acting upon those old attitudes, are essentially "I"-atti-
tudes—the individual's wishes are separated in his consciousness from
those of other members of his family. Such an evolution implies that
the new values with which the individual gets in touch are individualistic in their meaning, appeal to the individual, not to the group as a
whole; and this is precisely the character of most hedonistic, sexual,
economic, vanity-values.[1]

While Thomas and Znaniecki's description of the process
of family disorganization is essentially based on the large
family group characteristic of Polish peasant life, it reveals
a process not very different from that which occurs where
the family relation includes but two persons. It is necessary,
however, to describe this process with more strict reference
to the marriage relationship.

Let us mean by family disorganization, then, so far as it
concerns the relationship between husband and wife, that
series of events which tends to terminate in the disruption
of the marriage union. It is, in other words, the individualization of behavior in marriage relations, as contrasted with
family organization, which is the tendency toward identification of behavior in marriage relations.

The disintegration of the family may be thought of, ac-

[1] *The Polish Peasant in Europe and America*, IV, 41–42.

cordingly, as a loss of family consciousness, i.e., a disintegration of the familial attitudes which make up the family complex. Divorce and desertion are but forms of family disintegration, and may be taken to indicate the completion of the process of family disorganization, i.e., that series of events leading to the breakdown and discontinuance of the family relationship.

Such a process conception of family disorganization, however, implies an organic relationship between the several elements in the process. Is it not possible, then, that studies of family disorganization from this point of view will necessitate the working out of a method of analysis which recognizes the organic relationship?

THE CASE-STUDY METHOD

A method based upon the assumption that human behavior constitutes an organic system has been introduced, in fact, into the analysis of family disorganization through the study of cases. The case-study has come, as a method, from two diverse sources: history and case-work.[1] Historians, with their wide reaches of facts about society, have resolved their data into descriptions of trends and tendencies. A case for analysis becomes, thus, for them an epoch, a generation, or a century in which each trend is organically related to every other. Case-workers, on the other hand, though often relying upon the statistical method in the analysis of their problems, have been constrained by the

[1] This is not to be interpreted to mean that these are the only sources from which the case-study method has been introduced into the analysis of other social problems. Indeed, to the psychiatrists and the psychoanalysts belongs the credit for introducing it into the analysis of behavior problems of the individual, and to Le Play for showing its possibilities in the study of family life.

nature of their work to take a smaller unit as constituting an organic system, namely, the individual.

The case-study eliminates one of the shortcomings of statistics, which have been found largely futile for solving the problem of family disorganization. Part of this failure has been attributable to poor statistical technique and to slackness in defining concepts in fundamental terms. But may not part of the failure be attributable to the use of a method which assumes the atomicity of human behavior?

Studies of family organization, it is true, have recognized, at least by implication, that human behavior constitutes an organic system. But this assumption gains strength in the analysis of family disorganization through the use of the case-study method, whether attention is directed toward historical trends or toward tendencies in the individual.[1] May not the case-study method, with its concentration upon processes rather than upon isolated traits or events, contribute the solution which statistics failed to give?

[1] Obviously, there are some logical differences between these two approaches. The organic system to the historian consists of all of human life from the beginning. To the case-worker the individual is the organism. The two ideas, however, are not mutually exclusive except in the extreme form where the first becomes an organismic conception of society and the second a biological conception of the individual. The fallacies in the writings of Spencer and Lillienfeld, for example, like those in the discussions of so-called "individual" psychologists, lie in the assumption that either society or the individual constitutes an organic system to the exclusion of the other. Both. as Cooley has pointed out (*Human Nature and the Social Order*, chap. i), seem to be but aspects of the same system.

CHAPTER VII

SOCIAL FORCES IN FAMILY DISORGANIZATION

The introduction of the case-study method[1] into the analysis of family disorganization, as has been suggested, may be credited to two sources: (1) attempts of historians to describe what appeared to be trends and tendencies with reference to family disorganization, and (2) efforts on the part of social workers to diagnose and treat instances of family disintegration.

Tendencies or trends in the sequence of temporal events, or in the movements of thought, the historians have called "social forces." Some of the most important, as they affect the disorganization of the family, are the great movements

[1] By the case-study method is meant a systematic analysis of the relationship between attributes as they appear in combination in any particular instance of a given phenomenon. The unit for study, as Professor Giddings has pointed out (*The Scientific Study of Human Society*, p. 94), may range from one human individual or simply an episode in his life to, let us say, the life-history of a nation or an epoch of world-history. The logic of the procedure is that for some reason or another attention is directed in analysis toward the combination of attributes rather than toward their distribution.

The procedure in the case-study method is in many respects not unlike that of casual observation in that reasoning is inductive rather than deductive. The collection of material is, of course, more systematically prosecuted where the method is that of case-study than where it is of casual observation. In any instance, however, it is often difficult to determine how much the writer's conclusions are the result of one or the other of these two methods of study. Not infrequently one supplements the other.

There is, nevertheless, a decided difference in one respect between the methods of case-study and casual observation. Documentation is an essential aspect of the former method giving to it precision and acceptance which casual observation does not have. Documents may be prepared by the person making the analysis, or he may depend entirely upon the documents of

of modern times, the Reformation, Romanticism, and Individualism. These movements culminate and find their most characteristic expression in the Industrial Revolution and in urban growth. In the cosmopolitan districts of our great cities, we shall expect to find, therefore, the freest operation of the social forces making for the disintegration of the family.

No comprehensive study of the rôle of social forces in family disorganization has yet been essayed. Yet certain books and articles offer at least the essential background for such an inquiry.[1] Moreover, intimations and common-sense

others. In either instance the negative cases are not so likely to escape his attention as when he depends entirely upon casual observation.

While Professor Giddings seems to assume that the case-study method leads to more concreteness in the analysis of attributes than does statistical analysis, because it treats them always in combination with other attributes, such is not necessarily the case. It is true, of course, that one may confine his attention to finding out the relationship between all the attributes within a single case and so be concerned primarily with its uniqueness; one may also do quite otherwise. In fact, the investigator may become so engrossed in observing the resemblances between the combinations in one case and those in others which he has noted as to fail to notice whatever uniqueness exists. Or he may, because he is interested in arriving at abstract combinations, neglect as insignificant certain unique qualities and attend only to those which seem to be significantly similar. In this sense the relationship between attributes becomes of greater importance than the attributes themselves in the case-study method. In this way the case-study method leads to abstractions and generalizations just as surely as does the statistical method. Such generalizations, however, will be in terms of "organic" rather than "atomic" relations.

The description of trends on the part of historians is an illustration, though incomplete, of how this method may be used in arriving at generalized descriptions of sequences. The incompleteness of such historical analysis lies in the failure to carry the method far enough—probably because of lack of data, for so far, at least, history has proved quite fragmentary.

[1] Georg Simmel, *Die Grosstadt und das Geistesleben;* Robert E. Park, "The City," *American Journal of Sociology* (1914–15), pp. 593–609; L. C. A.

appreciations of the play of social forces are to be found in many of the studies of divorce and desertion. These intimations, however, are largely in terms of changes in the economic organization of society rather than in terms of the dominant attitudes resulting from these changes. Lichtenberger devotes a chapter to the analysis of the causal relation of the economic development of the United States to the increase in the divorce rate.[1] Calhoun points out that the flux of modern civilization makes for family disintegration.[2] Cooley's discussion of individualism and romantic love, however, introduces a new note into the analysis of social forces in family disorganization,[3] though there are hints of it in Calhoun, in Goodsell,[4] and even in Lichtenberger.

The impact of certain social forces, individualism, restlessness, the romantic complex, mobility, upon family life might be described either in their historical perspective or in their present-day manifestations. It is perhaps feasible, at least as an experiment in methodology, to combine these two types of approach in a description of the component elements of the *Zeitgeist* of American society.

INDIVIDUALISM AND MARRIAGE EXPERIMENTS

Individualism as a social force is the tendency toward the complete freedom of the individual from social restraint. That is, individualism, as Thomas says, "means the personal

---

Knowles, *The Industrial and Commercial Revolutions in Great Britain during the Nineteenth Century.*

[1] *Divorce: A Study in Social Causation*, chap. x.

[2] *A Social History of the American Family*, III, 266–70.

[3] *Social Organization*, pp. 362–67.

[4] *A History of the Family as a Social and Educational Institution.*

schematization of life,—making one's own definitions of the situation and determining one's own behavior norms."[1] This emancipation from the group is, of course, never completely accomplished.

Individualism in America, like democracy of which it is the beginning, has been accepted in political and economic relations for a longer period than in social relations. However, it could not but penetrate even into this realm of human life.

Individualism in political relations means that each person reserves to himself the highest degree of autonomy and self-determination consistent with the necessary minimum of social control. In economic relations it means that each person is free to work for his livelihood in accordance with his own interests and wishes without the arbitrary interference of his fellows. Carrying the same ideal into family relations, the individual asserts his right to seek whatever union will give him the greatest opportunity to express his personality and to dissolve as freely marital ties when they become oppressive.

It is in the Reformation that we have to look for the beginning of individualism and for the roots of the disorganization of the family of today.

The Renaissance and the Reformation worked out in the elevation of the individual and tended to cause the decline of the family as a social unit. Every man was to stand on his own feet. Laxity of opinion and teaching on the sacredness of the marriage bond and in regard to divorce goes back to continental Protestantism of the sixteenth century. It was reflected in the laws of Protestant states in Europe and in the codes of New England.[2]

[1] *The Unadjusted Girl*, p. 86.

[2] Calhoun, *op. cit.*, I, 43–44.

Calhoun's explanation, however, does not directly take into account the change in the economic organization of society. As the result of the Industrial Revolution the family changed its economic basis. Even in the rural environment of the New World the family was an essential economic unit. A family was an asset to a man rather than a liability. The wife played the part of a partner in wresting a livelihood from the soil. Woman found her true sphere in the home as a wife and mother. Spinsterhood was feared because there was no place for the single woman except the status of household drudge. The prime motive in marriage was to have a home, to be economically secure.[1]

Specialization in industry and the movement of population from the country to the city took away almost all the economic functions of the home and led to the "emancipation" of women. The multiple opportunities in urban life for a woman to become self-supporting have released her from economic dependence upon a man. Hence marriage is not so imperative as formerly. And after marriage, the woman can break the family relation without necessarily endangering her livelihood.

The degree of this economic change may be indicated by statistics of the employment of women in industry and the professions. Chart XII[2] shows the increase in percentage of

[1] Cf. *ibid.*, chap. v.

[2] The dotted line in Chart XII probably shows more accurately the percentage of women ten years of age and over who were gainfully occupied in the United States for the year 1910 than does the continuous line which represents the Census figures. This inaccuracy in the Census figures is explained in a footnote of a bulletin published by the Women's Bureau (No. 27, 1922) under the title, *The Occupational Progress of Women*. The footnote reads as follows: "The decrease during the decade 1910 to 1920 in the proportions of all women 10 years of age and over who were gainfully occupied is to some extent apparent only and may probably be attributed to three main causes:

CHART XII

PERCENTAGE OF WOMEN TEN YEARS OF AGE AND OVER GAINFULLY
OCCUPIED IN THE UNITED STATES, 1870–1920

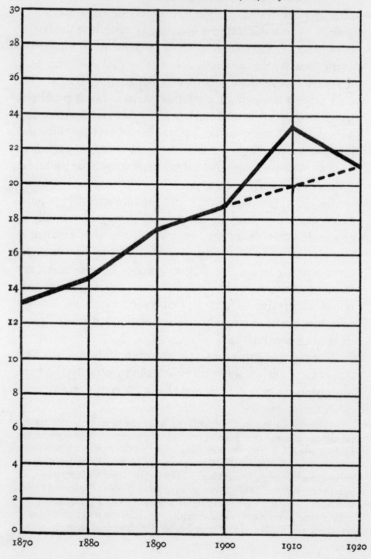

women engaged in gainful occupations in the United States since 1870. Chart XIII reveals that in addition to a definite increase in the employment of women there has been a pronounced shift from domestic and personal services to other occupations.

With the advent of women into industry and the professions where she can support herself and at the same time have the status and prestige which she could have in marriage, the desire for security[1] has become less significant. She finds that almost all the wishes can be satisfied, nearly if not entirely as well outside marriage as in, except those intimately connected with sex. It is to marriage that she looks

---

(1) The change in the census date from April 15 in 1900 to January 1 in 1920—, from a very busy farming season to a time of the year when all farming activities are at the lowest ebb. This change would probably result in a great reduction of the number of women returned in agriculture, forestry, and animal husbandry, tho the returns for men were apparently effected to a less extent by the same circumstance (2) An overstatement in 1910 of the number of women engaged in agriculture. . . . . The Census Bureau in 1910 estimates this overstatement at almost half a million, and suggests that it may have been largely the result of an instruction issued to census enumerators to return every woman working regularly at outdoor work as a farm laborer. . . . . (3) A great decrease in the employment of girls 10 to 15 years of age. . . . ."—*Op. cit.*, p. 8.

1 "The desire for security is opposed to the desire for new experience. The desire for new experience is, ... emotionally related to anger, which tends to invite death, and expresses itself in courage, advance, attack, pursuit. The desire for new experience implies, therefore, motion, change, danger, instability, social irresponsibility. The individual dominated by it shows a tendency to disregard prevailing standards and group interests. He may be a social failure on account of his instability, or a social success if he converts his experiences into social values,—puts them into the form of a poem, makes a contribution to science. The desire for security, on the other hand, is based on fear, which tends to avoid death and expresses itself in timidity, avoidance, and flight. The individual dominated by it is cautious, conservative, and apprehensive, tending also to regular habits, systematic work, and the accumulation of property."—Thomas, *The Unadjusted Girl*, p. 12.

CHART XIII

Percentage of Women Engaged in Domestic and Personal Service of All Women Ten Years of Age and Over Gainfully Occupied in the United States, 1870–1920

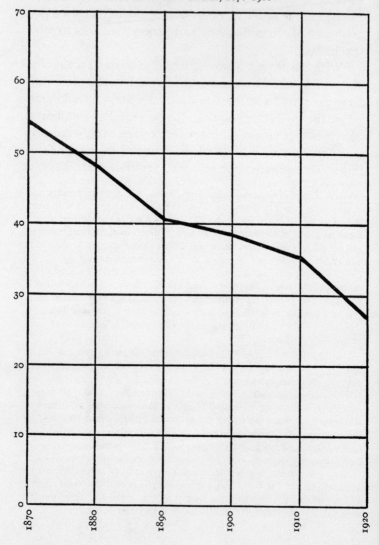

for love and affection, and whether for biological or social reasons is of little importance. Under the present social order, at least, the marriage relationship offers the only medium for the continued satisfaction of these intimate demands for the average woman, if not also for the average man. ⌐The woman's dependence upon a man is now primarily in terms of what Thomas calls the "wish for response."[1] The selection of a husband is in terms of response attributes, i.e., love and affection. Whether or not she remains with him, once married, is determined primarily upon the same basis.⌐

It is thus out of the changed conditions of modern life, which find their most pronounced expression in the city, that there has developed a new outlook upon the marriage relation. The desire for response has supplanted that for security as a predominant motive in marriage, and upon the basis of its satisfaction a marriage relation is judged in terms of the wishes of the individuals alone. This leads to an individualization of behavior in marriage tending toward experiments in marital relations. These may take unconventional or even illicit forms, or through the medium of divorce provide a conventionalized way of passing from one union to another.

The case of Fannie Hurst represents an experiment in marriage relations which allows both husband and wife the maximum of "freedom."

Being firmly of the opinion that nine out of ten of the alliances I saw about me were merely sordid endurance tests, overgrown with a fungus of familiarity and contempt, convinced that too often the most sacred relationship wears off like a piece of high sheen satin damask, and in a few months becomes a breakfast cloth, stale with soft-boiled

[1] "The desire for response . . . . is primarily related to the instinct of love, and shows itself in the tendency to seek and to give signs of appreciation in connection with other individuals."—*Op. cit.*, p. 17.

egg stains, I made certain resolutions concerning what my marriage should not be.

First of all, I am anxious to emphasize that my marriage was neither the result of a fad or an ism, but simply the working out of a problem according to the highly specialized needs of two professional people.

We decided to live separately, maintaining our individual studio-apartments and meeting as per inclination and not duty. We decided that seven breakfasts a week opposite one another might prove irksome. Our average is two. We decided that the antediluvian custom of a woman casting aside the name that had become as much a part of her personality as the color of her eyes had neither rhyme or reason. I was born Fannie Hurst and expect to die Fannie Hurst. We decided that in the event of offspring the child should take the paternal name until reaching the age of discretion, when the final decision would lie with him.

My husband telephones me for a dinner appointment exactly the same as scores of other friends. I have the same regard for his plans. We decided that, since nature so often springs a trap as her means to inveigle two people into matrimony, we would try our marriage for a year and at the end of that period go quietly apart, should the venture prove itself a liability instead of an asset. . . . .

On these premises, in our case at least, after a five-year acid test, the dust is still on the butterfly wings of our adventure. The dew is on the rose.[1]

As for those cases in which one union is terminated to be succeeded by another, scarcely a week goes by but that the newspapers record the third or fourth divorce of someone.[2]

RESTLESSNESS OF WOMEN

The changes in city life which have been the source of individualism have also made for restlessness. The transition from the handicraft stage of industrial production to the factory stage has shortened the hours of labor; but it has

[1] *New York World*, May 4, 1920; quoted by Thomas, *op. cit.*, pp. 92–93.
[2] The case of Peggy Joyce, for example.

also made work monotonous and irksome. The result is that not only does the individual have more time for play activities, but he tends likewise to select those which are highly stimulating in compensation for the dull hours he spends in the factory and in the office.

In the small and spatially isolated communities of the past, where the influences were strong and steady, the members became more or less habituated to and reconciled with a life of repressed wishes. The repression was demanded of all, the arrangement was equitable, and while certain new experiences were prohibited, and pleasure not countenanced as an end in itself, there remained satisfactions, not the least of which was the suppression of the wishes of others. On the other hand the modern world presents itself as a spectacle in which the observer is never sufficiently participating. The modern revolt and unrest are due to the contrast between the paucity of fulfillment of the wishes of the individual and the fullness, or apparent fullness, of life around him. All age levels have been affected by the feeling that much, too much, is being missed in life. This unrest is felt most by those who have heretofore been most excluded from general participation in life, —the mature woman and the young girl.[1]

It is the woman, then, who has been swept farthest from her moorings. In the large realm of life which has suddenly opened to her there are few, if any, norms of behavior which apply to her. Behavior is tolerated in a woman which would not be in a man because the chivalric attitude toward the woman tends to continue in the changed situation.[2]

Not only has the woman been freed from the restraints of the past, but she has also been freed from the necessity of performing any sort of work except, perhaps, for a short period before marriage. From the standpoint of something to serve as a ballast in the changing world of experience, the

[1] Thomas, *op. cit.*, pp. 71–72.

[2] There is, for example, no technique for dealing with a woman who refuses to await her turn in line.

young man has this advantage that after a variable period of schooling he is expected to earn his living. The girl, though she has won the freedom to do the same work as does her brother, is either not required to do so or begins later in life to earn a living. If she marries, she is almost certain to be supported on the salary of her husband, though she may live in an apartment hotel and have no work except the care of her personal possessions. ⌈While the married woman of yesterday had a home to care for, and often several children, her married daughter of today has little else to do, at least among certain classes, than to spend her time seeking new stimulations. She has no children to care for, no house to clean, and no meals to cook. Her leisure-time activities become her all-absorbing interests—interests which often lead her away from her husband rather than to him.⌋

Nothing works more for sanity and contentment than a reasonable amount of necessary and absorbing labor, disciplining the mind and giving one a sense of being of use in the world. It seems a paradox to say that idleness is exhausting, but there is much truth in it, especially in the case of sensitive and eager spirits. A regular and necessary task rests the will by giving assurance, while the absence of such a task wearies it by uncertainty and futile choice. Just as a person who follows a trail thru the woods will go further with less exertion than one who is finding his way, so we all need a foundation of routine, and the lack of this among women of the richer classes is a cause of restless, exacting, often hysterical, spirit, harassing to its owner and everyone else which tends toward discontent, indiscretion and divorce.[1]

Restlessness leads to indiscretion, and divorce grows out of a social situation which fails to give wholesome direction to the activities of women.[2] The avenue of escape which is

[1] Cooley, *op. cit.*, p. 368.

[2] "Wife Attempts Suicide after Intimacy with Cabaret Friend," *Chicago Herald and Examiner*, March, 1919.

most accessible is commercialized recreation. Few other leisure-time activities have the strength of appeal which is
found here, for the control of the primary group is no longer
felt. The bars of convention tend to be down, and social
intercourse becomes more free. Indiscretion easily follows,
and the so-called "triangle" situations develop where a man
and a woman meet without knowing or caring whether or
not the other is married.[1]

Because much of the married woman's leisure time must
be spent without the company of her husband, she is tempt-
ed to find the companionship she craves in association with
male admirers who frequent the places of entertainment
which cater to her interests. Under the community type of
social organization she would have had neither the time nor
the desire for these outside diversions away from the control
of gossip, for she would have found in association with her
children the response she now seeks elsewhere.

The following case of Mr. and Mrs. K illustrates how
separate contacts in leisure-time activities lead to indiscretion on the part of the wife.

Mr. and Mrs. K are about twenty-five years old and do not have
any children. Before her marriage Mrs. K was considered "fast." Her
family was prominent in church work, but this did not interest Mrs.
K until just two years ago when she tried to get into "society." She
has a wonderful personality and almost everyone likes her from the
beginning. After she knows a person well, however, she imposes upon
him. She always took part in the many plays given by a woman's club
to which she belonged. It was there that she met Mr. K, who was playing a minor rôle, but one that threw the two together a great deal.
They began to practice together and finally became engaged. After
that the two always selected rôles that would bring them together.

A year later they were married. As Mr. K had a good position in

[1] "Asks for Divorce after Wife Relates Cabaret Adventures," *ibid.*,
February 29, 1920.

his father's business, he was able to furnish a comfortable home in which they took a great deal of pride. After two years of married life, however, Mr. K began to go down town more often and Mrs. K began to associate again with some of her old friends. Mr. K refused to go out with her as before, but wanted her to mingle with his friends while she preferred her old group or the church group. He absolutely refused to have any contacts with this latter group, often calling for her at the church in his old greasy clothes. Sometimes, in chagrin, she would not ride home with him. At such times he would make remarks construed as "hardly proper" by her church friends.

Mr. K refused to take part in any more plays. Mrs. K, however, seemed to care for them more than ever. While in a play she met a young man—they played in two plays together. Mrs. K told him that Mr. K was a "brute" in their marital relations, while she craved attention, affection and caresses. She told her admirer that her husband refused to allow her to have a child; she wanted a child for she felt it would help to draw her husband back to her. At first she refused the advances of the other man. She said she wanted him to make up for the romance that her husband lacked. After a time, however, they started going out together; then they would drive out to a nearby town. They continued going out together until the man moved away.

After her lover left town Mrs. K began to show her husband more attention and for a time he responded. He was not seen down town so often. Soon, however, Mrs. K took up another play and they drifted apart again. But Mrs. K did not form any close attachments this time and she soon turned her entire attention and time to church affairs.

Mr. and Mrs. K "get along." He goes his way and she goes her way. She now has her own car so she can go where she wishes without asking her husband. They have never had an open break. They rarely go out together since Mr. K refuses to accompany his wife to any of the social affairs he once attended.[1]

THE ROMANTIC COMPLEX

Closely related to restlessness, but more widespread, is the romantic outlook upon life which is characteristic of

[1] Unpublished document (manuscript).

America. Modern civilization, represented in its highest form in the city, is external nature, artificial and standardized. Everywhere the individual tries to escape beyond the horizon of this perfect material paradise which modern man has constructed. In his endeavor to emancipate himself from the repressions of the material environment he has tried to throw off the restraints of his social environment as well. In this process the new and the unusual (often the bizarre) become the supreme values until there is little left but incoherent, chaotic movement—analogous to the attempts to escape of a newly caged wolf. All this effort to escape conforms to the romantic ideal.[1]

In general a thing is romantic when, as Aristotle would say, it is wonderful rather than probable; in other words, when it violates the normal sequence of cause and effect in favor of adventure. Here is the fundamental contrast between the words classic and romantic, which meet us at the outset and in some form persists in all the uses of the word down to the present day. A thing is romantic when it is strange, unexpected, intense, superlative, extreme, unique, etc. A thing is classical, on the other hand, when it is not unique, but representative of a class. In this sense medical men may speak correctly of a classic case of typhoid fever, or a classic case of hysteria. One is even justified in speaking of a classic example of romanticism. By an easy extension of meaning a thing is classical when it belongs to a high class or to the best class.[2]

Hulme has put it somewhat differently, though not without the same implication, when he says:

Here is the root of all romanticism: that man, the individual, is an infinite reservoir of possibilities; and if you can so re-arrange society by the destruction of oppressive order then these possibilities will have a chance and you will get Progress.

One can define the classical quite clearly as the exact opposite of

[1] In the village this romantic ideal becomes institutionalized.

[2] Irving Babbitt, *Rousseau and Romanticism*, p. 4.

this. Man is an extraordinarily fixed and limited animal, whose nature is absolutely constant. It is only by tradition and organization that anything decent can be got out of him.[1]

While romanticism colors almost every form of activity in modern America, nowhere has its effect been more revolutionary than in family relations. Whether or not the romantic ideal is unattainable, as some have intimated,[2] need not concern us here. Enough that it has had a decided effect in changing the attitudes of individuals toward marriage relations.

The romantic ideal of marriage is a natural development out of the romantic conception of life which is current in America. Not only does such a conception imply freedom of choice in marriage, unhampered by the authority of any group, but it also implies freedom to construct one's marriage relations according to any pattern which suits one's fancy.

The "Romantic complex" may be defined as that complex of attitudes and sentiments which regards the marriage relation as one exclusively of response. This romantic attitude pictures the marriage relationship in terms of love—sexual attraction in a large part—and sets up a standard according to which success in marriage is measured by the satisfaction of a highly idealized desire for response.

The romantic attitude is further characterized by the beliefs: (1) that in marriage will be found the only true happiness, (2) that affinities are ideal love relations, (3) that each may find an ideal mate, (4) that there is only one, and

[1] Thomas E. Hulme, *Speculations: Essays on Humanism* (essay on "Romanticism and Classicism"), p. 116.

[2] "But the awful result of romanticism is that, accustomed to this strange light, you can never live without it. Its effect on you is that of a drug."—*Ibid.*, p. 127.

(5) this one will be immediately recognized when met, i.e., through love at first sight.

Romance, moreover, demands constant demonstration of affection—love, caresses, constant wooing. When work tires the husband so that he neglects to caress his wife, she is unhappy, for her day has been spent in anticipation of such attention as the ideal form of married life.[1] Although romance divorces love from passion, there still tends to be a high correlation between sex relations and the heights of happiness, though this relationship may not be admitted even by the persons themselves.

Attention has often been called by medical men to the fact that the sexual desires of men are not like those of women. In the male the sex impulse is relatively localized, while it is widely diffused in the female. Periodicity is much more marked in the female than in the male so far as direct sexual impulses are concerned. But there is little correlation between physiological and psychological periodicity in the female at least where the romantic attitude enters into the situation. The desire for indirect sexual response—affection, caresses, attention—is relatively constant in the female. In the male, however, the indirect is more closely associated with the direct. This conflict in sexual impulses is accentuated and becomes a more active irritant because in the romantic attitude the physiological basis is not recognized, or if recognized, pushed out of mind.[2]

In the romantic scheme there are no shadows, but only lights and darks. If there is not happiness—supreme happiness—there is despair. To the romantic-minded life is a series of dismal separations. Separations are from necessity rather than from choice—for one must at least pretend to

[1] See p. 232 of chap. xi.   [2] Cf. Malchow, *The Sexual Life*, chap. ix.

want the constant presence of the other. To wish otherwise is to be a traitor to one's romance. The rut of regular married people is the nightmare of all romanticists.

Anniversaries are therefore events of great importance, to be remembered and celebrated with special showing of affection. The letters which were written during the courtship must be treasured until at last the sentimental attachment to bric-a-brac and presents remains to torture one after love has flown.[1]

It is this romantic conception of the marriage relation which becomes the focal point in marital discord at the present time.[2] Where the ideal is not realized in the first marriage, without the pressure of the primary group to the contrary, the tendency is to seek for its realization elsewhere.[3]

This romantic attitude is represented from one angle in the following letter introduced into the evidence in a suit for divorce by the man who had not been the romantic husband which his wife had expected.

MY DEAR, DEAR GEORGE:

I have waited for two weeks for my "little bit of heaven," and the relaxed tension of my nerves is almost an agony. Oh, George! If you only knew how I longed for it—a little token that I am really dear to you instead of the recipient of your sympathy.

I am sure of myself from now to eternity. But I could only take actions as a guide where you were concerned—until the time came for us to separate. Then I know that you were also sure of yourself. . . . .

I was very unhappy when you left. I am like you—I cannot stand separation from those I love. I cried, but I was all right when I got to your home. I spent the evening there, and mother read cards. She

[1] Cf. p. 250 of chap. xi.

[2] See "The Diary of Miriam Donaven" (chap. xi).

[3] "Husband Asks for Divorce after Finding Wife with Affinity," *Chicago Herald and Examiner*, May 3, 1919.

laughed and said I was going to marry the best man living one of these days.

Next day the Other Party had a talk with me—said I loved you —and you loved me—that it showed in our faces when we looked at each other—said he noticed it the other night. I said if we did, we had been unconscious of it and that now you were gone I realized that I cared all the world for you. . . . .

You are all my thots constantly and I go with a prayer on my lips all day. God will surely hear my prayer, sweetheart, and we will be happy some day, I am sure. I try to picture you in camp but my constant companions are memory pictures of our happy times together. Do not forget WOMAN is there with you and she is just as lonely as you are. I have read and re-read your letters and gleaned every bit of love from every word you wrote. There is nothing between you and me now—I am already divorced from him in spirit, soul and heart.

I never will do anything to injure your reputation, for I love you too well—a pure, clean, true love that seems to carry me up to higher and better heights.

When you can feel that HOME is in my heart, George, then it is certain that the real love of your life has come to live with you—a love that even your mother, dearly as you love her, could not change.

Even from evil, good can come. Be patient. Be brave. Remember, dear, that I am having my full measure of unhappiness, too, dear, but I can fight if I have any hope of the future. God help us both.[1]

The increase of leisure time for the modern woman has given her more time to read and dream—to idealize life. The result is that much of her time is spent in attempting to realize that ideal either directly or vicariously. Because of the externality of the situation she tends to idealize the persons she meets in her play activities and so to become dissatisfied with the characteristics of her own husband. Thus she makes other alliances which promise to give the satisfaction craved.[2] Considerations which held the family together in the primary group—status in the community,

[1] *Chicago Herald and Examiner*, May 3, 1919.

[2] See, for example, the case of Mr. and Mrs. K on pp. 157-8.

security, the care of children—seem, thus, of little importance where the romantic ideal becomes the basis of measuring success in marriage.

Thus one is able to indicate certain trends which are presumably correlated with the increase in family disorganization. Individualism, the restlessness of women, and romanticism or the romantic complex have been selected as representative of this method of study. In essence these concepts represent abstract descriptions of concrete events in so far as there is any uniformity in the changes from a simple agricultural and handicraft world to a complex one in which machinery furnishes the dominant note.

The difficulty with such concepts as these is that they fail to offer any explanation of the phenomena which they are used to describe. To say that family disorganization today is the result of individualism, or the restlessness of women, or the romantic complex, leaves still unanswered the question: Why are men and women more individualistic today than heretofore; why are women more restless and romantic than of another age? One of the explanations commonly given is, of course, machinery.[1] According to this explanation, the Industrial Revolution has transformed life in the modern world. But how has it changed life? By changing the material conditions and so altering the economic organization of the world. But again this explanation offers only a description of the change in physical organization and still fails to show how these material changes modify the behavior of human beings.

Cooley's[2] distinction between the primary and secondary

[1] Cf. Chapin, *An Historical Introduction to Social Economy*, pp. 170–260.

[2] *Op. cit.*, chap. iii. It is true, of course, that Cooley does not use the term "secondary group" in this reference, yet the distinction under consideration is implied.

group with its accompanying differentiation of social contacts offers an explanation of the phenomena which have been described.

DECLINE OF PRIMARY-GROUP CONTROL

Urban life is not essentially different from rural life, except that all of the life-processes have been speeded up. That is, the processes of adjustment of the individual to his environment are of the same kind in urban life as in rural, but adjustments must be made more rapidly and in a more complex situation. Take, for example, the satisfaction of the play impulse. The process of adjustment between the impulse and the material conditions offering satisfaction is of the same order in both rural and urban life. But in urban life the adjustment is not so simple nor made so leisurely as in rural life. Recreation in the city is more stimulating, but more fatiguing. The difference, however, is relative, and one of degree rather than of kind.

There is a principle in biology known as the "law of organic growth." It describes the way in which a large majority of organic processes have been found to grow or change. These changes follow a geometrical progression. That is, at regular intervals of time, each new value will be a constant percentage or ratio of that value immediately preceding it. Professor Ogburn's recent book would seem to confirm the application of this law to all social change.[1] In urban life it would seem, then, that all the processes of rural social life have changed or grown by a constant ratio.

Many attempts have been made to measure this growth. All have been relatively unsuccessful because they have had to do chiefly with changes in the economic structure of the city. The significant thing is that these economic changes

[1] *Social Change with Respect to Culture and Original Nature.*

produce changes in the contacts and stimulations which affect everyone. Under such conditions life increases in mobility. There is no longer a mass of social habits which furnish appropriate adjustments to all one's contacts and stimulations, many of which are as new to the group as to the individual.

The first effect of this multiplication of contacts is to disorganize the individual by breaking down his personal relations upon which morality is based.[1] Relations become casual and specialized. Association is upon a basis of specialized interests where but one phase of one's personality is known. The individual, to a large degree, determines his own behavior norms. The externality of his contacts makes it possible for him to pass from one group to another even though the norms of the several groups are in conflict. All this is made possible by the increase in secondary contacts and a growing tendency to substitute them for primary contacts.

The multiplication of contacts does not necessarily mean social disorganization. Social disorganization is the result of a lag in what Professor Ogburn calls the "adaptive culture" of a group.[2] The family had worked out a fairly satisfactory

[1] If the individual has been reared in the city he is still likely to have had the rural type of organization, even if in a modified form. He does not, necessarily, become so highly disorganized as does the rural migrant to the city, and he is probably more proficient at passing from one group to another. It is possible, of course, that eventually individuals and groups will work out codes of morals based upon a rationalized conception of social relations which will take the place of that based upon personal relations. But such a thing has not yet been done, except, perhaps, within very limited groups. The city-bred person, accordingly, may, and often does, become disorganized as highly as does the country-bred, once he is freed from the restraints of his family and of the neighborhood.

[2] *Op. cit.*, pp. 240-45.

adjustment to conditions under earlier agricultural life. The behavior of the individual was quite definitely controlled by the family, the church, and the community.

In the old rural society, custom reigned. It was custom to live with one wife; it was custom for the wife to be submissive and for the husband's authority to overrule incompatibility. Moreover when people spent their entire lives at the place of their birth, the sentiment of their neighbors acted with telling force. A man that formally broke up his family or a woman that formally deserted her husband had to take into account the antagonism of the neighborhood and the bitterness of its frown. City life is a great solvent of custom: neighbors do not know each other or, if they do, they are tolerant, or the problem may be solved by moving. Hence one is free to follow fancy in matters of divorce.[1]

Much of present-day disorganization of the family is the result of this change from primary to secondary relations, without the necessary adjustment in control. Many of the attempts to control, however, are of the same kind which worked in rural society. One of the most effective ways of giving permanence to an institution in the primary group is to buttress it with the sanctions of religion. This type of control is a technique worked out under an autocratic philosophy where the rights of the individual were of small importance and the interests of the group were paramount. Religious sanction preserved the institution from the forces of dissolution by creating belief in the final destruction of those who refused to conform. But in America, from the first, marriage was conceded not to be a sacrament, but merely a civil contract. This could lead to but one conception of the family—that it was not a sacred institution, and should be formed upon the basis of the needs of the individuals concerned. Each in his own way would find, accordingly, that

[1] Calhoun, *op. cit.*, III, 266–67.

certain aspects of an institution sanctioned by religion were not to his liking. The result we see about us—experiments of all sorts in family relations, with dissolution of the marriage bond if found unsatisfactory.

The method of social control characteristic of the primary group is what Thomas and Znaniecki have called the "ordering-and-forbidding" technique.[1] This was satisfactory in a more elementary grouping because the possibilities of satisfaction of the wishes in other groups were limited by the physical limitations upon movement. Today in the city the situation has changed. Many groups compete for the allegiance of the individual. The "ordering-and-forbidding" technique fails by driving the individual to another group where his wishes may be satisfied. The result is that the individual seeks satisfaction for many of his wishes in groups where there is considerable promiscuity; that is, in groups where contacts are primary but upon a secondary basis.

This "emancipation" of the individual from the control of the primary group has been facilitated by the rapid increase in the population of urban areas. Chicago may be taken as illustrative of the changes which are going on in the city. Chart XIV shows the increase in population for Chicago since 1860. This growth has been largely the result of the movement of people from the country to the city and the influx of immigration rather than because of the natural increase of births over deaths. This rapid increase in population has meant a constant shifting of persons from one part of the city to another. Each change in the economic structure of the city has meant an accompanying change in its social structure. The result is that not only do primary contacts become broken up but the constant change of persons from one set of surroundings to another has prevented the

CHART XIV

INCREASE OF POPULATION IN CHICAGO BY DECADES, 1860–1920

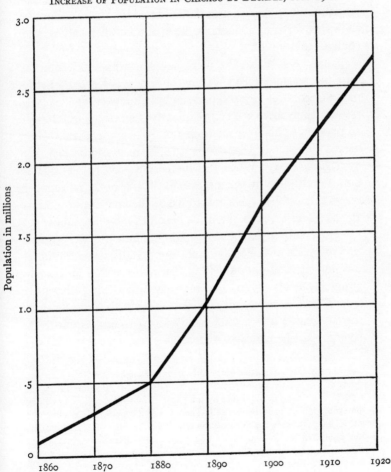

building up of neighborhood ties and of intimate personal bonds, and has led to the substitution of more transitory contacts.

The development of secondary contacts in the city may be indicated by the increases in newspaper circulation; attendance at public dance halls, theaters, motion-picture shows; advertising; telephone calls; automobiles; radios; and changes in address.

Chart XV shows the increase in newspaper circulation for Chicago since 1884. Within four decades the daily newspaper circulation per 100 persons has almost tripled. At the present time there are approximately 8 newspapers for each 10 persons or about 4 for each family of 5 members.[1] This means, of course, that many people read more than one newspaper a day. When this increase in newspaper circulation is multiplied by the increase in the size of the newspaper issues themselves, the significance of the increase of secondary contacts through the press becomes more apparent.

The result is that many groups compete for the specialized interests of the individual. But because the individual can find satisfaction only for a few of his wishes in a single group his relationships become casualized. This allows for a considerable anonymity. The result of this anonymity in the city makes it possible for individuals to live double lives. Every year in Chicago many cases are recounted in the

[1] The reader is cautioned against taking these figures too literally. The daily newspaper circulation does not go only to readers within Chicago. What proportion of the total is outside the city cannot be secured from the reports of circulation published by the papers, and while not a factor to be disregarded, is still relatively small. There is also a considerable reading of a single paper by more than one person as well as a circulation of daily papers not published in Chicago which would increase the true daily newspaper circulation. How nearly the two latter qualifications offset the first is only a matter for conjecture.

CHART XV

INCREASE IN AVERAGE DAILY NEWSPAPER CIRCULATION
PER 100 POPULATION IN CHICAGO, 1884–1923

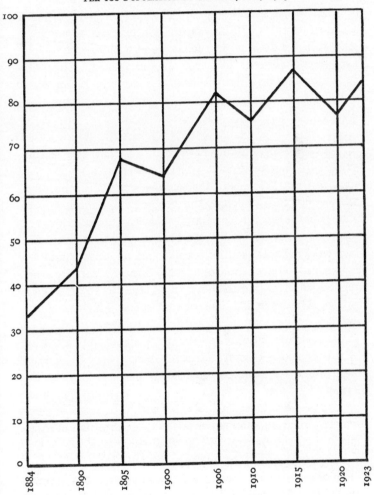

courts of men who have established two homes—an impossible achievement in a primary group.[1]

Thus in the city the individual is freed from the old controls exercised through gossip which are dependent upon primary contacts. In his marital relations this means freedom to the individual in the choice of a mate and all that such freedom implies, i.e., marriage contacts and obligations in conformity with the wishes of the individuals concerned and without reference to any other persons or groups.

SOCIAL FORCES AND PERSONAL INTERESTS

Social forces in family disorganization may now be considered in their relation to other methods of studying this problem. Social forces in the sense here used are tendencies which combine to define the general trend of historical change in the prevalence of family disorganization. But such forces affect every family. To explain why in a given case one family becomes disorganized and another family remains integrated one must show how in the latter case other tendencies counteracted those which tend toward disorganization. The result is a lack of conciseness which would be eliminated if attention were directed to the way in which these tendencies appear in the experiences of individuals.

For purposes of control, then, it is necessary to think of social forces as somehow objectively embodied in the behavior of persons. Research into the processes by which attitudes are developed in the experience of persons in their marriage relations offers more adequate descriptions of social forces than the charting of historical tendencies.

The study of historical trends, after all, charts only mass

[1] Allard, "Jailed When Bride Finds He Is Father of 5," *Chicago Herald and Examiner*, May 30, 1923.

influences of institutions and fails to show how these forces take form in the experiences of persons. Such an analysis of family disorganization serves, thus, as a method of orientation preliminary to the description of processes within the experiences of persons. Case-work, the other source of the development of the case-study method, begins with the individual as the unit for analysis, and so offers a methodological development better suited to the discovery of causal relations.

CHAPTER VIII

CASE-STUDY THROUGH RECORDS OF SOCIAL AGENCIES

The use of the case-study method by social agencies in the diagnosis of family disorganization has been chiefly in the study of desertion rather than of divorce. This may be accounted for by the fact that desertion has long been recognized as a major factor in charity cases, while divorce has been relatively negligible. The exigencies of social case-work have made it imperative that some sort of record be kept of cases both for the sake of knowing what had previously been done and to serve as a basis for determining future policy with regard to each case. Out of this accumulation of records arose the attempt to analyze them for the light they might throw upon the solution of future problems in desertion. This analysis determined the common factors in a large number of cases, and in several instances gave the frequency of each.

There was at first little comprehension that this approach constituted any departure from the orthodox statistical method. In fact, aside from the inadequacy of the number of cases of statistical treatment, the only justification one has for including the study of Brandt, *Five Hundred and Seventy-four Deserters and Their Families*, in a chapter on the case-study method is that her analysis was based upon case materials, and in it she happily hit upon a description of type situations revealing the possibility of viewing cases organically.[1]

[1] This does not mean, obviously, that characterizing the case as a whole, as Brandt often does throughout her study, is entirely an orthodox statistical

CLASSIFICATION OF FACTORS

Classification of factors in family disorganization is common to studies of desertion and divorce. In both cases the logic of the procedure is essentially the same whether the basis for the classification is casual observation or case-studies. Each is intended to indicate the range of causal factors in family disorganization of the particular type studied,[1] even though it goes no further than to fix the responsibility.

Several definitions of significant factors in divorce and desertion have determined their classification. These definitions are by implication, of course, rather than by any direct statement, and may be classified as follows: (1) factors pertinent to the fixing of responsibility; (2) description of overt behavior and circumstances contingent upon such behavior; (3) conscious motives on the part of the person making the break; (4) environmental and personal factors.

FIXING THE RESPONSIBILITY

Classification of factors in an attempt to fix the responsibility is an outgrowth of rationalistic psychology, now generally discarded in principle by all persons dealing habitually with problems of family discord. Nevertheless, it still creeps into much of the popular literature upon the subject. Interpretations of divorce statistics where the distinction is

---

procedure. In so far as this treatment is not strictly statistical it may be taken as justification for including Brandt's study in this chapter. Some of her tabulations, however, were strictly of the statistical type, such as those of religious affiliations, number of children, etc.

[1] Brandt's insistence that her classification is of "explanations" and not of causes is only her way of saying that further study may reveal more adequate factors. In a sense each new classification is likely to do that. Her distinction is, accordingly, somewhat redundant (see *op. cit.*, p. 38).

made as to whether the divorce was granted to the husband or the wife often either affirm or imply the determination of who was responsible for the break-up of the family. Miss Brandt's classification of "explanations" (see Table XXXIV) which follows uses this rational principle explicitly as the basis of her major classes as well as implicitly for the subdivisions.

TABLE XXXIV*

I. Apparently chiefly the man's fault:

Laxity of ideals in regard to relations with women	78
Laziness or shiftlessness, often increased by habitual dependence on others	53
Intemperance	31
Intemperance combined with gambling or laziness or some other bad habit	16
"General worthlessness"	17
Loss of interest in family	13
Unwillingness to share domestic difficulties	13
Desire to escape the consequences of crimes or debts	12
A roving disposition	5
A passion for gambling	3
Anger with wife	2
Morphine habit	1
Homesickness (for Poland)	1
Total	245

II. Apparently chiefly the woman's fault:

Intemperance, slovenliness, neglect of home and children, often accompanied by a trying disposition	21
Intimacy with other men	17
Extravagance	6
Unreasonable jealousy	1
Unwillingness to come to America	1
Total	46

III. Apparently equal responsibility:

Incompatibility.. 15
General low standards of both............................ 12
Intemperance and laziness of the man, bad housekeeping
   and disagreeable temper of the woman................ 8
Sexual immorality on both sides......................... 15
Ill-health and consequent irritability of both............. 1
Youth and inexperience of both.......................... 1
                                                                               ———

Total... 52

IV. Chief responsibility in circumstances beyond the control of
    both:

Interference of relatives or friends...................... 16
Man probably did not intend to desert when he left home.. 15
Mental disturbance..................................... 6
Physical inability of man to support family.............. 3
Presence of wife's relatives in family................... 3
                                                                               ———

Total... 43

*Op. cit., pp. 41-42.

The difficulty of such a basis for classification of factors has already been indicated. Its assumption of a rationalistic psychology implies that the whole occurrence is an act of free-will to be remedied by showing the responsible person where he is at fault. Unfortunately, the latter is not so easily accomplished as one might wish and fails to work oftener than not when it is tried.

OVERT BEHAVIOR

While Miss Brandt's major classes imply an attempt to fix the responsibility for the desertion, her subclasses are based upon descriptions of overt behavior in some instances and upon conscious motives in others. Studies of divorce have more consistently defined significant factors in terms of overt behavior, or circumstances contingent upon it, than have those of desertion. The best illustration of this is in the assumption that the legal causes in divorce cases are significant. This assumption has already been disproved in another place.[1]

The fallacy of this definition of the significant factors lies in the failure of overt behavior to reflect the attitudes of the person. A man may desert his wife because she is extravagant, but why is she extravagant? A wife may divorce her husband because he beats her, but why does he beat her? The overt behavior is often the same where the attitudes are widely different. There is, in other words, no basis for control where the only thing which is known is the overt behavior of the persons.

CONSCIOUS MOTIVES

Classifications of factors have been built up from the statements of the motive by one party to the case or by the social worker. This step marks the transition from emphasis upon the descriptive to the explanatory. The former implies a moralistic approach to the problem; the latter, a scientific one. Some of Miss Brandt's "explanations" belong in this latter category. Causes listed by courts of domestic relations are largely of this sort.[2]

While definition of significant factors in terms of conscious motives reveals attitudes and so gives one a more adequate understanding of the situation, there is little in the attitudes themselves to show how they developed and therefore to indicate how they might be changed. All this is upon

[1] See chap. iii.

[2] For illustration see Patterson, "Family Desertion and Non-Support," *Journal of Delinquency*, VII, 304–10.

the theoretical assumption that the motives are known. In practice the motives are often inferred by the social worker in accordance with whatever preconceptions she may have regarding the causes of desertion. Further, motives are not necessarily conscious, or at least if so, may be vague and ill defined.

ENVIRONMENTAL AND PERSONAL FACTORS

More recent studies of family disorganization have built their classifications of causes out of factors in both the cultural and personal experiences of the persons. The most elaborate classification of this sort is that of Miss Colcord, which follows:

Contributory Factors in the Man and Woman

1. Actual mental deficiency
2. Faults in early training
3. Differences in background
4. Wrong basis of marriage
5. Lack of education
6. Occupational faults
7. Wanderlust
8. Money troubles
9. Ill health: physical debility
10. Temperamental incompatibility
11. Sex incompatibility
12. Vicious habits

Contributory Factors in the Community

1. Interference of relatives
2. Racial attitude toward marriage
3. Community standards
4. Lack of proper recreation
5. Influence of companions
6. Expectation of charitable relief[1]

[1] *Broken Homes*, pp. 24-48.

One of the obvious difficulties with such a classification is the confusion of descriptive categories with others which are primarily appreciative or moralistic. A second difficulty is the lack of any unifying principle. In the third place, one has no assurance that these factors are unique, that is, they may characterize normal families as well as abnormal ones. The classification is, in other words, one of common sense as are most analyses growing out of concrete attempts to solve specific social problems.

THE TYPICAL CASE

Because the classification of factors often developed out of the study and analysis of cases it may be considered one trend in the use of case material for the analysis of family disorganization. It is not, however, the only trend, Where the analysis depends upon the classification of factors each is treated as a discrete unit. As long as the factors which are considered consist of those necessary to fixing the responsibility, characterizing the overt behavior, or expressing the conscious motive of the deserter little difficulty is encountered in pigeon-holing each case under its appropriate head. When, however, the emphasis is transferred to the environmental and personal background of the two persons concerned in the disruption of the family a second trend develops. Here the procedure becomes that of defining sequences of events or combinations of factors.

The first evidence of this trend to be found in a study of desertion is Miss Brandt's description of the typical deserter.

The typical deserter is not a figure to excite admiration, nor even much interest. He is young, able-bodied, more or less dissipated, capable of earning good wages, but rarely in a mood for making the exertion, and, above all, he is lacking in the quality which makes an obligation to others outweigh considerations of personal comfort or preference. This combination of characteristics makes him susceptible to the attractions of various sorts: it incapacitates him for dealing in a philosophic spirit with the elements of discord which exist in every household; and it prevents him from resisting with even an average will the restlessness that is apt to call every one at times away from the ordinary prose of life. He may be, withal, though he is not always, of a personal attractiveness that makes him a coveted comrade and gives him an advantage with women.[1]

While this description is little more than a rhetorical way of summarizing what Miss Brandt considered the most outstanding factors in desertion, it does suggest the beginnings of the attempt to define in case-studies series of events or combinations of factors which culminate in family disintegration. But a composite picture loses the precision and completeness which the description of the behavior of a single deserter would give.

DESERTION TYPES

The second step in the trend toward the definition of a series of events or combinations of factors culminating in desertion is that of finding typical cases. According to this method, types grow out of groupings of cases by similarities. The typical case becomes, then, one which contains all the essential similarities of the group to which it belongs.

Eubank[2] in classifying more than six hundred cases from the records of the United Charities of Chicago was able to differentiate five major classes:

A. The Spurious Deserter
B. The Gradual Deserter
C. The Intermittent Husband
    a) The Periodic Deserter
    b) The Temperamental Deserter
D. The Ill-advised Marriage Type
E. The Last Resort Type

[1] *Op. cit.*, p. 63.   [2] *A Study of Family Desertion*, chap. v, pp. 37–49.

The basis of this classification, according to Eubank, is "the nature of the problem presented by the different groups of cases and the fundamental characteristics common to each group." In this connection two problems arise: (1) Has the basis of classification as given by the author been adherred to? (2) Is the basis itself fundamental?

As a basis for an answer to the first question two types of cases may be contrasted: the spurious deserter and the ill-advised marriage type. Eubank gives in illustration of the spurious deserter the following case:

William Morris and family came to the attention of the society for the first time in June, 1908. Although Morris was a sturdy and able-bodied fellow, various streaks of bad fortune made it impossible for him to furnish his family at all times with the necessities of life. For five years, intermittently, they were fed and clothed by the society. Morris seemed to regard the society as equal to every emergency, and worthy of all confidence. His faith expanded as time passed. Attempts to care for the family's needs himself seemed less and less worth while. At length further aid was refused as the only means of placing the responsibility upon Morris, where it belonged. Two days after the ultimatum, Mrs. Morris came to the relief office with an absolutely new tale of woe. Morris, of all men, had deserted and left his unhappy family to starve! However, her unqualified refusal to coöperate in prosecuting him was in itself suspicious. A month later she again refused decisively to take action against him. A visit made about this time, in spite of the distressing picture conjured up by the story, revealed no distress although aid had been refused all the while. An unexpected visitor still later trapped the careless Morris within his own home, and he could do nothing but acknowledge the deception.[1]

This case clearly illustrates one type of problem with which a social agency is confronted. The type which it illustrates is, then, based upon an implied definition of the significant factors arising out of administrative needs. The

[1] *A Study of Family Desertion*, chap. v, pp. 37–38.

fundamental characteristics common to all cases of this type are accordingly those which are considered fundamental from the point of view of the administrator. The practical problem is, Shall the family be given aid or not? This type serves as a warning to social workers that some "deserted families" have not been deserted, and therefore should not be aided. That this case gives the essential events leading up to the "desertion" upon the basis of which similar cases may be recognized may be questioned.

The ill-advised marriage type may be illustrated by the description which Eubank gives of a forced marriage:

Jacob McDaniel and Mary Murphy were reared in the uninspiring atmosphere "Back of the Yards," and grew up in a community not conducive to highest morals. In fact, the fathers of both were drinking men, and Jacob's father, especially, had the reputation of being unkind to his wife. The couple had been neighbors and school mates from infancy but were in no sense betrothed at the time Jacob became engaged to another girl who had moved into the community. Before the day set for their wedding, however, Mary's mother discovered that her daughter was pregnant and that Jacob was the one responsible for her condition. Pressure was brought to bear, and five days before her baby was born Mary Murphy became Mary McDaniel. Aside from the gloomy satisfaction of giving the child a name the marriage was a farce, for Jacob never pretended to make a home for his wife and baby. He continued his attentions to the other girl, who was receptive. Eventually they eloped, going to a large city of the middle west where they lived as man and wife.[1]

This case also illustrates a type of administrative problem confronting social workers. But it is more than that. It gives something about the social background of the couple which may serve as a clue to the cause of the desertion. If these facts are fundamental it is for some other reason than that they warn the social worker of the futility of trying to

[1] *Ibid.*, p. 46.

keep the couple together. For this type of case the factors chosen, while they have some bearing upon the administrative problem, have been determined largely by what, in the mind of the writer, seemed to explain the situation. In other words, the basis of classification has not been held to with any high degree of consistency.

The point has been made throughout the discussion of the two cases quoted above that classification has been made upon the basis of the essential factors from the point of view of the administrator, although such a definition was not exclusively adhered to. The difficulty with such a classification seems to be that it gives the administrator the answer to but two questions: (1) Shall the family be aided? (2) Is there any hope of reconciliation? It fails to define accurately the series of events leading to desertion upon the basis of which probable desertion may be predicted, and it gives little or no basis for understanding and solving the problem.

In so far, however, as the cases in Eubank's study contain factors which are not consistent with the administrator's immediate needs they reveal the introduction, into the case-study method, of data which are more fundamental from the point of view of human nature. It is assumed, of course, that the interests of the social worker are limited to those arising out of the immediate problem, namely, the giving of economic aid, directly or indirectly, to the deserted family.

SOCIAL DIAGNOSIS IN SOCIAL WORK

Social diagnosis in social work has also played a part in the development of the case-study method. While social workers have been primarily concerned with the solution of immediate problems, they have, through the development of an elaborate method of making case records, accumulated data which may be used to define the series of events or combinations of factors leading to desertion. Miss Richmond has indicated the scope of such records in her elaborate questionnaire for the study of desertion cases.[1]

While from the point of view of Miss Richmond's outline the following case-study is wholly inadequate, it does represent the type of data which the case-worker obtains and which is available in the records of social agencies:

Five years ago the L family was referred to our agency because of domestic difficulties. Since then the case has been active with us uninterruptedly. The trouble at bottom is: Mr. L is a confirmed gambler. He is a baker by trade, and a very good workman, but works only two or three days a week. He would make sufficient money to support his wife and two children adequately with the two or three days' work per week were he not to gamble away all his earnings. Mrs. L is a very sick woman—has been a patient at a convalescent home and since her discharge has been under observation at the dispensary. A report two months later reads as follows: "Upon patient's return from the convalescent home her condition was much improved. Her diagnosis is mitral stenosis (valvular heart condition in the mitral area) and her cardiac reserve is poor. Mrs. L is to return for observation."

During the months of March and April our visitor has been in constant touch with the family and although Mrs. L goes to the dispensary regularly her condition apparently seemed to be getting worse. Early in March the dispensary had advised that Mr. and Mrs. L be separated as Mrs. L's condition was becoming worse, and we are working on this very suggestion, but so far have not gotten anywhere.

On April 28th Mrs. D, a neighbor of the L's, telephoned stating that Mrs. L was very ill. A doctor from the dispensary called at the home. On May 1st our worker called and found Mrs. L sick in bed. A doctor did not arrive until the next day. At the time we knew nothing of arrangements that were being made for Mrs. L's admittance to the hospital. We were promised a written report and recommenda-

[1] *Social Diagnosis*, pp. 396–400.

tions. Today Mrs. L telephoned stating that she had been notified to enter the hospital as arrangements have been made for her. She will go as soon as the children, a boy of eleven and a girl of seven, are placed.

Later.—During Mrs. L's stay at the convalescent home the children were cared for by Mrs. S, sister of Mr. L. Now the S's are unable to take the children as Mr. and Mrs. S are having domestic difficulties and are a case in our office. Mrs. L, Sr., is an old woman, partially deaf, and unable to care for the children. Mrs. L requests that the children be boarded out away from the relatives and Mr. L will pay for their board during her stay in the hospital.

Later.—Our visitor called. "Found Mrs. L home with both children. Mrs. L stated that she expected to go to the hospital again on Saturday. She has found a woman, a previous caretaker of the home finding society, who will take the children for $10.00 a week. She feels that this arrangement will be satisfactory as she would prefer to have her husband spend his money that way than lose it playing cards. She would have made her own arrangements but the worker of the home finding society told her that that society would take care of the children. Since Mrs. L can and is willing to make her own arrangements I told her that we would not take care of them.

"Called at the hospital on Monday and found that Mrs. L was still there. They do not know when she will be able to go home. Have been unable to see her since she has been there until today. She is a very pleasant woman, uncomplaining, good-natured, and easy to get along with. It is therefore my opinion that the clash comes from something outside of that in personalities."

The social agency diagnosed the case as domestic difficulty due to the gambling of the husband. At the dispensary, however, Mrs. L finally told the doctor that her husband demanded sexual relations more often than her weakened physical condition would allow. When she refused he retaliated by refusing her money. The doctor thereupon diagnosed the case as sexual incompatibility.

This case represents several points of inadequacy often found in the case records of social agencies: (1) the economic bias, or the tendency to ignore other than economic factors; (2) overemphasis upon immediate problems; and (3) the lack of any fundamental conception of what facts are pertinent to the understanding or solution of the problem.

Desertion cases are looked upon as hopeless by the average social worker. She is likely to see in the situation little more than the financial problem created by the desertion. If she goes into the motives of the deserter it is to determine whether it is worth while trying to get the husband to assume once more the support of his family. Because this is the immediate problem to her she is likely to assume that it must have had something to do with the desertion. As a result her interpretation of causes is likely to be economic.

The sort of facts which the social worker selects reveals the lack of any comprehensive attack upon the problem. A great deal of attention is given to elaborating the description of the financial situation from every angle possible: physical examinations; opinions as to what were the motives; impressions of social workers regarding the personality of the wife; history of interviews and telephone calls; accounts of previous desertions, if any; and perhaps, in some cases, brief statements of the domestic difficulties of the parents. Little or no attention is given to the personal and cultural background of the family, to the genesis of the attitudes which receive superficial expression in the external behavior of the individuals.

CULTURAL ANALYSIS

Two more studies representing a somewhat different attack upon the problem of defining the circumstances leading to desertion require consideration. These are the studies of Thomas and Znaniecki[1] and Miss Sherman.[2] Seeing, apparently, the practical difficulties involved in getting a complete description of the social and personal factors in the genesis of the desertion case, both have resorted to interpreting the cases of social agencies in the light of the cultural background of the husband and wife.

Thomas and Znaniecki confine their analysis to the Polish group. Their cases were taken from the records of the Chicago Legal Aid Society. They find that after the general decay of the institutional significance of marriage there are five main factors leading to the actual break of the marriage relationship. These factors are (1) temperamental misadaptation of husband and wife, (2) individualization of sexual interests, (3) economic demoralization, (4) interference of relatives and neighbors, and (5) interference of the state.[3]

The type of case which Thomas and Znaniecki use as well as their method of analysis may be represented by the following case in which the main factor leading to the disruption of the marriage group was sexual interests:

Minnie and Stanley Michalski were very young when they were married. Shortly after their marriage a friend of Stanley's, a young man named Frank Kornacki, came to see them. He called about a half-dozen times. One Monday in January, 1912, he came to the house at noon-time. Young Mrs. Michalski was at home alone doing the washing. Whether or not he forced her to have sexual relations with him it is hard to say. She later claimed that she resisted him, but that he held her mouth with one hand so firmly she could not scream and as she was 5 months pregnant she did not dare struggle to prevent him. She did not tell her husband of this. The child was born and named Helen.

[1] *The Polish Peasant in Europe and America*, Vol. V, chap. iii, pp. 221-70.

[2] "Racial Factors in Desertion," *Family*, III, 143-47, 165-70, 197-201, 221-25.

[3] *Op. cit.*, V, 253.

One Sunday in August of the same year, Kornacki and Michalski were gambling together in a saloon. Michalski had won $8 when Kornacki, half drunk, offered to tell him "something" for the return of the $8. He then told of his intercourse with Mrs. Michalski. Michalski went home almost crazy and choked his wife until she told him the truth. His fury knew no bounds. He would not believe that she had been without fault in the affair and ordered her to have Kornacki arrested for rape, refusing to live with her unless his former friend was punished. The warrant, however, was refused. He was especially enraged because the attack had happened during her pregnancy, and as she was at this time again pregnant she had an abortion performed to pacify him. He thereupon allowed her to return and they lived together for 2 years more. Then he left her, promising her $5 a week for the support of the child.

Mrs. Michalski appealed to the Legal Aid Society to assist her to get more money from her husband. Michalski answered in person the society's letter and made a very good impression on the interviewer, a new and inexperienced girl who was "very sorry for him." He insisted he loved his wife dearly but could not live with her. She had admitted to him having relations twice with some man and he simply could not forget that. Besides, every time he went out with her he imagined she was flirting and making some engagements with men. He concluded by offering to bring his wife to the office of the society "to talk the matter over." This he did. He refused more money and urged Mrs. Michalski to get a divorce, nobly promising to produce conclusive evidence of his unfaithfulness to her.

Nevertheless, the Michalski family lived together once more, rented a flat and bought new furniture. After 2 weeks Stanley Michalski left and his wife went to the Legal Aid Society to complain that he was running around with another woman and giving her only $5 a week. She was now willing to get a divorce. Nothing was done in the matter, however. Six months later she again applied to the society. The night before her husband had come to her flat and threatened to kill her and Helen. He turned on the gas and tried to choke her into unconsciousness, but she screamed so loudly that he became alarmed and left, seizing a photograph of himself that was hanging on the wall and taking the child with him. Mrs. Michalski called a policeman, arrested him and got the child back.

Shortly after this, Michalski, who had become manager for the company he was working with, gave his wife a job in his office at $7 a week—this to avoid paying anything toward the support of the child. She soon lost her work and he did not resume payments. The Legal Aid Society sent for him. He said he was unable to work, that he had contracted syphilis from some woman he lived with, was undergoing treatments for it and would probably have to have an operation. He insisted that his wife was living immorally and told of catching a man partly undressed in her closet once when he called at her flat with a policeman. He wanted to arrest the man but was afraid of involving his wife. Some months later, Michalski went to the office of the Legal Aid Society and demanded the record of the case. He wished to see whether the record contained any admissions by his wife of her immorality, meaning to use such admissions as the basis for a divorce. When this request was naturally refused, he became very much excited and charged the society with always "shielding the woman."

Another six months went by. The divorce had been granted without a contest. Much testimony had been produced as to Michalski's good character and Mrs. Michalski's immoral conduct. Michalski's brother and a young girl had testified that one evening they had all been drinking and were playing hide and seek when Mrs. Michalski invited an 18 year old boy into her bedroom and had intercourse with him. At first Mrs. Michalski denied this and offered to bring the boy in question to court to refute the story, but when more closely questioned by the Legal Aid attorney and shown the dangers of perjury she admitted it was true. But she implored the society to get the order of court giving the custody of the child to its father set aside. She said, with tears in her eyes, that the child meant everything in the world to her. When, a few days later, Michalski took the child from her, her despair was so real and so pitiful that the society determined to contest the divorce for her. The decree already entered was set aside on a preliminary showing of Michalski's bad habits. In preparation for the final hearing the Legal Aid attorney called on the girl for whom Michalski had left his wife. She did not resent the suggestion that she come to court to tell of her relations with Michalski. She "felt sorry for poor Minnie and would be glad to help her out," but it was a most inauspicious moment, as she was suing her own husband for a divorce and she not did wish to be placed in the situation of telling the same

Judge in Minnie's case that she was an immoral woman and in her own case that she was an irreprochable wife, seeking separation from an undeserving husband. She finally agreed that if her own divorce "went through all right," she would consider helping "Minnie." But on no account was she to be subpoenaed, for if she was forced to testify against her wishes she would tell so much that neither Minnie nor her husband would be allowed to keep the child. A few weeks later Mrs. Michalski said Stella refused to help her, for Stanley had promised to marry her if he should get another decree of divorce. This was not the only promise of marriage that Stanley made pending his divorce.

Mrs. Michalski was allowed by the court order to see the child and once she kidnapped it. The Legal Aid Society obtained a court order allowing her to keep it. Neither Michalski nor his attorney appeared in court to contest the matter.[1]

Thomas and Znaniecki interpret each type of cases in terms of the mores of the Polish immigrant group. This method may be illustrated by a summary of their interpretation of the group of cases to which the one quoted belongs, i.e., the group in which the main factor leading to the actual disruption of the marriage group was sexual interests.

Under the traditional Polish system sexual life possesses a secondary rôle. Among the Polish peasants sexual tendencies were regulated in the interests of the large family rather than in the interests of morality. Sexual contacts were significant only as they affected the marriage possibilities of the individuals. After marriage the sexual life of husband and wife had no more social significance, being essentially a private matter. Conjugal infidelity was indecent because it introduced into the family system an essentially private matter and tended to weaken the family.

When, in America, the large family and the marriage group lose their institutional significance the check upon sexual tendencies is lost. Only the bearing of sexual indul-

[1] Thomas and Znaniecki, *op. cit.*, V, 232–35.

gence upon the family system made it condemnable. In America sexual relations in the Polish group tends to become looked upon as purely a matter of personal choice and no longer subject to social regulation.

In general, however, for the individual, sexual interests have not become dissociated from other conjugal interests. Most immigrants are inclined to look upon marriage as the normal way of obtaining sexual satisfaction. Even where there is loss of sex interest, jealousy tends to persist and to provoke conflict where there is infidelity. It is, thus, where there is identification of sexual interests with other marriage interests that the extra-conjugal satisfaction of sexual desires leads to the break of the marriage bond.

There has been, then, a change in the significance of sexual life through the loss of its social character and its transfer from group to individual concern. There has also been a change in the significance of the marriage group through the loss of control by the larger family. Personal association of sexual interests with other marriage interests still persists, but without the re-enforcement of group control. But so long as this identification of interests still continues, it remains a potential cause of family disintegration in a group where sexual contacts have become individualized.[1]

Thomas and Znaniecki's method, as illustrated by the interpretation of the group of cases to which the case of Michalski belongs, is the use of the cultural background of a nationality in interpreting the cases of social agencies. They attempt to find an explanation in the cultural background for the facts set forth in the case records, upon the assumption that each individual is essentially a product of that cul-

[1] *Op. cit.*, pp. 255-61.

ture. One limitation of this method is that it does not take into account the way in which conflicts in culture affect the individual. The description of the cultural background becomes, thus, a hypothetical interpretation of the facts revealed by the case-studies rather than an explanation derived from objective concrete description of family interaction. As such it lacks the precision and definiteness which is necessary for defining sequences of events leading to the dissolution of the family.

The method of study used by Sherman is somewhat comparable to that of Thomas and Znaniecki though her emphasis is upon the individual rather than upon the group. While she gives some attention to the cultural background of certain nationalities in her study, she is more concerned with their ethnic traits. Interpretation is in terms of racial characteristics, which, apparently, are assumed to be inherited. She attempts to define the personalities of the persons in the cases used and to explain them, rather than to define sequences of events leading to family disintegration. Without raising the question as to whether or not the emphasis upon individual and racial characteristics is misplaced, the method seems to be definitely open to question in assuming that there is sufficient homogeneity in the racial characteristics and culture to furnish explanations for the cases of family disintegration. The method further fails to differentiate types of sequences leading to family disorganization, and so does not provide a basis for prediction and control.

The case-study method in the analysis of the case records of social agencies has progressed from a naïve interpretation of obvious facts about desertion to attempts to state factors more objectively, to define types, and finally to interpret desertion in terms of the culture of the inclusive group.

Records of social agencies at their best, however, are naturally and perhaps necessarily concerned more with facts bearing upon the apprehension and the treatment of the deserter than with facts of human nature bearing on the underlying causes of desertion. They are, therefore, inadequate in many respects for analysis by the case-study method.

The studies of Thomas and Znaniecki and of Sherman, however, indicate that in the past the cultural background of immigrant groups has been almost entirely ignored by social workers in not only the analysis of cases but in the diagnosis as well. A further development of the case-study method both in sociology and social work suggests that increasing emphasis is being given to descriptions of behavior that reveal the interaction of persons, social attitudes, and human wishes.[1]

It is to the classification of cases in terms of the interactions of persons, then, that one must turn for a more fundamental analysis of family disorganization. The classification of family tensions represents such an attempt as this, and will be the subject of the next chapter.

[1] See, for example, the following: William Healy and Augusta F. Bronner, *The Judge Baker Foundation Studies;* Ada E. Sheffield, "Clue Aspects in Social Case Work," *Survey,* November 12, 1921; E. W. Burgess, "The Trend of Sociological Research," *Journal of Applied Sociology,* VIII (1924), 131-40; E. W. Burgess, "The Family as a Unit of Interacting Personalities," *Family,* VII (March, 1926), 3-9.

CHAPTER IX

CLASSIFICATION OF FAMILY TENSIONS

Family disorganization as defined in chapter vi furnishes the unifying principle, lacking in common-sense analyses, necessary for an adequate classification of cases. Classification may proceed, then, by the discovery of typical situations in which family discords arise—situations described in terms of the attitudes of the marriage group. These conflict situations, as has been suggested, may be thought of as arising out of differences in attitudes which create tensions in family relations.

Meroney has worked out an elaborate classification of tensions. "The repression of the wish for response," he says, "by any of the following factors has a tendency to produce tensions in family life:"

I. Economic Factors
   1. Poverty
   2. Financial Reverse
   3. Economic Independence of Wife
   4. Occupational Conditions
      a) Employment of Both Husband and Wife
      b) Mobility of Occupation
      c) Stability of Occupation
      d) Occupational Standards
      e) Sex Contacts Required by Occupation

II. Health Factors
   1. Sickness and Disease
   2. Physical Deformity
   3. Physiological Changes Due to Age
   4. Psychopathic Conditions

III. Personal Factors
   1. Temperament

2. Appetites and Habits
3. Sex Attitudes
4. Age Variance
5. Philosophy of Life
6. Personal Behavior Patterns

IV. Social Factors
1. Race
2. Social Class
3. Religion
4. Status
5. Child-Complexes
6. Social Control in the Family Group
7. Relatives[1]

Meroney does not, however, give cases illustrating how each of these factors causes tension. The intensive study of one hundred cases of family disorganization led to the following classification of types of tensions: (1) incompatibility in response, (2) economic individualization, (3) cultural differentiation, and (4) individuation of life-patterns. Each case does not necessarily represent a single tension, but the assumption is that there is in each case one type of situation which is predominant in the conflict between husband and wife.

The following description of tensions is necessarily tentative and will undoubtedly be shown to be defective in many respects when a more adequate technique is discovered for getting more complete case-studies of family disorganization. But the tensions defined here will not be substantiated alone by case-studies of family disorganization. If they are fundamental descriptions then they must stand the test of furnishing complementary types of accord which can be verified by the study of cases of family life where adjust-

[1] *The Town Church and the Modern Family* (M.A. thesis, University of Chicago), p. 77.

ments between husband and wife have been successful. This, however, does not come within the province of the present study except as a theoretical possibility.

INCOMPATIBILITY IN RESPONSE

Incompatibility in response includes what is known in common sense as "sexual incompatibility." The sex factor is probably more commonly the cause of family discord than would appear on the surface. People are not accustomed to talking frankly about sex. Even between husband and wife there is often a decided reserve in any discussion of this sphere of their relations. It is doubtful if the average husband and wife themselves realize the importance of sexual adjustment in promoting harmonious adjustment in other relations.

Sex should not be too narrowly defined, however. In both the male and the female there are primary and secondary erogenous zones, though sex feeling in the female is much more widely diffused than in the male. But here sex is defined by implication wholly in physiological terms. In the experience of the individual the sex impulse becomes overlaid with traditional attitudes and with reactions to one's own sexual contacts. All the "love" elements have their origin in sex, but nowhere today do they constitute purely physiological reactions. Especially in the female there is an overlaying of the sex impulse by sentiment, emotional attachments, and the like. One of the most baffling of loyalties is that of a wife to the man with whom she has had all her sex contacts and for whom she has borne children even though he may have deserted her for another woman. Social workers constantly find their attempts to punish deserters frustrated by such an attitude.

It is sex in this composite meaning of sense and sentiment

which is at the basis of compatibility in response. and for which Thomas has substituted the term "desire for response."[1] Sexual attitudes vary, therefore, with cultural groups as well as with individuals. Incompatibility in any particular case depends to a large degree upon what the two individuals expect in the way not only of direct sexual contacts but of indirect as well, including all those ways conventionally accepted as appropriate for the demonstration of affection.

In every marriage there are factors which tend toward incompatibility in response and lead to differentiation of love interests between husband and wife. The sex impulse itself is never quite the same in strength for both, and no two persons, perhaps, ever have exactly the same emotional attitudes toward love contacts. Sexual excesses and sexual anaesthesia tend to accentuate this latent antagonism.

Incompatibility in response has its origin in rather a wide diversity of circumstances. Differences in sex impulse between two persons may be primarily physiological; they may be the result of differences in temperament; or the differences may be simply those of culture. Poor health is often the origin of physiological differences. Either the husband or the wife may feel a repugnance toward sex relations which acts as an inhibiting force. The puritanical attitude toward sex still finds its followers who insist that intimacy even in marriage should never be experienced except for the purpose of reproduction.

Diversity in the desire for response often is due to a difference in the desires for direct and indirect sex contacts.

[1] "The desire for response," Thomas says," . . . . is primarily related to the instinct of love, and shows itself in the tendency to seek and to give signs of appreciation in connection with other individuals."—*The Unadjusted Girl*, p. 17.

The wife may wish caresses and attention rather than the more direct sex stimulations. She may even recoil at the latter, especially if it does not include the former. The husband, on the other hand, may find the caresses and attentions which he gave his wife during courtship boresome now that relations may be more intimate. In certain cases dulling of passion leads to perversions which make the whole relationship repulsive to the wife.

Interference with established habits of intimate relations by circumstances such as the pregnancy of the wife or the absence of the husband may give rise to differentiation of sexual interests.

Fear of pregnancy is often a real terror to newly married couples. The husband fears it either because he does not care for children, or because he cannot afford them. The wife fears the pain in addition to the fears complementary to those of the husband. And still there may be little or no disposition on the part of the husband to refrain from intimacy, even though that were possible. But even when he co-operates it often creates restlessness and irritation.

Refusal to have intimate relations is also often the origin of conflict though it may arise out of the fear of pregnancy on the part of the wife. Especially is this true where there is a lack of frankness, and married couples are often not very frank when it comes to these relations. But even though the motive is quite clear, there may be discord due to jealousy. Human beings are not entirely the rational beings so often assumed by social reformers. Frankness alone is not a complete solvent of jealousy and suspicion arising from the refusal to have intimate contacts.

Discord in response relations is often prevented, of course, by transference to other interests of the attention ordinarily given to these relations. The wife often finds it possible to substitute response from her children for that which she has failed to get from her husband. This substitution is more easily made, however, in the case of the wife than of the husband, and it may even go so far as to take the place of sexual intimacies. But with the husband the interests substituted are often of another type, having in themselves conflict elements. Gambling and carousing often represent such substitutions; or the husband may substitute the association of other women. In either case, the result is likely to be the same: absence from home, suspicion of infidelity, discord.

In some cases the sex impulse becomes diffused in women to include the desire to experience pregnancy, child birth, and nursing of the baby. Failure to find satisfaction for all phases of this diffused desire creates dissatisfaction. Impotency or the use of contraceptives may be the origin of this failure, as well as abstinence.

Other interests may absorb the attention of one or the other of the two to such a degree that the response relationship is forgotten. If this redirection of energy into other channels is not mutual the dissatisfied party tends to turn elsewhere for response.

The following case illustrates incompatibility in response. While there was no direct break in the marriage relations, all the essential elements are present except that the wife was unwilling to forego her security in order to satisfy the desire for response.

American woman, forty-five years old, married. Husband is a prosperous real estate broker, and member of many clubs, a church warden, director of several corporations, a typical business man of the type termed "successful," a good citizen "without one redeeming vice."

She is a beautiful woman, albeit tired and faded. Her hair is prematurely white, her youthful face with deep-set brown eyes has a wistful contradictory appearance. Has many sides to her nature, can play ball with her boys as well as she can preside at a meeting. Is a good companion, has many friends, and leads a busy life as head of a prosperous household. Has five children, four boys and one girl. One would not guess that she is an unsatisfied woman; her friends all think her life ideal and, in a sense, she does not deny it. This in substance is her view of married life though not literally word for word:

"I suppose there can never be a school for marriage—how could there be?—yet how sad it is that every one must begin at the same place to work out the same problem. I had a good father and mother. They did not understand me but that was probably more my fault than theirs; I never confided in my mother overmuch. My father considered my mental progress at all times and I owe much to him for the manner in which he made me think of myself, strengthened my views, and guided my education. When I left finishing school I played in society for two years and many of the men I met interested me, though none compelled me. I had never been given any clear conception of what marriage should be in the ideal sense. I knew vaguely that the man I married must be in my own class, good and honorable, and rich enough to maintain a dignified household, I had more of a vision of love at sixteen than at twenty-six, the year I married, though I was sure I loved my husband and I do—that is he is as much a part of my life as my religion or my household conventions. He is wholly a product of civilization and I discovered too late there is an element of the savage in most women. They wish to be captured, possessed—not in the sense the suffragists talk about; it is really a sense of self-abasement, for it is the adoration of an ideal. They wish to love a man in the open—a fighter, a victor—rather than the men we know who have their hearts in money making and play at being men. Perhaps it cannot be remodeled, it is only a bit of wildness that will never be tamed in women but it makes for unhappiness just the same.

"My sex life had never been dominant. I had a commonplace adolescence with physical longings and sensations which were not explained to me and which did me no harm. My relation with my husband was perfectly orthodox, and vaguely I longed for something different. My husband was shocked at any demonstration on my part.

If I was impulsive and threw myself in his arms he straightened his tie before he kissed me. Once at our cottage in the mountains I suggested that we spend the night in the woods. I saw a possibility of our getting nearer to each other physically and spiritually if we could get out in the wilderness away from the restraints and niceties of our luxurious household. That was the first time I ever felt like a traitor. He told me quite sternly to go to bed, I was not a wild Indian and could not act like one. I went to the nursery for the night and snuggled close to my little boy and was glad he was young and slender and hoped he would never grow fat and complacent. I had noticed for the first time that my husband was growing stout, like any other churchwarden.

"Since that time I have never been wholly happy. It was not the foolish incident, it was the fundamental principle and underlying our civilization. Our babies came rather closely together and I was glad that the mother element in me needed to be uppermost. My husband was perfectly content with life, I satisfied him at dinner parties, I could dress well and talk well, managed the household money to advantage and was at hand—tame, quite tame, when he wished to kiss me. I do not mean to sound sarcastic and bitter. It is not what my husband is which troubles me, but what ne is not; I think I speak for many women. I am more mated to the vision of what my children's father might have been than to the good kind man whom I teach them to love and respect.

"Perhaps you have guessed I am coming to a confession: I met the man in England two summers ago, but he is an American and is in this country now, a friend of ours whom we both see quite often. Something in both of us flared the very night we met. He and Lawrence (my husband) get along famously; they both believe in many of the same ideals and discuss kindred subjects, but my brain and his supplement each other in a way which is hard to explain. I did not mean to love him. It is an upper strata of myself; I love Lawrence; I mean I belong to him, am part of his very being and he of mine, but I am myself when I am with this other man and I refuse to think what a different self it might have been had I known him before. The very morning after I faced the awful fact that I was thinking of a man other than my husband, Lawrence put a bouquet at my plate at the breakfast table. It was a red geranium, a tiny pink rose, and some leaves of striped grass. Poor Lawrence.

"Our adventure in love came rapidly. He understood me perfectly and I knew that he cared. We have never told Lawrence for we do not intend to do anything more that is wrong. He has spent several evenings at the house when Lawrence was away. There was no deception about this—it just happened and we have talked and kissed and faced life in the open. We decided quite calmly, and without passion, that we would have each other entirely just once. I wanted the complete vision of what my love could mean. If it is wrong I cannot think so; at any rate I would not give up the memory of that time. It was only once and it was a year ago. We both knew there could be no continued sex relation. When I have an opportunity I kiss him and he me. Lawrence never kisses my lips, so they belong to him. He has helped me to be more patient, and understanding of my life as it has been and must be. I have my children and must live out the life for their sakes and for Lawrence who loves me, tamed and domesticated.

"If life could be—what it would mean to give him a child, but life in its entirety cannot be—for me. Probably that is the creed of many women."[1]

In the foregoing case there was no break in the marriage relation as there undoubtedly would have been had the wife not been willing to dissociate her response interests from those involving her security and had she not been willing to forego further sexual relations with the other man. She has also found it possible to substitute response from her children for that which she failed to get from her husband.

Whether or not any type tension culminates in family disintegration depends upon the dominant interests of the persons and their ability to dissociate one type of interest from another. If the dissatisfied person is willing to forego the satisfaction of one group of desires for another group, or

[1] Smith and Cabot, "A Study of Sexual Morality," *Social Hygiene*, II, 532–34; quoted by Thomas, *op. cit.*, pp. 27–30.

if there is sufficient dissociation of interests to allow the relationship to continue upon the basis of certain interests without the others, family disintegration does not materialize.

In the modern marriage relationship, however, the desire for response tends to dominate all the rest of the wishes. It is thus the most stabilizing element as well as potentially the most fertile source of conflict in the modern family. This conclusion seems quite in accord with the facts, for out of the one hundred cases upon which this chapter is based 40 per cent represent incompatibility in response.

ECONOMIC INDIVIDUALIZATION

Economic individualization is probably more commonly found in the relations of husband and wife among the lower and middle classes than among the upper classes. Where there are ample resources for every possible need of the family, even though the economic interests may become individualized to the extent of the wife knowing scarcely anything about her husband's business, individualization does not create friction, necessarily, so long as the wife's security is not threatened. Upon more thorough analysis, however, it may appear that the interests in security and status are as much a part of what may be called "economic interests" of the married couple as are the vocational interests. The admonition made to newly married couples that they share with each other some portion of the economic problems which trouble the husband is simply a recognition that this is an effective technique for minimizing the tendency toward economic individualization.

In every marriage there tends to be some individualization of economic interests. This tendency arises out of the differences in attitudes toward economic matters, which is primarily the result of differences in training and in personal experience. Differences in standards of living, the individualization of spending, differences in attitude regarding whether or not a wife should work, vocational separation, and economic independence are all factors in this tension.

Change in the standard of living to a lower plane involves the change of habits which have, in many cases, become second nature. The result is a feeling of irritation and hopelessness. Tension often arises, also, because the husband feels that as he has earned the money he should have the privilege of spending what he wants to as he wishes. If there is anything left, it can go to his wife. Or the husband may feel that the world owes him a living, and no matter where the income comes from he may see no reason for being concerned about it. His economic interests may thus become wholly centered in the sort of security which requires the least personal effort.

Differences in conception of the rôle of each in the economic process often leads to conflict. Under rural conditions the pattern of adjustment in this realm is fixed within rather narrow limits; in the city it becomes highly individualized. Vocational interests which tend to separate the husband and wife for certain periods of time are potential sources of conflict. Not only does this tend toward differentiation of economic interests but other interests as well. Where both parties are equally competent in the economic field the attempt to make adjustments to the diversity of opportunity offered to each is always potentially a source of conflict and tension. Such situations necessarily involve a high individualization of economic interests and, if this necessitates constant separation, differentiation of other interests invariably follows.

The following cases represent economic individualization:

I am 29 years of age. Hubby is the same age. He makes $41 every two weeks. Now there is where the trouble is. He thinks I can live on this. I do the best I can with it. We pay $36 a month rent, then electric and gas bills have to be paid and the children have to be looked after and fed. Half the time we are hungry. We don't know what it is to have warm clothes or take in shows like others. Haven't been to a show in two years, as Hubby thinks I should live on this. I really do the best I can. Forgot to tell you I owe on my furniture which is $10 every month. All this has to come out of the $82 a month. Don't know what I will do, as this is the only thing that is making our home unhappy. Sometimes I feel like running away when Hubby thinks it ought to do us; then I think of my little ones—what would they do without me?[1]

Agnes and Jack became acquainted during the few visits which Jack made to Agnes' home town as a traveling salesman. Both were extremely romantic and against the wishes of Agnes' parents, they were married. Jack had practically no other income than the salary which he received as a salesman and so the two found it necessary to go to live with Jack's parents. Jack succeeded in obtaining a position in the shops of the company for which he had traveled, but his salary was no higher.

Agnes had been accustomed to having plenty of money before her marriage, and the reduction in her spending money soon became irksome to her. She began to think that Jack was lazy and did not earn as much as he should, and she also thot his parents denied her comforts which she should have. She began to nag the whole family, and created such a feeling of hostility between herself and Jack's parents that she and Jack were asked to look for an apartment for themselves. Agnes rebelled at this action, which she felt was an injustice, but she and Jack soon found a small house of their own. The added expense made a great hole in Jack's salary and Agnes found it impossible to manage the expense, so that everything could be paid for. Jack was irritated at Agnes' lack of ability in managing the houshold expenses, and began to threaten to send her home.

About a year after their marriage Jack was brought home from work in an ambulance, and Agnes was told that Jack's eye had been

[1] *Chicago Herald and Examiner*, November 24, 1921.

put out by a piece of flint which had flown up and struck it. Her spirit of loyalty seemed to rise at this time, and during the following weeks, she cared for Jack faithfully. The doctor bills were large and when Jack returned to work again the two young people found themselves heavily in debt.

Shortly after this a son, Jack, Jr., was born and to the debt which had already piled up, was added the expense for hospital and doctor bills, and the two young people began to feel that they could not meet their bills. When Jack, Jr., was about six weeks old, Jack told Agnes that he could not support her any longer, and so they gave up their home and Agnes took Jack, Jr., to her parents' home. After about six months, Agnes felt that it was time for Jack to be sending for her to come back, for she thought he could have saved enough money by that time to have paid off their debts. She wrote him that she was coming back, and went to his parents' home, but there she received only a cold welcome, while Jack informed her that he didn't care to have her come back, as he couldn't support her as she cared to live. After a great deal of urging on her part, Agnes succeeded in getting Jack to consent to try again, but the next few months showed that Agnes could not live within Jack's salary, so he sent her home again.

At regular intervals for the next two years Agnes tried to go back to live with Jack, but their efforts always failed and at last Jack told Agnes he didn't want her to come back again at all. He refused to send her any money, and left her and the baby to be supported by her father. Now Agnes is applying for divorce on the ground of non-support.[1]

CULTURAL DIFFERENTIATION

Cultural differentiation has its source in the diversity of cultures to which the two persons have been subjected. These differences are chiefly in the religious, racial, and educational folkways and mores of the groups in which the two persons grew up. Conflict generally centers about questions of right and wrong, proper and improper conduct. Social contacts are made upon the basis of cultural characteristics. Cultural differences thus become bound up with preferences

[1] Unpublished document (manuscript).

with regard to friends. It is in this realm of life to which belong recreational and leisure-time activities wherein contacts tend to lose their conventional character. Diversity of cultural background becomes, then, a source of irritation which leads to loss of sympathy and of common ideals.

While cultural differentiation does not necessarily lead to individualization of other interests, it always tends to. How far it involves other interests depends, perhaps, largely upon the amount of time the two persons have to devote to cultural interests.

Differences in folkways are not only the source of differences in habits, but also make for diversity in the choice of social contacts, and are therefore potential causes of conflict. Differences in cultural and recreational interests likewise tend to lead to differentiation of social contacts. The personalities of the two persons develop under the influence of social contacts which, if widely divergent, may lead to changes in personalities and to a breakdown in common interests and sympathetic relations between husband and wife.

Cases of cultural differentiation are not uncommon. They tend, however, to include other tensions as well, as the following illustrate.

The wife grew up in a small town and is now a manicurist in a barber shop. She is a Gentile and her husband a Jew. He comes from a good family and has many friends. Husband and wife separated three weeks ago, following frequent quarrels. There are no children. He went out often with his Jewish friends. At first she accompanied him, but she was the laughing stock among them and soon refused to go out with him. Whenever she became angry at her husband, she called him a "Jew." This her husband resented. Besides feeling that she did not belong to his crowd, she felt that he should save some of his money instead of spending it all on good times, and leaving her alone so often until late at night. Since their separation he has been going out with other women and she thinks it is likely that he had done so before. At the time of the separation he advised his wife to get a divorce and recommended a lawyer to her. "She was never meant for me," the husband said.[1]

The H family was composed of husband, wife and a baby one year old. The parents were both young people, having been married but two years and a half. The girl was brought up in a small city, the daughter of a minister, and all her relatives are very cultured people. She herself is a college graduate, and a very refined young woman. Mr. H was brought up on a farm, in a neighborhood which is far from being cultured. He is also a college graduate, and a graduate of a dental college and is successful in his profession. They met in college and had many good times with other young people. Since they were seldom alone, but usually out with a crowd, the differences in their folkways and mores did not stand out, for the crowd usually acted together. Even later when they separated and corresponded for a year there did not seem to be any vital difference. The next year they were in the same city, and became engaged almost at once. As they were now frequently together alone, the differences in cultural standards became apparent. The girl found herself annoyed at the way he held his knife at the table, in his lapse into poor English when he was embarrassed, and most of all at the friends he had made in the city. He was a broad-minded, deep-thinking young man, with high ideals, and she equally intelligent and with equally high ideals. She really loved him and realized that she was letting unimportant things come between them—for he was not conscious of any such infractions of the cultural code. She put aside any annoyance she felt and he never suspected it. As long as they were alone she was satisfied, but she grew more and more ashamed to take him among her own friends. She did not enjoy his friends, who were chiefly men, and their wives, whom he had known in the dental college. But she was quite sure she loved him and he was devoted to her.

Within a year they were married. When they were in their own home Mrs. H discovered many more things which offended her tastes,

[1] Case heard by a social worker in the Complaint Department of the Chicago Court of Domestic Relations, December 5, 1921.

and tho she tried to make him see that things he did were not cultured
he could not quite get her point of view. "Why not do things at home
as you want to?" he would ask. Soon she gave up reforming him as
hopeless, she stopped asking him to do things differently, but she always had to suppress her feelings. He went on unconscious of what
was wrong, only realizing that she was often cold toward him, when
at first she had been very demonstrative.

One day when there was company and he had come to the table
without his coat she was very much chagrined, and when they were
alone she burst into tears and said, "You'll just have to get another
wife, even if I do love you!" He was perfectly astounded. Finally he
made her tell him what he had done and gradually they went on as
before. But her story was out; they both became self-conscious at
home and they avoided going out together, if at all.

The tension was always present. She was conscious that she had
allowed petty things to spoil their happiness, and had hurt her husband's feelings. He was conscious that thru no fault of his own he had
offended his wife, and was doing so all the time.

They went on, both determined to forget it and be happy anyway,
but it was impossible. He was always sure he was doing the wrong
thing, and if he was, his wife tried in vain to overlook it. When their
child was born, it looked as if things were going to be more agreeable
for them, and for a while they were. But now that the child is getting
old enough to learn even a few things, the old question of whose ways
it shall learn is coming up again. She has come to the point where she
tries to avoid having him embrace her at all and a real estrangement,
physical as well as spiritual, has taken place. She is conscious that she
is at fault, and therefore is determined that they shall not separate.[1]

INDIVIDUATION OF LIFE-PATTERNS

There is in the individual a schematization of all his
habits which gives to them a consistency and unity Each
individual, more often unconsciously than consciously,
works out for himself an outlook upon the whole of life
which takes the form of a philosophy. This schematization
which may be called his "pattern of life," determines the

[1] Unpublished document (manuscript).

general attitude or bias with which he will approach any problem. Where there is too great diversity between the patterns of husband and wife there tends to be conflict or tension.

Individuation of life-patterns may originate in differences at the time of marriage, or in those which arise out of later experiences of the individuals. Whether the pattern of life is primarily based upon temperamental characteristics has not yet been determined, though the probabilities are that it is. Personal experience, however, modifies very greatly the development from the temperamental background. In many persons there tends to be considerable change with age, and severe crisis situations produce in many cases profound effects. In the analysis of cases it often becomes very difficult to distinguish clearly between this tension and that of cultural differentiation. In fact, it is probable that the former tends to accentuate the latter.

The essential elements in the distinction between cultural factors and patterns of life may be illustrated by imagining two twins, both of whom have grown up under what seem to be the same environmental influences, one of whom is an introvert and the other an extravert, that is, one has an objective approach to life and the other a subjective. These two imaginary twins could hardly be said to have had a different cultural background, and still their outlook upon life and the general schematization of their habits would be quite different. In fact, the differences might be so great as to make intimate association impossible. So it is with husbands and wives.

Differences in life-patterns often go unnoticed until certain age periods are reached or some severe crisis accentuates the latent attitudes. Differences in age and experience of husband and wife are also factors in the individuation of life-patterns, all of which become easily accentuated by vocational separation. While there are other tensions in the case of the S's, individuation of life-patterns seems to have been the chief source of conflict. This difference tended to differentiate the approach to all interests in life, culminating finally in the entire loss of common basis for marital relations.

Dr. S met his wife when he was a senior in a small coeducational college in the Middle West. Mrs. S, the daughter of a well-to-do Southern family, entered the school as a freshman the year her husband was graduated. During her first year in college she fell in love with Dr. S, who was the instructor in one of her classes. They became engaged just after Dr. S took his degree.

The next year Dr. S went to Yale to take his Doctor's degree in zoölogy. He was able to create a very favorable impression in meeting and dealing with people, being a smooth, fluent and interesting conversationalist. Dr. S was well received at Yale and was sent to Peru to do some field work for the department of zoölogy. When he returned from this expedition he finished his scholastic work and received the degree of Ph.D. Immediately after this Dr. S married his fiancée and they went to Cleveland to live, where he secured a very good position in an educational institution. While here he became interested in social problems and associated with a group of "radical" thinkers in this field.

When Dr. and Mrs. S were first married he was an ideal husband. His wife was madly in love with him, and she thought that he was in love with her. Everywhere they went their friends remarked, "What an ideal couple." He was all tenderness then, and oftentimes in the evening would sing little lullabies to her.

Then the children came,—two boys and a girl, each about two years apart. Their father took great pride in them. When the children were about to enter school Dr. S was sent to Samoa to lead an expedition. With the prospect of the father's being away from home for several years, Mrs. S took the family to Paris where she studied and kept the children in a very strict day school. Dr. S seemed to feel no restraint in leaving his family for he could always rely on her family to help her out in any way possible.

With her marriage Mrs. S gave herself up entirely to her husband, her children and her duties as a mother. She loved her home and exerted all her energies to the task of making it attractive both to her family and to her friends. The result was that many visitors came to her home. Her husband likewise, through his entertaining speech and pleasing personality, drew many friends to his fireside, where he expounded to them at will his pet hobbies, theories of society and religion. Mrs. S, though she disapproved of her husband's atheistic beliefs and the application of a laissez faire system to social life, nevertheless treated him with indulgence and heard his radicalism with amusement, maintaining the rather maternal attitude that he would "outgrow them." These ideas, however, persisted, encouraged by his "radical" friends.

During the years that his children were in school, Dr. S spent little of his time at home. He was home for a few months before going to new territory to do field work. With each furlough home Dr. S seemed to be delighted to be back with his family. He was continually planning evenings for himself and his family, such as dinners, the theatre, the opera, and almost any sort of exciting amusement which would keep him out of his own home and among pleasure-bent crowds.

Gradually Dr. S began to develop a strange antagonism toward his elder son. At first the son only mildly irritated him, but as he was at home for longer periods of time the aversion became stronger. This caused some antagonism between him and his wife. Her maternal instinct was thoroly aroused by her husband's unfatherly conduct and she could not endure her son to be subjected to such uncalled for abuse and neglect. With all the tact possible she endeavored to bridge the breach between the two, but with little success. In spite of her husband's conduct she never ceased to care for him.

About this time the elder son married a woman of good social and financial connections. She had been known to the family for a number of years. At the same time Dr. S without any explanation moved his personal effects to another part of the city and refused to have any further connection with his family, with the exception of his younger son with whom he dined occasionally.

Mrs. S, shocked and grieved, gave up her house and took an

apartment, where she and her unmarried son and daughter lived. Mrs. S at first refused to give him a divorce, for she thot that some day he would see his folly and return to her. She has since learned that he had many affairs with other women. When he first asked for a divorce he would have married a woman in Cleveland had Mrs. S given him his freedom. Mrs. S feels that no one woman can satisfy her husband.

Looking back upon the situation, Mrs. S now says that she might have been able to "hold her husband" had she always been his companion in those first years. But that was impossible for she was tied down with a growing family and her husband was going on frequent expeditions.

In spite of her husband's conduct Mrs. S has never ceased to care for him. She had early built up a romantic dream world about him. He was older than she and more advanced intellectually. In the beginning she was wonderfully happy and she still holds to that romantic dream world, saying that the man who now exists is not the man she married and loved.

Mrs. S does not regard her husband as immoral but unmoral. He has lived hard. There have always been women. And he has been fond of drink, tho he never becomes intoxicated. Of late years he has had little contact with his children and has appeared indifferent toward them.

A few years ago Mrs. S divorced her husband. She lives with her son and daughter, moving in practically the same circle as before her divorce.

A few months ago Mrs. S received word that her husband had re-married. This came as a shock for in spite of her divorce she seems to have held to the belief that some day he would return to her. She said that had he re-married soon after his divorce she could not have endured it. She could not stand to think that another woman had taken her place! "It is a blow," she said, "for a woman to know that she cannot hold her husband, but it is still more of a blow for a woman to know that another woman has taken her place—especially if she still cares for the man."

Mrs. S says that she has no desire ever to re-marry. She feels that there is a certain "biological loyalty" to a man for whom a woman has borne children. In spite of all her unhappiness, Mrs. S feels glad that she had married. For a time she was intensely happy and she "still has those memories."[1]

Definition of family disorganization in terms of type tensions marks a clear transition to the objective classification of causative factors. It also gives to such a classification the logical consistency necessary for science by defining these factors in terms of attitudes. In this way interaction becomes the unifying principle and thus satisfies the logical demand that the classification, in its complementary aspects, shall also serve in the analysis of family organization. For example, it is quite apparent that compatibility in response is as much a factor in conditioning harmonious relations in marriage as is incompatibility in response a factor in causing discord.

It is necessary, however, to carry the analysis of a phenomenon beyond the classificatory stage before any high degree of control can be obtained. Mere classification of tensions, therefore, is not sufficient, but only preliminary to the discovery of sequence of events or processes. While each type tension represents, presumably, a process or a group of related processes, it does not describe, and so does not explain, the sequence of events tending to culminate in family disintegration. The next step in the analysis of family disorganization becomes, then, the description of family discord in terms of typical sequences of events, i.e., in terms of typical processes.

[1] Unpublished document (manuscript).

CHAPTER X

BEHAVIOR SEQUENCES IN FAMILY DISORGANIZATION

The description of family discord in terms of typical behavior sequences has not made much progress for two reasons: (1) Students of the problem have not always had a clear conception of the logic of all science. (2) Sociology has not yet equipped itself with an adequate terminology for the description of behavior. Both of these difficulties are in turn the result of the complexity of human behavior. The behavior of molecules is quite simple in comparison to the behavior of human beings, and still it is only recently that the scientist has been able to predict with any degree of accuracy what chemical elements would do under the simplest conditions. And it has been even more recently that he has come to understand the logic of the processes by which he has made these predictions.

THE LOGIC OF SCIENCE

The first problem with which the logic of science is concerned is that of perception. The natural scientist takes much the same point of view which characterizes common sense with regard to this problem. That is, he assumes a dualism between matter and mind as well as the "reflex-arc" system of psychology which has been discredited by a growing group of psychologists under the leadership of Professor Dewey.[1]

We appear to receive from without, during our waking hours, a continuous stream of sense-impressions leading to what we call the

[1] John Dewey, "The Reflex-Arc Concept in Psychology," *Psychological Review*, Vol. III.

perception of external objects and events, or grouped sense-impressions. These perceptions succeed one another in time, and change with greater or less rapidity. Although our percepts are in a continual state of flux, the changes in them are not entirely haphazard, but exhibit a considerable degree of regularity or sequence, of such a kind that we possess a certain amount of power of prediction of their future course. . . . . We find, moreover, that we possess certain powers of classifying and sorting out our percepts, or forming by abstraction from them permanent concepts, under which whole classes of our percepts are subsumed.[1]

This type of experience is, as Professor Hobson says, that which characterizes what is called "common sense," and constitutes the essential condition for any action upon the part of human beings. Natural science, however, elaborates and refines this view of the world of matter.

It is a part of the view of the nature of Natural Science, or the Science of physical percepts, which I propose to develop, that Science is essentially a purposive continuation of the formation of what I have called common knowledge, but carried out in a more systematic manner, and to a much higher degree of exactitude and refinement. The earliest stages in the formation of scientific knowledge are of the kind which may be described as classificatory. Physical objects are arranged in classes, in accordance with observed similarities in the objects assigned to any one class; physical events or sequences of events are classified in accordance with observed regularities or similarities in those events or sequences. There is, however, always a certain degree of arbitrariness involved in the selection of the precise similarities or regularities which form the basis of the classification. . . . . The result of this process expresses itself in the formation of abstractions or concepts, which are not identical with any of the perceptual objects or happenings which conditioned their formation, but which serve as a conceptual symbolization or representation of those aspects of the latter which we regard as alone relevant for the purpose of classification.[2]

[1] E. W. Hobson, *The Domain of Natural Science*, p. 23.

[2] *Ibid.*, p. 25.

Such a conceptual description of perceptual sequences is then used for purposes of predicting what will happen under conditions which are not identical with those from which the description was obtained, but in which there is a high degree of similarity. The adequacy of this method thus depends upon the reliability with which predictions of future occurrences may be made.

In the attempt to discover a scientific law, a selective process is requisite in regard to the percepts, some greater or lesser part of what is perceived is ignored, as irrelevant to the purpose in hand; this selective procedure amounts to a process of abstraction, in which some elements of our actual percepts are removed, and not attended to. . . . . A scientific law is accordingly always, in some greater or lesser degree, abstract, in the sense that it represents only a part of what is in any individual case actually perceived; it describes a particular sequence of physical events which, in an actual case is accompanied by other percepts or events in relation to which the law has no application. . . . .[1]

These statements, then, describe in brief the procedure of the natural sciences. It would seem plausible to assume that a similar procedure would produce comparable results in the field of sociology, in general, and therefore in the study of family disorganization. The difficulty lies, however, in the assumption in natural science that the rôle of the subject in perception is passive. Such a methodological assumption is justified in the natural sciences where no account is taken of psychical events. In sociology, however, the matter is not so simple. It is generally recognized that human beings often "think" one way and act another.

The fundamental wishes, we may assume, are the same in all situations. The attitudes and sentiments, however, in which the wishes of the individual find expression are determined not merely by

[1] Hobson, *op. cit.*, p. 29.

these wishes, but by other factors in the situation, the wishes of other individuals, for example. The desire for recognition is a permanent and universal trait of human nature, but in the case of an egocentric personality, this wish may take the form of an excessive humility or a pretentious boasting. The wish is the same but the attitudes in which it finds expression are different.[1]

It is about this problem that a great deal of the present conflict between the behaviorists and introspectionists in psychology centers. In so far as sociology has become psychological in its approach it also has had to take sides in this controversy. One way out of this conflict, with the difficulties which are immediately suggested by taking either of these extreme approaches, is for the student of family disorganization to take a middle-of-the-road point of view. According to this latter approach thinking is as much a form of behavior as is acting. It is recognized, of course, that there is a distinction between overt and incipient or truncated behavior, but the distinction is one of degree rather than of kind. From such an approach to the study of family disorganization the same logic would apply as that which characterizes the generalizing in the natural sciences.

It follows from this process of reasoning that the student of family disorganization will search for sequences of behavior which he can describe conceptually in such a way as to serve as a basis for prediction. But the actual working out of such sequences depends upon the definition of the essential behavior units or events which are to be the terms in his formulas or sequences. This requirement is, however, not the only logical demand which must be met. Behavior sequences are not only disorganizing with regard to family relations but they are organizing as well. The two pro-

[1] Park and Burgess, *An Introduction to the Science of Sociology*, p. 439.

cesses, family disorganization and family organization, referred to in chapter vi, may thus be reduced to a common
denominator by thinking of them as types of sequences
within the flow of attitudes between husband and wife, i.e.,
interaction. Thus, there is obtained a process analogous to
metabolism in physiology or the flow of consciousness in
psychology. Whatever differences there are in the process of
organization, or identification, as compared to that of disorganization, or differentiation, are differences first in kind,
but ultimately only in degree.

It follows, then, that one of the problems in the study of
family disorganization is that of ascertaining the causes determining the flow of attitudes in any particular way between husband and wife. These causes will be defined necessarily in terms of sequences or combinations of events, i.e.,
in types of processes. It will be expected, of course, that
these types of processes will be the same, except in degree
and combination, whether the flow of attitudes between husband and wife, i.e., interaction, results in identification or
differentiation, just as in psychology it is assumed that there
is no fundamental difference in the mental processes in the
sane and in the insane except from one of degree or of combination.

Obviously, this description of behavior must go beyond
mere overt behavior. And here it is that the distinction between the natural and the social sciences becomes apparent.
The natural scientist is concerned only with what Hobson
has called "perception of physical objects." It is these percepts which are classified and fitted into an abstract conceptual scheme called a "scientific law or sequence." In the
description of interaction, however, it is the relations between individuals, in this case between husband and wife,

in which the sociologist is interested. These relations he describes as forms of behavior. But he cannot observe such relations; he can only infer them. He is forced thus to conceptualize his data even before he has classified it. The result is that his abstract descriptions of sequences are farther removed from the data of observation, the percepts, than those of the natural scientist.

With this definition of method, one may proceed to the analysis of an attempt to define abstractly a sequence of events culminating in almost complete disintegration of the marriage relation.

A CASE-STUDY IN TENSIONS IN FAMILY LIFE[1]

Mr. and Mrs. L had been married about four years when I first came to know them. They had but one child, a very beautiful girl of three years.

Mr. L was a man of very ordinary ability and mentality, rather small of stature, of the middle-class clerical type, with about a high school education; somewhat anti-social, retiring in disposition, high-strung, unsuccessful, unsmiling, relentless, and apathetic.

Mrs. L on the other hand was a gentle, sweet, rather beautiful woman of refinement and culture. She was much Mr. L's superior in

[1] E. T. Krueger, unpublished study (manuscript). In incorporating this study into this chapter the writer in no wise assumes responsibility for the organization of the materials nor the interpretation of the case. This study is introduced because it presents a departure in interpretation from the static conception of family disorganization in terms of typical discord situations to a dynamic conception in which several discord situations are linked together in a sequence. The value of the study lies, therefore, in this departure in method, rather than in the materials presented and interpreted in common-sense terms. In fact, much of the description and interpretation is too subjective to meet the requirements of science. Also, the interpretation contains much material which should have been introduced into the description of the case if one is to observe strictly the division between fact and inference. Nevertheless, this case reveals more sympathetic insight into the causes of discord than is ordinarily revealed in the procedure of those who habitually handle cases of family discord.

mental ability but had about a like schooling. Her reading, however, since school-days had been wide and educative. She was highly idealistic, had approached her marriage with a sense of the divinity of the new life, and was full of anticipation for its fruits. Her temperament was artistic and she had some musical ability. She found her greatest happiness in mutual love, and seemingly did not care for ostentation. She was even-tempered, kind, gracious, and full of friendship. In many ways she was one of nature's attempts to form personalities around which the world of personalities might be organized and civilization held together. She was almost an ideal mother and woman. Her friends felt that she had married far beneath her.

Mr. and Mrs. L had begun their married life by taking up a homestead claim. For three years they lived in a pretty home built at the head of a coullie, which broadened out from the hills into the great range and through which ran a small stream which found its way to the Little Beaver. At the end of three years they had proved up their claim and under the urging of Mr. L they planned to leave the homestead and go the the city. Mrs L was very well satisfied to remain where they were. They were quite happy, living much out in the open; the mystery and beauty of the range country fed her idealistic sense of values, and the duties of the new farm kept them busy.

Mr. L had learned the photographer's business and to him the ranch was irritating, overwhelming, and too great a struggle. They moved to the city and Mr. L secured a position as the photographer of one of the large local drug stores. This work was not quite what he had anticipated, but he found that the photographers already in business in the city had equipment and outfits which he could not procure in his present financial state. His work was largely commercial developing and printing, enlarging and reproducing.

Mr. L made few friends. In fact, he seems to have made but one friend, a man of about equal ability to himself, but even more crude, high-strung, and exacting. This man owned a house which he arranged in such a way as to permit small double living apartments. The L's came to live in the second apartment, the owner of the house in the first. The wife of this friend was more or less crude, unrefined, high-tempered, and insensitive.

Mr. L had no prestige in the city, no standing, very few friends, and an inferior position; the inferiority, however, was due in part to the man. The photographic vocation is capable of both extremes of status; it can be one of the great vocations or one of the most inferior.

Mrs. L made many friends, took up church work—such had been her girlhood—and found that her husband resented her friendships, opposed her church work, and finally ordered her to break her church relationships. In despair she turned to certain phases of Christian Science to secure for herself the food her spiritual, personal nature demanded. Mr. L. had been identified with a church when he was a young man but seemingly had not integrated any philosophy of life sufficient to see him through his present stress.

Mr. L clung to his one friend and went into fancy poultry raising with him as a side line. He tried to make the social life of these two families meet the needs of both himself and his wife. But this close neighbor family could not satisfy the refined and sensitive tastes of his wife. Their isolation from the church, from cultured friends, broke her spirit.

Gradually husband and wife drew apart. He seemed to love her almost desperately, and yet had not the means to hold her love. Almost insensibly she developed a sex antagonism in which her husband's advances sickened her and made her nature revolt. My last knowledge of the state of affairs in this family was that the wife was attempting to understand her situation and to formulate a plan of action. She had two courses from which to choose: she could take her child and leave her husband; or, rather than face the publicity and violation of the mores and folkways, subdue her own spirit and submit to the repression of herself. Her troubles were making inroads upon her health.

INTERPRETATION

This case involves change in status in the move from rural to urban environment, the marriage of unequals, the idealism of the wife which mistakes the ardency of a man for idealism, the change from outdoor healthy life and activity to the confinement of a photographer's basement shop, economic depression, religious conflict, sex antagonism, family disintegration, and ill-health.

The change from the farm or ranch to the city involved many factors. Ranch life was isolated. It drew the family together, neighbors were few and far, and there was little opportunity for Mrs. L to measure her husband against other men. As a consequence the family status was, as far as it went, on a par with the general run of families on the range. In the city the family had an inferior economic status which no doubt increased the natural irritability of the husband and caused the wife to make mental comparisons and contrasts which belittled her husband in her eyes. She probably rationalized her attitudes at first, and had not other situations developed the economic status alone would not have caused her to discount her husband to the exclusion of natural sex life.

Mrs. L was indeed too fine-spirited a woman not to have sympathized with her husband in his economic difficulties. Her values were primarily of human and spiritual worth. On the ranch she had a far different life. There, there was economic co-operation, she shared in the life, the work, the plans; she could guide her husband's thinking and planning. In the city all economic co-operation was destroyed. She sat in her home; she cooked, baked, scrubbed; her life was a monotonous round of impossible days. The ranch, with its trees, its mountain stream, the great, mystic range country, the sunsets, the out-door life, the unity of the home and family interests, the sharing in the common objects of planning and work, had given depth to her life, satisfied her idealism, fed her spiritual values. On the ranch her husband lived out-doors; in the city the physical activity which he needed was almost entirely lost. There can be little doubt that the new, city life was making the husband less vital physically, that his loss of economic status and rather insufficient financial returns were wearing on his morale and probably caused a state of mind which sought relief in constant sex stimulation, to the horror of the wife.

We need also to go back to the apparent cultural differences of the husband and wife. Had they remained on the farm these differences would probably not have become a disruptive influence, unless there should have followed an economic failure, which would have tended to accentuate difference in culture. We have here a situation in which the wife is of distinctly finer pattern than the husband, where the wife is idealistic and refined, looking upon her husband with eyes that saw the ideal, not the actual. Had crises not arisen, this state of mind on the wife's part might have lasted for life. Life in the city disabused her mind of the values she had accorded her husband. Turning to church work was natural for her, but it was not long before the church became a spiritual necessity to her. The life in the city had become the crisis which brought in its train the force of circumstances which were destroying the idealism and anchorages of her soul. Consequently the church tended to give her a substitute set of spiritual values upon which she pinned her faith.

As time went on she realized more than ever that her husband lacked not only cultural values but idealistic values; his narrowness, his smallness of calibre, his inability to make friends, his dislike of the church, his lack of ability to succeed,—all these caused her deep misgivings for the future. Full loss of respect for her husband did not develop until the accentuation of sex stimulation and satisfaction appeared. He wanted her desperately, but it sickened her to realize that he had no conception of the high character of sex life. Under the stress of apparent failure to achieve and under the physical strain of the loss of vitality and the enervation of the cellar-occupation downtown, he sought relief in sex relations. The frequency and violence of these disgusted her.

As the sex antagonism developed, his opposition to her participation in church life increased. This added fuel to her loss of respect for him. On several occasions he had accompanied her to church only to find that she vastly out-distanced him in social recognition. He was unknown and a nonentity; she was popular, people showered her with attention, and although she tried to introduce him and push him forward he shriveled within himself and made a sorry mess of it. In his bitterness and belief that things were against him, he gradually forced his wife to discontinue her church life; he could not bear to see her stand higher than he stood. When she turned to Christian Science, "new thought" ideas, to feed her need for inner life he became violently opposed to the Christian Science church and any participation in its doctrines. No family can long endure in our modern cities unless it surrounds itself with some social life. This antagonism to her friends, to their dropping in to visit, to any social life except that of the family in the other apartment, made her life dreary with isolation and loneliness. He was of no help to her and he refused her friends who could be of help.

It was inevitable, perhaps, that with church, friends, culture and status denied her, all of the resulting tensions should unite to accentuate the sex antagonism. This antagonism went so far as to cause a deep revulsion toward her husband. She debated leaving him. Her sensitive nature was at the breaking point. She disliked any thought of divorce with publicity and the inevitable explanations; but she was fast finding herself unable to enter longer into the intimate relations of sex life with her husband. Inevitably her health was beginning to break under the strain. Just how she solved her problem I do not know.

Here, then, developed a series of tension complexes out of life-pattern tensions; differences in culture led to economic tension under stress of removal from rural to urban life, led in turn to loss-of-respect complex, thence, to religious tension, then to sex tension and finally to health deterioration.

The process of family disorganization described in this study may thus be reduced to the symbolic representation:

Loss of respect→Pattern of life-tension→Cultural tension
→Economic tension→Loss of respect→Religious tension
→Sex tension

The adequacy of such a description depends, of course, upon the effectiveness with which the terms in the formula describe, though abstractly, the steps in the changes in the behavior of the husband and wife toward each other. The difficulty with such a representation, however, lies in the absence of any mechanism by which one type of tension passes into another. This difficulty arises from using as units in the description of sequences type tensions which are in themselves only groups or types of sequences.

The first stage of the objective study of any phenomenon is classification. Cases are grouped according to what seem to be their essential similarities. By a process of abstraction some conception of the group as a whole is obtained. But such conceptual elements are not the only ones with which science has to deal. Another type of concept is that which is formed by an effort of the constructive imagination for the purposes of the representative scheme of which it forms a part. Such concepts are hypothetical in character, and are justified only so far as they fill into the conceptual scheme of representation those elements which are not data of experience but which are necessary for the logical completeness necessary for prediction and control. Atoms in chemistry are such ideal constructs of the imagination; so also is the mechanism of compensation in social psychology.

The description of the foregoing case in an abstract way gains in logical completeness by the introduction, into the sequence, of elements which are hypothetical in character. In this way some account is taken of the transformation in behavior which is not a matter of experience as the description of the sequence in terms of tensions assumes. This case then, may be represented diagrammatically somewhat as follows:

Type of case: Husband and Wife of different cultural levels

Loss of economic and social status (resulting from move of the family from the country to the city)

Compensation:

1. Attempts to win recognition (wife competes for recognition in church group)
2. Attempts to win response (husband cultivates intimate association with neighbor)
3. Resort to stimulations
   a) Sensuous (possibilities: alcoholism, narcotics, etc.)
   b) Sensual (sex excesses of Husband)
4. Breakdown in morale (ill health of the wife, jealousy of the husband)
5. Development of rationalized philosophy of wife
   a) Personally developed (a possibility)
   b) Adoption of a cult (wife adopts Christian Science)

Such an attempt is, of course, open to all the objections which may be legitimately brought against attempting to abstract from one case. It is introduced here, however, to illustrate a method which may be developed as soon as adequate case-studies of family disorganization are at hand for such an elaborate analysis. Any successful attempt to prevent family disorganization must have as its basis conceptual descriptions of typical sequences of abstract units or events of some sort.

Two problems are therefore introduced by this method of approach: (1) the definition and classification of the significant events in the interaction culminating in family disorganization, and (2) the discovery of the sequences in which these type events occur. Both, however, await the accumulation of cases in which the description of interaction is more complete than in the current literature on family disorganization.[1]

The formulation of typical behavior sequences, however, is only one part of a complete study and explanation of family disorganization. Family disorganization must be studied also with reference to the forces producing changes in modern life. If the L family had remained under rural conditions, tensions probably would not have developed.

The mobility of city life, with its trend toward "atomization" of the individual, has broken down the control of the community. At the base of this transformation are certain changes which are going on in the economic organization of city life. How all these forces condition the behavior of individuals in their marriage relations is also important in the explanation of family disorganization.

Furthermore, it is necessary to analyze the attitudes of husband and wife in relation to their behavior. Two persons

[1] "The Diary of Miriam Donaven" (chap. xi) represents, though inadequately in some ways, the sort of material needed.

living under what seem to be the same community influences act differently, nevertheless. Even an attitude has a life-history, part of which is unique for each individual, and part common to all of a particular cultural area. The origins of attitudes, and the wishes of which they are reflections, are therefore important in the understanding of human behavior in family relations. To become intelligible, then, the explanation of family disorganization depends upon the discovery of ecological forces which condition changes in social forms and upon the interpretation of attitudes in terms of their origins in social experience in addition to the description of behavior sequences.

CHAPTER XI

THE DIARY OF MIRIAM DONAVEN

Documents for such a detailed and exact analysis as was suggested in the preceding chapter, unfortunately, are not available in sufficient numbers to yield conclusive results. In venturing upon such an attempt one is forced, therefore, to be content to apply the method to the most detailed account available with the caution that the results are of the most tentative sort.

Not only is there a scarcity of intimate documents available but those which may be had are in many respects too superficial and sketchy to be of much value. Students of human behavior are just beginning to take an objective view of the study, and so have not yet developed a method for obtaining accurate descriptions. Too often rationalizations are taken naïvely to represent the objective portrayal of factors conditioning human behavior. The result is that case-studies often tend to be artificial and forced. A better view can be obtained from such naïve documents as diaries, autobiographies, and letters. Of these three the diary, perhaps, represents the best medium now available for analysis.

While the analysis of a diary must be made with all the reservations suggested, it still offers a medium through which an appreciation and understanding of the causes of family disorganization may be realized. The cycle of events in the diary of Miriam Donaven is a group phenomenon rather than an individual experience. Other cases show the same cycle, as does common-sense evidence. It is, of course, because the diary conforms so closely to common-sense knowledge that it loses some of its value as a document for scientific purposes. Yet it serves, in the absence of a more scientific description, to indicate a more complete, even if still tentative, methodological approach than has been presented thus far.

THE DIARY[1]

The diary opens during the seventh week of married life, December 1, 19—. Miriam Donaven is already beginning to find disillusionment in marriage.

December 1.—The past month has been one of happiness to us both, and I would not write of what I did. Just a month ago today I have been living in this dear flat. . . . . Every night for over a week he [Alfred] has come home dead tired, crawled right into bed and after kissing me dutifully, goes to sleep with my head on his arm. One night there was no arm for my head to rest on, and not even a good-night kiss, so I turned over and cried myself to sleep. Oh, I wish my husband knew how much I want to be loved. I tell him, but he does not realize that I mean all the time, every minute he is with me. He loves me, though, and last Sunday night never seemed to love me quite as much as he did just then. It is very seldom he is so fierce, but he was that night and this Friday night. Poor boy, he is sick and cross sometimes, and I fear that I forget often to make allowances. His mother, dear little woman, says that there must be two bears in our home—Bear and Forbear.

[1] Sometime Saturday night, March 6, 19— (eight years after her marriage to Alfred Donaven), Miriam Donaven, a divorcée, shot Robert Timmins, an advertising man, in her apartment in Westfal, a mid-western city, and then turned the gun upon herself. When the police entered the apartment the following Tuesday they found both bodies in bed very much as though two persons were asleep. A diary, which Miriam Donaven had kept, was discovered in the apartment and was included in the evidence taken at the coroner's inquest. This diary opened soon after the marriage of Miriam Patterson and Alfred Donaven. It closed with an entry at nine o'clock Saturday morning, the day she died, apparently. The account which is given in this chapter, and upon which the interpretation in the following chapter is based, is a summary of the diary from the beginning to the time that she and her husband separated. It gives, therefore, a picture, as she saw it, of the conflicts and of the discord in her married life.

Thus it is that married life begins with the Donavens. Alfred is tired when he comes home from work and only demonstrative when his passion is aroused. Miriam wishes to be loved fiercely and all the time. Her only approach to harmonious relations with her husband is embodied in the injunction of his mother—"Bear and Forbear." The first quarrel soon follows (a day later).

December 2.—This A.M. we had words about money. Oh, how I wish we could live together and not have cross words every day.

Alfred begins treatments for an affliction, the symptoms of which suggest a venereal disease. His sickness makes him cross and keeps him away from his wife.

December 9.—Oh, I was so lonesome tonight. Alfred was here, but he can't love me, now that he is sick. God speed his recovery.

December 12.—Alfred home at 8:30 A.M. Slept till three, and got up like a bear. He is just breaking my heart with his cross words and indifference. Every time it simply widens the gulf between us. I don't love my boy less, but I cannot love him more as I should. Oh, God, wake him up, make him kind and considerate all the time. Is it because he is ill that makes him so fierce tempered sometimes, or am I really to blame? . . . . Oh, I must be wrong, but if so, why does God let me live? Life is unbearable to me now, and if things don't go better, something happens.

Miriam is not quite the ideal girl which Alfred's mother thought he deserved as a wife. So Alfred tries to control her conduct in his mother's presence. That procedure causes ill feeling.

December 25.—Alfred and I took a walk to 59— [the home of Alfred's parents] and we played and sang for some people there. Damn it, anyway, I am not stuck on that. I am just chuck full of things I should not have and I broke loose this A.M. Alfred was sore, but I can't help it and I am tired of acting like an angel around his folks. I told him a lot of things that I have only been thinking so far. He ought to know how I feel, anyway, about those things. Anyway, I wish we were out of town, so that all we could do was write to our relations. That's enough for me, thank you.

Soon after this Miriam discovers that she is pregnant. But Alfred does not want a child yet; she easily acquiesces and has an abortion a little later. In the meantime Alfred becomes jealous because Miriam goes to see an old sweetheart.

Jan. 10, 19—.—Mary and I went to see Harold in his office. Seemed queer to see him, and Alfred was sore when I told him. Gee, I like to see the fellows I used to go with, and then go home to Alfred. Oh, he is so much better in every way than the others.

A few days later Miriam becomes ill, the symptoms suggesting a venereal disease, though she does not seem to realize the probable source of infection. This does not bother her so long as Alfred is thoughtful, but he soon comes to think that she blames him.

Jan. 14.—Up at eleven. I felt so badly it was bed again for me all day. Alfred phoned Joe and Harold not to come. God knows what I have, but it is awful; believe me, I'm sick when I can't eat. My boy is so thoughtful, brought home candy and cream and a paper for his little girl and I felt so rotten I couldn't even get the kid a thing to eat. Bed early. Not up from bed all day.

Jan. 15.—Well, here I am, still in bed, and feel worse, if anything. God, please make me well for my boy's sake. . . . .

Jan. 16.—Saw Robinson, will be fixed up tomorrow and Saturday. Went out to see Ma, fine today. Alfred is sore because he thinks I blame him.

They get along somehow for a time. When Alfred is kind Miriam is happy, and when he is inattentive she prays God to wake him up. Miriam goes to work and Alfred changes jobs. Both resort to petty thievery in the struggle for a living. But always for Miriam the desire for attention overshadows all other interests.

Apr. 22.—Mother's birthday. Alfred and I have decided we are altogether indifferent toward one another. I wonder just how my life with him will end. Ever since Sat. eve about seven there has been something missing when he spoke to me of his dad and mother the way he did, making me feel like a thief which I am or a convict or most anything that is not good enough for his father and mother. Last night we sat in the dark and he opened up and told me a lot about his folks. I don't like my mother-in-law any better than she likes hers, and I feel exactly the same toward his. Would be happy if I never see her again. I hate her. She is mean and hateful and whining and spiteful and Mr. Donaven is O.K. and if anything happens to him his wife will never live where I do or even near me. Alfred is on to her I think just as I am only he won't own up. There is no reason why we should like each other. I am not her kind and she is not mine. I wonder why Alfred and I don't get along. Do we need a child, money or simply to be rid of his folks? It seems to me that if we lived far, far away where we would run no risk of seeing Mrs. Donaven, we would be O.K. I can't stand her and God knows I tried at first but the everlasting complaining gets on a fellow's nerves and so I quit trying to be sympathetic and it works fine.

Oh, God, how will our life end? What are we coming to? Last night Alfred was kind to me when I cried. I could not hold in any longer and he quieted me and put my head on his bare breast and kissed me. Oh, how thankful I was for that attention and of how I needed it and do now. He told me he wants a pal, his little girl, and wife back again and misses her oh so bad. Oh, God, when has that part of me gone? Is the fault mine, his or ours? He says I have changed the last three weeks in what way I can't understand because I feel right toward my boy. Last week one night when he came home I cried and told him I had been lonely all day and the Saturday before Easter Sunday we kneeled and prayed to God to make us happy and Easter he said would be Little Girl's day and every Sunday thereafter, All that was less than three weeks ago, was his ideal gone then? Well, while I was crying my heart out to God I asked Alfred what he wished to do, if we could go on and he suggested separation. All of a sudden I seemed to really know what that would mean for me and I thought I would go mad. I certainly am an unhappy woman with him now sometimes, how should I feel without him?

Not only does Alfred feel irritated because Miriam cannot come up to the ideal which his mother sets for him, but he thinks her selfish because she prefers to remain idly at home instead of working. Miriam feels that they have each other and that is enough—there is no need therefore to worry about finances. She sees her friends who are ideally happy, and she envies them.

May 9.— . . . . Guy and his girl Edith were here. She's nice good kid. I am glad he got that kind. Tuesday night Alfred and I were heavenly happy. Its queer how happy, exquisitely happy we are and then when we are angry how unhappy, tragically unhappy we are, and last night I did not sleep with him for the first time. I noticed how kindly, almost lovingly, Guy looks at Edith, and it makes my heart ache and my soul hunger for Alfred's kind attentions. God help us to be happy all the time, not part.

More quarrels about Alfred's parents follow, and Miriam determines to have nothing more to do with them. "Spats" become more frequent; "nearly every day we have a fight." Miriam goes to work; she steals clothes for her husband.

*July 19.—*This diary seems like an old friend I am talking to. By the way I have been at Bell's in boy's department steady since June 24th earning a little money to keep us going. I like it very much. I have "gotten" Alfred a lot of things, shirts, ties, gloves, handkerchiefs, collars, garters, etc., and myself a shirt, silk and gloves. I wish God could tell me what is wrong. I don't understand it anything. It was just about a week ago tonight that I cried for over an hour, what from I don't know unless pure weariness. Of course I realize that fear has a great deal to do with it and then the noise is tiresome. But I will stand it, if others do why not I? But I shall go mad if I am asked, if Alfred insists on my seeing his folks. I can't stand that, won't even try to. It's kind of lonesome now. Alfred, my boy, Gee, it makes me cry. (I cry at the least thing now, at almost everything. I can't see to write now.) Alfred is sitting on the other side of the table drawing. He wants to be somebody, know something and is going to spend his spare time drawing. Oh, God help us.

Thus the first year of married life ends in despair.

October 18.—Well, dear diary, I have an ache in my heart and a tear in my eye this dreary day after our first wedding anniversary. I feel the need of gentle words and strong arms to soothe me. I'm short. Alfred and I seem to be growing farther apart day by day. Whose fault is it? I am always ready to love and be loved and Alfred is so busy with cutting articles from newspapers concerning baseball and the president, that he does not care to spend his precious time kissing me. I just wonder a year from now what I will be writing in this book or if I shall be here to write at all. Oh, God, Oh, God, if you only knew how my heart is breaking, how hungry I am, how I suffer. If I could only harden myself to his cold treatment and I should be able to suffer in sickness, but I love my husband and I want his attention. I never think for a moment that he cares for some one else. I would swear that he doesn't. Why should he when I love him so. God knows I devote all my time to my boy and do all I can for him. So, my diary, I leave you feeling better for the little chat we have had, least why, my God, if I couldn't write down all these things here, I should have no comfort at all. A baby, a baby, my baby? What does that mean to a girl? It means something to love and care for, something that trusts and turns to you for its every need.

Last night we dined with Helen and her husband and Alfred and he left to get beer and were gone the greater part of the evening, near three hours. It makes a girl feel good to have her husband whom she loves so far away on the night of their first anniversary. Well, maybe by the time the second comes around she won't care any more than he does now. Oh, God, I hope not, I pray not. If I didn't care for him so I should go out, have a good time with other fellows, but I love my husband, so help me God.

Nov. 19.— . . . . Told Alfred I would go with him to see his folks. However, they can never be anything to me and I resent their kind feeling (?) toward me. I simply cannot endure his people, not even for his sake. I know Alfred thinks less of me because I do not care for his mother but I cannot even pretend to like or tolerate her. Oh, diary, every day I am steeling my heart against the little slights I get and I am thankful I can say that they hurt less each time. I wonder if it is because I am becoming used to them or if I am really hardened.

My husband most likely does not mean that but I have told him and told him. For a change I am trying letting him come to me for a kiss. After all the nice clothes I have taken the risk to get him he ought to be mighty good to me. . . . .

A little later she telephones to an old friend and Alfred becomes jealous. Then there is the roomer, Jim, whose company Miriam finds interesting when Alfred is at work.

January 29, 19—.—Alfred has just left after insulting me more. That's all I get now and am getting used to it. Its a long story and not fit to tell. It began when we were first married and Alfred used to pull his hand away from me when I would slip mine under his in a dark nickel show. Oh, God, how it used to hurt, but that is gone now and there is only the vivid remembrance. You see I don't give him a chance to turn from me now and then I could not keep away from him but now, Oh, God, I've been pushed away so many times that I have grown up. It took a long time, didn't it, Diary, but then I was a fool and I loved him, God knows, I loved him, and still do! He cannot have my respect or any decent thoughts. I would to God, Oh, no, I can't say that. If I had never seen "my boy" I would never have loved. Maybe it would have been better, our love is so shattered now that it doesn't have the slightest resemblance to love, to real love.

February 1.—Saturday. Jim has gone. Alfred is so jealous that he or rather Flo [Miriam's sister] told him to go. Thursday was his last day here. He and I had a pleasant time. Alfred's folks came for dinner. My mother was here the night before. Jim left after dinner Thurs. night. . . . .

Then follows a serious quarrel over Jim. Miriam tries to see Jim and stays out late. Alfred gets drunk. Miriam goes out with Jim. Finally, Alfred relents and asks Jim to stay, only to abuse him and tell him to go the next day. This time Miriam does not interfere; she wants to "get in right with Alfred for once."

February 6.— . . . . I have discovered much to my annoyance and sadness that I want to go out, I mean shopping and to see people. I must not be idle or alone. . . . . Alfred thinks I am for the men and drinks and that is not it. I have lost something that I feel will never be mine again and in desperation I seek consolation and diversion if that's in anything handy.

Feb. 9.— . . . . Another whole day on my hands with nothing to do. Last night after going to bed we talked it over. Alfred says I am not happy. I am but something is lacking. . . . . He is very kind and tries to console me. He loves me but not as he used to and God knows I love my husband, yet something is lacking. . . . . Oh, dear Lord, I know we were too happy for it to last. Alfred and I both take a half hearted interest in things now. . . . .

Feb. 10.—I am selfish. It's queer how when I feel sad and neglected and lonesome I think of God and wish to write in my diary. When I am happy I don't think of God. I share only all my sorrow with Him. Alfred thinks more of cutting things out of magazines than he does of keeping his wife's love and wanting her attention. It's only because I love him that I notice the neglect. If I did not love him I would not wish him to be with me as I do. He just came to me and kissed me and asked me to write something nice about him. I will. I love him and I know he loves me. He's a dear good kid and I shall stick to my husband. Oh, he's such a boy, so young. I was just thinking about being married. Why because I am married should I be happy without going out and seeing people and things when Alfred pays so little attention to me sometimes. I am here alone all day. When he comes home is it not natural that I should wish to talk to him or sit quietly on the lounge with his arms about me, listening to him telling me nice things? Never get tired of that or of him. But, dear God, as much as he loves me, he does tire of it, otherwise he would sit and spoon with me. Anyone I care for I want to be with, look at, touch. Is that not natural? I don't wish to be a fool or have foolish feelings.

Miriam's birthday comes, and Alfred is inattentive on this day of days! Tears. Then three days later:

Feb. 13.— . . . . I awoke last night to find Alfred putting my hand on his shoulder and I went to sleep again, very happy. So everything is all right again. I can't understand his moods. The poor kid doesn't feel well at all.

Alfred and Miriam have a fight a few weeks later out of which Miriam comes "with only a scratch." She writes that the next time Alfred strikes her, "I wish to God let me drop dead at his feet." And then:

March 30.— . . . . Alfred and I have been living in the same home and yet apart. That Saturday has made a great, and I believe and yet hope not, permanent change in me. The loss of Little Girl seems to surprise and anger Alfred. Well, it was over a year ago I began telling him she would go if she was neglected. I think I have forgotten how I used to act. It seems so long ago. It was so natural to me then, and now it is so very unnatural. I would have to be taught how to love that way again. I can never go back to the same way again. I may do better than I am now doing, but I can never be the expert I once was. I never think of unpleasant things any more. You say how can I help it? Well, I just don't think I would let myself become wrinkled and red eyed from crying. I love Alfred still. I want to be good to him and have him still look up to me for I believe he always has. There are all kinds of love and mine for him is the natural kind; that is, tender as well as passionate. Am I really so changed and hardened? Billie [the cat] is on my lap and makes me very happy with all his attentions. Does God send this dear Billie to lessen my sadness? I have some pretty clothes now and will think of them. Alfred has gone to get a new "job." The telephone Co. no longer needs him. At the flour mills he may get something. I pray God he may get something, anything.

April 11.—This is just another regular day. . . . . Alfred has an awful boil on his knee. Last night I wondered (it came to me suddenly) if I should have kept the first child God sent me. It, oh, it was a love child such as can hardly come now because I am so much older and wiser. I believe I really regret it, and God may punish me yet, though at the time I did it for the best. Mama has made some insulting insinuations and I don't wish to see her. Helen's baby is 9 months old and darling. I wonder if I want one.

Miriam stays away from home for a night after Alfred has insulted her. Then they make up. She sees more of Helen's baby and wishes for one.

May 5.—Last Monday night Alfred came home, kissed me and that was the last time I had till Thursday night. Alfred gets very angry at nothing. Oh, dear Lord, help me to be all that I wish. I must help myself too, I know. It has rained all day today and I long for the sunshine and dear Alfred to cheer me up. There is an ache in my heart all the time now for things in general. Everything seems to be so bad. There are lots of things to think about. The trees and shrubs are lovely. The leaves are bigger than dollars and bright and green and fresh. I wish I were as fresh as they. Somehow I feel old and faded, though I know I look young and am not faded. I believe I am absent-minded and nervous. I have a great desire to sing. If I could, it would be a means of unburdening my soul. As it is I can only write and very poorly at that. Very often I relax and cry. I often wonder if having a baby would help me any. I dread the duties of motherhood, while I long for them. The hardest part would be before and having Alfred so indifferent all the time. If I could only count on him to always be kind (I don't say loving), I believe I would wish one now. If I had money to spend I would seek diversion in shows and shopping, but as I have none I read books and maybe that is better anyway. I would like to go in the country now and spend my day roaming through woods and wading down streams and gathering flowers and eating eggs and milk and feeding chickens. Oh, God, would I tire soon of a life like that? That is the real life, it is to live, but I could not be content without Alfred to love me. How very dependent I am on him. . . . .

Two months pass with little change. Alfred and Miriam still have their "little tiffs."

July 13.— . . . . Honestly, I do get lonesome sometimes and wish to be comforted. I wonder why it is that girls don't like me. I believe I am truly not very lovable. Dear God, I am so tired telling Alfred to put things away. I wonder if I am really tired of living. That is not impossible.

August 22.—Oh, all this week I have been sick from Dr. Mean's arsenic. He said they would rid me of my hickies and instead I have been sick. . . . . Alfred has been very good to me since I have been ill. Lester Cohn, God bless him, sent me a doz. beautiful red roses. Think of poor little nobody me and roses. It makes me so happy. Les is the most thoughtful boy I ever knew and I just got a couple of sheets of music this afternoon too and here I am taking two weeks to draw him a head.

Money becomes more scarce and Miriam goes back to work.

Sept. 23.—Well, Diary, I have been working at Gordon's for nearly a week. I rather like it for a change. Alfred is perfectly willing, nay only too glad to have me down there—I mean so that I can meet him at noon.

Oct. 7.—Working doesn't seem so bad now. Several times I have come home feeling good, but Alfred does not seem to appreciate it.

Oct. 10.—Alfred has gone to see his folks. I feel very badly when I think of him being perfectly willing to leave me alone here when I have been working out all day. It certainly does hurt. . . . . I get so angry with myself when I sit here alone and cry for Alfred if he goes out a couple of hours.

Oct. 25.—Well, Alfred and I have been married two years and nine days. It doesn't seem possible, does it, Old Diary? You and Billie are the only two I tell my troubles to. I don't know which is the most comforting. To a woman love is life; to a man, it is simply an event. I have written and heard from my mother for which I am grateful. I owe her a lot I cannot repay, no matter how hard I try. The pictures she sent me of herself I love and kissed and cried over when I got them. I seem to think that I don't care for her, but I do, God know how much. I will never know unless a time comes when we must part. Of course, I would take Alfred, who is dearer to me than all else, and a child. Oh, My God, what happiness will be mine when little soft arms twine about my neck and rosy baby lips murmur so softly. I can barely hear "mother"—that one word I have never heard. Oh, how I should worship, yes, worship my child, and I hope it will be a daughter. There will be mutual sympathy between us.

The new year comes, and Miriam goes on an escapade with another man. Alfred is jealous and makes a dramatic attempt to arouse her pity.

January 1, 19—.—Well, I am glad we have a New Year. I am going to be very good. Was out with Helen and two fellows we picked up on the thirtieth. Alfred was wild and Bob [Helen's husband] came here and called Helen a pig's ass, and she nearly died laughing. Alfred is sore at her because if she hadn't come down, it wouldn't have happened. I have promised to do the straight and narrow, and I will. Alfred seems to care more for me than ever. It seems good to be home again. I suppose by the time I get the house straightened out I'll be back at it again. . . . . Last night Alfred lay in the bathroom with the gas turned on. I guess I won't forget that for a while.

After that they talk of divorce, though Miriam still insists that she loves Alfred and writes, "I will never live to see another man who could make me really love him." Alfred becomes more kind for a few weeks. There are flirtations with other men, and a proposal which Miriam does not take seriously. More quarrels.

May 7.—Bill Crane and Jim came over Sunday and stayed until three A.M. Alfred and Jim went to get some beer and Crane made love to me. I told Alfred after they left. He said Crane was drunk. I certainly have given him no encouragement, but he seemed to need none. Yesterday he phoned and repeated plea that he should be allowed to call some afternoon. I called him a silly little boy, and told him to stay away from married ladies. I suppose he has heard about Jim and me, and thinks he will try his luck. I simply detest him, and he will have no luck with me, so there. . . . .

May 13.— . . . . I just looked out the window and saw a nigger go by driving a red racer—can you beat it? Here am I, cultured, beautiful, longing and still sitting at home unattended, while a man as black as night runs an auto. What are we coming to? . . . . Monday afternoon Mrs. Martin and I were sitting here quietly enjoying some brandy, when the bell rang, and I opened the door to Roscoe Johnston who was in such a dilapidated condition he was not allowed to enter his room. . . . . We took him over and soothed him as one does a child (and a drunken man) and soon he slept. He asked me if I would like to have him buy me a yellow auto. What a proposal!

June 10.—About two weeks ago Alfred packed the suit case and almost left here after we had had some trouble. It was not furious or raging, but was just quiet—sad explanation. Well, I made a fuss and he stayed. If he had not, I wonder how far I would have sunk by this time. . . . . Johnston is married by this time, I expect. I am glad I didn't take his offer up for I really believe he was serious. God help the girl who falls in with a man like that! Sometimes my longing for a baby becomes so terrible that I almost decided to have one. One reason I do not want one now is because I am not satisfied with myself or with my Alfred. I wish to improve before I have a child to depend upon me, and then I am not worthy to be a mother.

More engagements with other men.

July 15.— . . . . Friday before last saw my downfall. Ha! Ha! I wonder if anyone can understand that. Mr. Johnston the agent has taken us riding twice. First time we went to the Dutchman's and the last time Mrs. H. was with us and we went to the Red House. . . . . In the ice box Alfred found two bottles that Johnston sent up and we had a big fuss.

Sometime during the summer Miriam and Alfred move to the East Side.

Sept. 26, Sat. Night at 10.—Diary, dear, the very first thing I write is to say to you how unhappy I am. Howard, I met him the other day, is coming to take me out, and Alfred has left to live with his folks. Gee, I'm a happy guy. I just put a few curls up while I wait. I must look pretty. Heaven help me. I would feel lots better if I had a dog here to keep me company, and believe me, I almost had one. I saw it alone on the street as I was walking to the car with Alfred. We just nodded good bye, didn't even shake hands. What a funny world! The kid, bless his heart, brought me some plantation drops when he came home. I thought it was fine of him. . . . . Alfred will give me about 60 a month and I get 3 a week from my roomer. Alfred says he never liked this apartment, but I think it is fine. . . . . I wonder if Alfred feels as badly as I do. . . . . Mother is in N.Y. I wish now I had gone. Jim asked me if I wanted to go when the war is cooled down. You know I want to go. I'd go anywhere with anyone I like. This winter I would like to do all the sports, learn to skate and swim, and anything else possible. When I go to bed it will seem mighty strange to be alone. God help me and keep me a little good—just a little good.

Then follows an orgy of dissipation and adventure, ended by Alfred's return.

Oct. 8, Thur. Eve. 8:10.—Alfred has been back since Mon. before last. I thought he would come home, but not quite so soon. The phone rang after I talked to Harold that night and it was Howard, who did not go to the Cambridge. I met him with another couple. Drove out within 2 miles of White Owl, and then we saw a sign outside a road house. Went in and everyone was satisfied, so we went back to the West Side. Took a girl home, had lunch in a little place and drove over and got a nice girl out of bed at 3 A.M. Went to golf links and got tickets—then slept in auto and missed our turn. Then we went to small links and waited and then I decided to go home. Howard put me on car, and I was here at 9 A.M. Met Mr. White just going out. Fed Bill and myself, and dolled things up, then went to bed with my clothes on. Slept till 1 P.M., then met Howard at 3:40 P.M., then dined on chop suey, tried to get Helen and couldn't, and then landed in Tap Room at 37th and Long Island. Jim and a lot of fellows came in and Howard and I went to Dutch Mill, Hammond's and to Green's, then home at 1 A.M. Went to sleep immediately. Oh, and I learned to smoke Sat. night without any trouble, coughing or anything. Why, its the easiest thing in the world. I'm a fiend by now. Harold came over Mon. night and we dined at the Briskway. When we returned at 8:30 I found at the door, cake and coffee cake and two eve. papers and two sheets of music, some of which Alfred had written on, saying he loved me. About 9 he phoned and came directly over here. His voice was so changed I hardly knew it. And when he came I saw he had been suffering keenly. His eyes were Oh, so sad and something, it seemed the very life had gone out of him. I kissed Harold for the first time that night. He said I have wonderful lips and seemed to like me altogether. Alfred and I have not had intercourse since he came back, and sometime probably two weeks before he left. My God, I couldn't give myself up to him as I used to do. I know now that is all men want. It is a hideous truth. Oh, God. I think of those things so much, and it makes me bitter. Sometimes I actually hate myself and the whole world. The people are all wrong, but I pity the poor animals. Tue. night Harold was here again and we dined at the Briskway. Alfred seemed to like him more than before. Howard thinks I have the prettiest profile of any girl he has yet seen. Hooray! Harold thinks my figure wonderful and also my passion.

Nov. 4.—Some old cat was on the wire this A.M. when I talked to Mrs. H. She made a noise all the time, and then when I said I'd tell the manager she said I wouldn't dare, she knows too much about me. . . . . She mentioned auto rides that my husband didn't know about, when I phoned to Alfred to tell him about her. My God, how can a woman be so mean and contemptible as to tell on another. . . . . I'm very unhappy now, as much now as ever, though Alfred is back and says he loves me. He doesn't act it, and won't kiss me. I suppose as long as he won't, others will. . . . .

But Miriam's romance is disintegrating, and disillusion-ment soon follows. Alfred is not satisfied, and continually threatens to leave. The New Year opens with Miriam in rebellion against life, which has lost its romantic hue.

January 4, 19—.—A New Year is becoming a very common thing to me. So far I have cried every day and when the whistles blew at 12 I was washing and getting ready for bed. Great time we had Xmas. Alfred gave me a bracelet I've wanted for a year, candy, cigarettes and creme de Yvette. I gave him a book, *Paths to Power.* . . . . Black was here New Year's Eve, and Smith came over. When 12 o'clock came Alfred and I were alone but not near each other. He came in the bath room and got me. I cried while the whistles blew in the New Year. The unjustness of everything is all I can think of. I don't be-lieve I can live and bear it much longer. I wish I could get away from it. No one phones me any more, and I am playing square with Alfred. . . . . Last night we walked to Hollis Ave., and back, and all the way talked of but one thing, our ideas of each other, and one moral stand-ard, which is the only one for me, and about the night Alfred saw me in Peterman's. He said he was with a woman that night. He spent about thirty dollars and I asked him why he didn't spend that much when he went out with me. I just had to get up and cry when I think of him that way. If my imagination were not so vivid and I could not picture what took place so well, I would not feel so badly. But when I shut my eyes I see the whole thing before me as though I had really been present. Oh, God. It is awful. Alfred went the limit that night, but I did not, thank God. He says he was drunk and governed by circumstances. I am sorry that I am not worth as much money as that woman. For the first time in my life I have had the desire to kill, to plunge a dagger in her heart. She's innocent. She didn't know he was married, and even so, she is not to blame. He is all wrong. I wonder if what I feel is jealousy. I think not. It is simply repugnance for the whole human race and their ideas, their unjustness. This is a man's world, ruled by men because they made it. Women simply fit in for man's convenience. . . . . Why cannot woman do as men do, or rather man do as woman does? How can the world go on? Oh, God, tell me. Let some one explain. Must I take all for granted just because they say to me "It is so"? Should I not ask "Why, why is it so?" Is there no answer—no reason? Is it right? Do you think, dost thou think it fair? Is there any answer but the one "Man makes it so"? Doesn't a woman count for anything? Is she nothing? What is there a woman can do that a man cannot do? Bearing a child is the only thing I can think of. All this is killing me, but thank God I want to go. I want and long to go home, to drop out of this earth where there is no place for me—where I don't want a place. Oh, if only I could believe as other women believe, accept things as they are and simply be ruled by the world's standards of right and wrong. Whatever made me different? It must be my fairness or my foolishness. I am sure people would look askance at me if they knew how I feel. I would enjoy meeting anyone who does truly believe as I do. It seems to me there is no sense to anything any more. Alfred says I go out with men, while he wants only the boys. Why do I? Because I cannot sit in a café without a man. Is that not ridiculous? It compels me to have a man when I don't really want one. I wish to God I could drop off the earth and just end my life, but it is not so. . . . . God make me patient and what? Good? True? I would love to be a mother sometimes, but could I bring up two children, a girl and a boy, and tell each different things? I should teach that one standard holds for both and be as fair as I can. When I die, all I ask is that I can lay my head on Alfred's shoulder and have his arms around me. I am more at peace now. I forgive him, but I can't forget, so I suppose it is not complete forgiveness. Oh, if I were not so bitter. If I did not have a mind of my own. If I could only take things as I find them. Alfred said early this morning when it was becoming light—he awoke to find me sitting up in bed with my arms over his shoulders and staring wildly at him and crying, my eyes wide open and yet I was asleep and have no recollection of the incident. He tucked me in bed, and I did not move again and went to sleep.

Thus her Prince Charming has become one of the lowest of human beings. Her romantic dream has been shattered completely. She tries to think only of Alfred's interests, and even says she is willing to step out of the way if Alfred wishes to marry the other woman. But she cannot so easily forget herself and her disillusionment.

Jan. 27, 12 p.m.—I have just crawled out of bed. I can't sleep. Alfred just came after me, and asked if he could do anything. The last rest is all I pray for now. Oh, God, how many times have I asked you to take me, take me, take me. Either I shall go mad from the thought I have, or I shall change my mind when I find an answer to the question I ask. Why should I be made to suffer for what Alfred has done? Before we were married he lied to me about himself. Simply because he knew I would believe him. Now that I am awake and know what he is, I suffer. Oh, God, the pain. I loved Alfred with the tenderest mother-love, and then to have my little god broken. Alfred is here by my side. 8:20 A.M. Alfred is very kind now, and I went to sleep on his shoulder last night. I am sitting here at my desk wearing Alfred's old trousers and a shirt of his. They are fine to work in. I wonder whether the girls Alfred went with before we were married laughed when they heard of me, or felt sorry for me. I don't suppose they have hearts enough for pity. They probably laughed and said I got what they left.

Feb. 15.—Monday night. Alfred is sore and has gone out without a word to me. I was preparing for the night. . . . . Saw Ada and the baby. God bless them, and help the little girl to be what—to be a good woman, as I *was*, and get what I got when I woke up. Is that what mothers wish for their daughters? But then, all of them have not views like mine. What is good for the goose is good for the gander, and God help and pity me for believing as I do. It has brought me much pain. . . . . Poor little Diary, I never come to you but to pour out my troubles. I never come to you to write down wonderful happi-

ness I have had. How can I? I never have any. Yes, a few moments
when Alfred is kind and then all the world seems good. The 15th of
this month [Miriam's birthday] was not a happy day. We did nothing,
not that I mind that, but Alfred was unkind. Alfred gave me a big
box of caramels, the kind I love. It was awfully sweet of him. . . . .
Thursday night Mama and I went to Peterman's. Alfred won't see
her, and I met a Mr. Greene I had seen there before with Alfred. He
bought our dinners, and Mama went home and he and I went to
Dago's, an old hang-out of Alfred's. Oh, I used to love my boy when
he was going to that kind of place, and I didn't know it. No wonder
he had no money saved when we were married. That is what makes
me know he kept it up to the last, for he certainly had no clothes. His
folks are supposedly Christians, but I hate them for not telling me
what he did. They knew, they knew, and never told. It would have
made a difference now if I had known then what Alfred was, that he
thought so much of physical sexual pleasure, that he did that, as they
all do. Fool, fool, fool! If I had only remained a fool. *If*, instead of
sitting here, wondering where Alfred is, I say to myself that I don't
care if he ever comes home, and I don't, so help me God. I don't.
I don't. . . . .

But Miriam is not sure that even yet she wants to lose
her Alfred. On March 4 they decide to separate on May 15.
Miriam tires of housework; "I don't feel that I am really
above it, but that I am not suited to it." She tries posing,
to which Alfred objects. This causes friction often, but she
refuses to quit; "It's decent and brings good money." They
also quarrel about Miriam's smoking, but why should she
not if he does, she asks. Miriam has a proposal of marriage
but she is not yet ready to give up Alfred. Even when she
does think of leaving him, she is hardly ready to consider
another man. They fight and quarrel. There are periods
even of sexual excesses. May 15 comes and still they do not
separate.

July 18.—Sun. . . . . Friday morning Alfred so far forgot himself
as to call me "Susan." He never says that when he is angry. I haven't

kissed him for three weeks today. He has never made one move toward reconciliation, and I never will. Usually I go to him and try to make up, but never again. I am sore and hurt all through. I feel that Alfred is unclean. Oh, if he had only told me about himself before we married. He had all the chance in the world when I confessed with much trepidation, about Alice he took it all in, with never a word about himself. God, what a cheap, cheap, cheap! and never once has he told me he is sorry. Even that would have been something. But no, not a word, and then after all that, he has not been kind to me. I wonder do men ever stop to think of the heartaches they cause on account of their sporting before marriage and sometimes after? Sometimes when I have held Alfred's hand to my lips, I suddenly wonder what that hand has done with another woman, and the knowledge of that has come too late hurts. It is a destroyer of all kind feeling and trust and respect and happiness. Oh, God, don't they ever understand and realize that it means as much to women as to men to love what is pure? But he never even said he was sorry. My heart is broken. May it never be healed. No, never, and I know that it never can be healed. . . . .

Alfred decides to leave again, but changes his mind and stays. Miriam thinks that though she can never love him again as she once did, if he is true and kind a "lesser love may come in time." But discord continues; "Alfred and I have an argument regularly, so that as soon as we come even near making up half-way, we are on the outs again." Miriam thinks of death. She tells herself that she no longer minds Alfred's indifference.

Dec. 11.—Trouble all the time. Alfred never believes me. Yesterday he was home ill, and some man phoned and Alfred was sore, and said I do not play fair. I told him that I do, but he doesn't believe me. I live simply from day to day.

Early in the new year Alfred starts night work and Miriam is more lonesome. At times they make up, then a quarrel estranges them again.

Feb. 1, 19—.—Last night Alfred kissed me, and as I did not respond, he went quietly to sleep. He kissed me about a week ago, for the first time this year. Neither of us miss anything like that any more. Thank God, because I cannot endure him now.

Feb. 27.—Mama has just left. . . . . We had what she said was a plain talk. I guess it was, for I told her she does not understand me. She blames Alfred for the way I treat her. How like her! Oh, God, why did I not die before I caused so much sadness and disappointment to my husband, mother and self? Yesterday at dinner Alfred flew into a rage. He said he loves me, and a smile flickered (it had no more time than to barely flicker) over my mouth and I was conscious of ducking my head and seeing a beautiful star. My right eye is very red and raw. It verged on blackness yesterday. . . . .

Early in June, Alfred tells Miriam to leave. She goes away for three days and then returns "on legal advice." Later she thinks of killing Alfred; then again of killing herself, even writing as much to her mother. Then Alfred agrees to give her cause for divorce.

Aug. 27.—Alfred offers 40 to pay storage. Also anything to get rid of me. He says Margaret leaves tomorrow for Cornwall. Oh, God, help me, give me strength. Alfred has been down in the basement for two hours looking things over. I went down and brought up the letters. Many of them that we have written to one another. I cannot throw them away, it would be like throwing something living, and yet as far as Alfred is concerned, everything is dead. My God, he is hard. I suggested that he move, and I should go away. I certainly cannot be here to see everything I love killed, torn to pieces, wrenched from my heart. It is wounded and bleeeding, now, and I can stand little more. Oh, God, give me strength.

Sept. 2.—At dinner tonight Alfred confessed that he never has loved me. God help me, I have given my all to a man who never loved me. He merely thought he did. It was no great surprise to hear that, as it accounts for the way he has maltreated me. . . . . No, Alfred Donaven has never loved his wife. . . . . and so after five years of thinking he loved me, and receiving the gifts of my beloved, he has finally decided that he never loved me. He must be decidedly slow to learn. . . . .

Alfred continues to urge Miriam to "get out." Finally, he signs papers promising to pay her forty dollars a month, and on September 13 she leaves. Alfred comes back to Miriam for a while the following spring after their separation, but they quarrel incessantly and soon he leaves. This ends the married life of Alfred and Miriam Donaven, though Miriam does not obtain a divorce until December.

After Miriam and Alfred separate, Miriam follows the scarlet path, making an easy living, but always restless and despairing. Later she enters into a free alliance with Robert Timmins, a married man who lives a double life. The same cycle of dreams, disillusionment, and despair which had characterized her life with Alfred Donaven are repeated, and finally end in suicide when she realizes that she is losing Robert Timmins.

CHAPTER XII

SOCIO-ANALYSIS OF A CASE OF FAMILY DISORGANIZATION

The following analysis of the diary of Miriam Donaven is presented as a tentative exposition of a method which it is contended will contribute to the understanding and control of family disorganization a more effective technique of analysis than currently found in statistics of divorce and desertion. Such a method of analysis, with the modifications which application to more cases will bring, should lead finally to the utilization of quantitative methods resulting in the precision of prediction and control now found in the natural sciences.

This tentative method of analysis may be divided into three parts: (1) influences of ecological and cultural forces, (2) conceptualization of the conflict between husband and wife into a process or sequence of events, and (3) interpretation in terms of attitudes and values.

SOCIAL BACKGROUND

Miriam Patterson was not an unusual sort of person. She was just an ordinary girl who had grown up in Westfal with much the same outlook upon life one would expect of a small-town girl. She was a high-school graduate, and had a fairly wide circle of friends. Her philosophy of love was typical of Main Street.

H. E. Patterson, Miriam's father, operated a grocery in West Heights during the early childhood of his daughter. When Miriam was about eight her mother and father were·

divorced. Her mother continued to live in West Heights, and it was in the area near the State Normal School that Miriam grew up. At that time this was an area of the *petite bourgeoisie*. The houses were chiefly of frame construction, each occupied by a single family. While the status of a grocer is not of the highest, it is a respectable business enterprise, and in Mr. Patterson's case seems to have been a successful venture. At the time the divorce decree was granted, Mr. Patterson placed sixty thousand dollars in trust with Mrs. Patterson for his two daughters, Miriam and Florence. Mrs. Patterson was to have the income but the principal was to go to the two girls when their mother died.

The parents of Alfred Donaven seem not to have lived in Westfal until the early part of the year in which Miriam and Alfred were married. Their home was in the Hamilton Park area, a quite urbanized section of the city at that time, characterized by the "white-collared" middle class. Mr. Donaven was secretary of a plate enamel company with offices just outside the business district.

Alfred and Miriam met at a Collegiate High School affair in the spring of 19— He was twenty at that time, and she nineteen. About five months later they were married. Alfred at that time was a clerk in a oil company's office. He seems to have been quite an ordinary man, no better and no worse than the average in the large city. He had acquired the usual vices of the typical urban youth in spite of his early puritanical training.

The young couple began housekeeping at 4— West Poplar Avenue. The process of deterioration had just begun in this district. The influx of Negroes brought in by the world-war had not yet made this neighborhood an undesirable place in which to live. At this time, however, it was becoming a rooming-house area. The Donavens themselves kept a roomer. Its proximity to the railroads and to the South Henry Street vice area made it, however, a much more mobile neighborhood than was either of the areas in which Miriam and Alfred had previously lived. During the latter part of their residence in this place there are intimations of the breakdown of primary group control in the references to automobile rides participated in by Miriam while her husband was at work.

During the summer of 19— Miriam and Alfred moved to the East Side, to Knollwood, an area of the comfortable middle class. Their leisure time, however, was spent in the nearby Hollis Avenue district, a "bright-light" area. Thus they became completely emancipated from the neighborhood friends of the West Side as well as from the control of Alfred's parents. It is here that Alfred left Miriam for the first time—an event followed by a wild escapade in which Miriam was out all night. Here they lived until their separation in the autumn of 19—.

SEQUENCES IN BEHAVIOR

The preceding section might be called an "ecological interpretation" of the Miriam Donaven diary; it attempts to show how changes in community influences and pressures facilitated the disintegration of the marriage relation between Alfred and Miriam Donaven. Further interpretation lies in the description and analysis of the tensions which characterized their relations and the abstraction out of the mass of concrete details of some conceptual description of sequences in behavior.

The first tension developed because Alfred did not give Miriam the response which she desired. He was too tired to

caress her; he did not measure up to her romantic conception
of a lover-husband. The first quarrel, however, was about
money. Illness, a little later, made Alfred cross and inattentive. The fact that the symptoms of his ailment suggest
venereal disease gives credence to the inference that his in-
attentiveness may have been largely the result of the absence of sexual impulses. Sexual antagonism thus developed
early.

The cultural tension arose out of the failure of Miriam
to adjust her conduct to the demands of Alfred's mother.
They quarreled about Miriam's inflexibility, which was a
constant source of irritation because it symbolized Miriam's
refusal to be dominated by the wishes of her husband alone.
It was this same difficulty that caused discord in the adjustment to economic interests. Alfred thought that Miriam
should work outside the home; she disagreed, but later
acquiesced.

Miriam went to work as a means of obtaining the response she craved from Alfred. At his suggestion, stealing
for him followed. But even this demonstration of loyalty
did not win the response she craved. When Alfred's sexual
impulses drove him to her, they were happy; otherwise, his
parents remained a barrier between them.

Failing to find response in her marriage relations, Miriam
turned elsewhere—and Alfred became jealous. This suggests, also, that Miriam's sexual impulses were not so strong
as Alfred's, though she craved more indirect response. This
failure to get the response she craved accentuated the latent
difference in philosophies of life. Miriam wanted to go out
in the evenings, while Alfred generally preferred to stay at
home.

Finally, Miriam learned about Alfred's relations both

before and after marriage with other women. In spite of all their quarrels she had believed him true to her. Disillusionment and loss of respect followed, especially as he did not ask for forgiveness or even say he was sorry. This omission on his part accentuated the response tension.

Thus the behavior in this case may be reduced to the following sequence:

Type of case: Husband and wife with different conceptions of the rôle of a wife (Miriam's conception of the rôle of a wife is Bohemian—a woman should be able to do anything a man does; Alfred's is conventional—"the mother-image")

Response tension (Miriam's failure to realize in marriage the romantic ideal)

Process of compensation:

1. Development of technique to secure response (Miriam goes to work —steals for her husband)
2. Attempts to secure response outside marriage (attentions of other men)
3. Resort to stimulation:
   a) Sensuous (escapades, drink, dissipation, automobile rides)
4. Breakdown of morale (shock and disillusionment upon learning of husband's past life)
5. Reorganization of philosophy of life (adoption of philosophy of life of lower order—relations with numerous men)

Further understanding of this case, as of all cases, lies in the analysis of the conflict of attitudes and of their genetic development. Thus one turns to the concrete description of attitudes and values and by inference to the wishes of the person.

ATTITUDES-VALUES[1]

In the analysis of a case of family disorganization, such as the diary of Miriam Donaven, in terms of attitudes and

[1] Thomas defines a value as an object, real or imaginary, having meaning, and which therefore may be the object of an activity. The attitude is the

values, one is handicapped by having only the direct expression of the attitudes of one person. In so far as the attitudes of the other person are taken into account, they must be inferred.

Dominating the life of Miriam Donaven was the wish for response. A husband to her was a man who loved one, caressed one, and was attentive at all times. As a value he was the product of romanticism. One went to him for response. But to Alfred a wife was one who gave herself to him sexually, and who played the conventional rôle—cooked, kept house, mended his clothes, etc. This conflict in attitudes seems to have been the basis of the discord throughout their married life. Slowly Miriam came to realize this difference in attitudes, though it was a long time before she could face it openly. When she finally came to recognize this difference Alfred lost respect in her eyes so far as her immediate relations with him were concerned, though this could not break entirely the sentimental attachments of the past. Thus the letters which he had written to her prior to their marriage remained to torture her with remembrance of this attachment.

Miriam turned to other men for response when she failed to get it from her husband because there was no one else to whom to turn. She seems not to have been companionable with her sister, Florence. She had many quarrels with her own mother. Other women did not seem to care for her, she complained, though she wished that they did. Sometimes she wished for a child, but the responsibilities of motherhood were too great—she and Alfred were not financially able to

---

tendency of the individual to act toward a value. Values represent the objective aspect of experience, while attitudes represent the subjective. Cf. Thomas, *The Unadjusted Girl*, pp. 232–33.

have a child, and besides she was not worthy to be a mother. Both of these seem to have been rationalization, for there are intimations that motherhood had become uncertain if not impossible for her.

Intimacies with other men seem to have been substitutes for the response which her husband failed to give her. Personally, she was attractive, though far from being the beautiful person she wished to be. Sometime during her married life Miriam painted an idealized picture of herself which was later reproduced by a calendar-maker. She seems to have been the type of woman who appeals to the *camaraderie* of men but who lacks the qualities which make for loyalty.

Alfred was dominated by quite different wishes. The wish for recognition seems to have been predominant. He was much more interested in "getting ahead" in the world than in caressing Miriam. The fact that he was always financially embarrassed suggests, however, that it was not security in which he was interested so much as recognition. His opposition to Miriam's smoking was prompted by the fear that as his wife she would cause him to lose status. He had much of the philistine in him in many ways. He did not like Miriam's mother because she was much more unconventional than his own.

Objectively, Alfred's behavior was similar to Miriam's; but the double standard was to him a value to be accepted and acted toward in the conventional manner. He drank, smoked, gambled, and was intimate with other women than his wife. To him there was nothing inconsistent in his doing all of these things and still denying his wife the same freedom. This conflict in norms was a constant irritant. Alfred's impulse was to dominate his wife. At times she allowed him to do so, apparently hoping thereby to gain the response she craved. When response was not forthcoming, she rebelled. It seems quite plausible that, if he had given her the attention, the caresses, which she wanted, he could have dominated all her behavior. But when he failed to caress her, she asserted her independence upon occasions by drinking a great deal, flirting with other men, and finally by smoking. Once learned, smoking became a symbol of her independence.

One writer, in commenting on the diary, has made a great deal of the fact that Miriam had no vocational qualifications. Her career in life was dependent upon her sex appeal—a dependence which became more marked, of course, after her separation than during her life with Alfred. She did not like housework. She could not see how Alfred could respect her when she had to clean the bathtub after him with her own hands. She seems to have known little about cooking when they were first married. Miriam tried several kinds of work: folding circulars, working in department stores, china-painting, posing for a corset company, etc. In none of these occupations was she particularly adept, nor did she like any of them very well. She spent considerable time drawing, but that did not give her response. She was ambitious to become a motion-picture actress. But she never really developed a vocation. As a result, much of her effort was expended in restless attempts to realize her romantic ideal —to be loved all the time, fiercely, passionately.

Miriam's appeals to God seem not to have been strictly religious. Her diary contains entries in which such an appeal and profanity appear in the same paragraph. The appeal was rather to the god of love, to "the blue bird" of romance. Her romantic ideals thus became objectified into a social object. Her diary and Billie, the cat, were also social objects. She talked to the diary much as she would have talked to a confidant. Her lack of appeal to other girls, her quarrels with her mother and sister, probably caused her to turn to the keeping of a diary during her school days. Then when discord arose after marriage, she turned easily to this school-girl practice. There are intimations, however, that at first she hoped that Alfred might read it—another attempt to get response.

Miriam Donaven's defeat in marriage was primarily a failure to adjust her attitudes toward the situation as defined by her husband as well as his failure to adjust himself to her attitudes. To what degree the romantic ideal of marriage is impossible one can hardly say. Enough that in this case the attitudes toward married life were in conflict. Romance was a value to both, but one which largely lost its importance to Alfred after marriage.

NEED FOR ANALYZED CASE-STUDIES

The analysis of the diary of Miriam Donaven represents an attempt to treat: first, a case of family disorganization with reference to the cultural and ecological background of the two persons; second, an analysis of the discord in terms of a process, or a sequence of events; third, an interpretation of the case in terms of attitudes and values. In its application to one case it represents a tentative method. Application to many cases will make the method more precise.

There is another difficulty in the use of personal materials which demands attention. Even a document such as this diary is incomplete in many respects. It was written too much in the spirit of the martyr who desires sympathy from the reader to contain always a candid account of the attitudes of the husband. As a document for the interpretation of the personality of a single person this is not a serious objection. But where the chief interest is in the conflict between husband and wife, a more complete account is needed to bring into relief the attitudes of the husband. Many references are made, also, in the indefinite terminology which characterizes the confidences of two intimate friends. The meaning of many phrases in the diary is therefore vague, because one does not know what were the associations in the mind of the writer.

In spite of these difficulties, however, this diary represents a more fundamental account than that found in the records of courts and social agencies, for it describes in intimate language the conflict of attitudes instead of giving a formal account of marital relations. It is from the analysis of cases such as this that there will develop an adequate sociological interpretation of the processes of family disorganization. Out of this approach one may look for a development of method and a definition of concepts and description of processes which may ultimately be measured and reduced to mathematical formulas.

Any attempt to prevent family disorganization, accordingly, must be based upon such definitions of concepts and descriptions of processes as may be expected to come from the development of such a method. Treatment of cases of family disorganization by social agencies at the present time is haphazard and ineffectual. No case is so discouraging to the average social worker as a "domestic difficulty." And the reason is because so little is known about the causes of family disorganization. There are, it is true, certain common-sense adjustments which can be made in some cases and seem to be successful at times. But whether the adjustment is accidental or due to the application of the common-sense technique is far from settled. Certainly, divorce statistics would confirm the impression that successful adjustments of more serious marital conflicts are the exception rather than the rule. What the social worker needs and what the courts need are descriptions of the typical processes of family disorganization made with such precision as to furnish a basis of predicting with some degree of accuracy what is likely to be the outcome of certain types of conflict in marriage relations.

To what degree it will be possible to reduce the description of processes of family disorganization to a quantitative statement one can hardly predict. All science is ever trying to become quantitative, and theoretically may be expected to become so ultimately. In the study of family disorganization, however, as in the study of other social problems, it may be expected that much of the analysis will remain in qualitative terms. Not only is this true, but it is likely that in many aspects little progress will be made in the immediate future beyond the classificatory stage of scientific analysis. This only emphasizes, however, the importance of attempting to discover tentative descriptions of processes of family disorganization.

If, for the present at least, there is more promise in qualitative rather than quantitative analysis of family disorganization, it would be expected that case-studies would offer the most adequate materials for the study of this problem. So long as the concepts with which one has to deal in the explanation of marital discord are not readily measurable, the statistical method, when utilized, compels one to turn to the measurement of concepts which lend themselves readily to mathematical treatment and then to depend upon the interpretation of the data to give a more comprehensive, and therefore more precise, explanation of the phenomenon.

Thus the introduction of the statistical method complicates rather than simplifies the analysis of the problem.

It seems only reasonable, then, to look for the present to the objective analysis of case-studies for the most useful description of causes of family disorganization. These descriptions of typical processes in family discord should furnish, therefore, not only a basis for the treatment of family discord, both preventive and remedial, but ultimately should give such definitions of concepts and descriptions of processes as may be reduced to measurement and treated statistically.

PART IV
CONCLUSIONS

CHAPTER XIII

THE CONTROL OF FAMILY DISORGANIZATION

Up to this point little has been said about the control of family disorganization, though, obviously, the desire to control has been the motivating force behind the collection of most of the materials analyzed. In fact, one may go even further and say that the discovery of methods of control has been the aim in all the studies of family disorganization whether consciously recognized or not. The only test there is of the adequacy of one's scientific findings lies in the degree to which one's principles furnish a basis for predicting future events. Prediction, inasmuch as it allows one to determine his behavior in advance with reference to certain known factors, leads inevitably to the utilization of such knowledge in the control of situations.

Advance in the physical sciences, physics, chemistry, astronomy, geology, biology, physiology, etc., in the last century has been the result of discovering principles which have given man control over the material world in a way little dreamed of a few generations ago. Those things which seem most to characterize modern material culture, the automobile, the telephone, the radio, the telegraph, the daily newspaper, the airplane, skyscrapers, and typhoid vaccine, for example, are the results of the application of scientific knowledge to the control of the material world. In the fields of the natural sciences control is no longer accidental but calculated and planned.

NEED FOR CONTROL IN THE SOCIAL SCIENCES

The social sciences, on the other hand, do not show the same high stage of development. Control is accidental to a large degree, or based upon "personality traits"—a term used to cover up processes which are little understood. Under this regime successes are often as unintelligible as failures. Rather than a known system of laws or principles, common sense, "personality," and trial and error are the only bases of control. Under these conditions even the most successful in dealing with human beings depend more upon "hunches" than upon methodical study of the problem and the application of scientific principles to its solution. And when an explanation for the success which follows is called for, such individuals fall back upon rationalizations as explanations.[1]

There is no reason, however, to assume other than that the social sciences can develop schemes and techniques which will secure adequate control over human behavior in just the same way as control over the material world has been secured in the so-called "natural sciences." Science is, after all, only an extension of common sense, but an extension which involves the purposive organization of experience in a systematic manner and with an increased degree of exactitude and refinement.[2] Science thus tends to become an end in itself without regard to the practical application of its principles. But this only means that it is more objective than common sense and less given to twisting the facts to fit into some existing conventional scheme which has become a part of the moral order.

Much of the backwardness of the social sciences is due to the failure of those interested in the control of human behavior to take an objective attitude toward their problems and the materials with which they have to work. Too often the practical demands of the situation, in terms of the ideals of

[1] Cf. Thomas, *The Unadjusted Girl*, pp 222–25.

[2] Hobson, *The Domain of Natural Science*, p. 25.

the past or the exigencies of the present, obscure the true relationships between the elements which must be recognized in order to control human behavior.[1]

In the physical sciences, on the other hand, there is not the emotional attachment to habitual ways of doing things which characterizes the social sciences. It is comparatively easy to see the advantage of an automobile over a horse-drawn vehicle, but to recognize the advantage of a growth-conception of social life instead of thinking in terms of never changing relationships is not so apparent. But more dangerous to the lay-mind is the thought that the acceptance of such a point of view may necessitate a complete reorganization of all those elements of personality to which the greatest emotional attachments are held. This tendency to avoid reorganization is illustrated by the recent flare-up against the doctrine of evolution.[2]

[1] Thomas finds that the chief obstacles to the growth of the science of human behavior are (1) our confidence that we have an adequate system of controlling behavior if we only apply the system successfully, and (2) our emotional attachment to the old community standards or norms. The average person who deals with human beings sees as his chief problem the discovery of how successfully to control behavior by regulating the wishes of the individual through the family, the church, and the community in the common-sense and customary ways. Such methods of control, however, assume a stability of the social framework which no longer exists. Advancement in the material world has been out of all proportion to that in the social world. So long as the social framework was relatively stable, the old methods of control worked fairly well. But in so far as the old order has disintegrated (and it has almost entirely disappeared in the city), it is necessary to recognize the need for new methods of control which do not run counter to new conditions. Cf. Thomas, *op. cit*, pp. 228–29.

[2] This emotional attachment to the standards of the past is not, however, an unsurmountable obstacle, for men have always objected to change of any kind. "There was strong condemnation, for example, of the iron plow . . . . on the ground that it was an insult to God and therefore poisoned the ground and caused weeds to grow. The man who built a water-driven saw-

The whole study of family disorganization in the past has been vitiated by this attachment to old community standards. Throughout the literature on the subject it is assumed almost universally that the traditional type of family organization should, if possible, be maintained against all disorganizing forces. Part of this attitude is clearly, of course, the result of idealizing the past and refusing to recognize that disorganization of the family existed at other periods of history. But much of it is due to the insistence that the family remain the same in spite of the changes going on in every other realm of life.

In this book an attempt has been made to define family disorganization objectively, without making any assumptions regarding its desirability.[1] In so doing it is not assumed that concretely family disorganization involves the same ele-

---

mill in England was mobbed; the man who first used an umbrella in Philadelphia was arrested. There was opposition to the telegraph, the telephone, the illumination of city streets by gas, the introduction of stoves and organs in churches, and until recent years it would be difficult to find a single innovation that has not encountered opposition and ridicule."—Thomas, *op, cit..* p. 229. As soon as this emotional attachment is recognized as leading to less rather than more adequate control of human behavior, it is likely to disappear, allowing research in the social sciences to proceed as objectively as in the physical.

[1] The question of the desirability of family disorganization, or of the organized family, is not, obviously, a problem of science, though this in no wise implies that it is trivial and unimportant. Society is, and probably always will be, interested in the preservation of the organized family. But in the realization of the desires of the group two tasks will need to be performed: (1) the study of the forces making for family disorganization in order to understand them, and (2) formulation of social policies with regard to the control of family disorganization upon the basis of such an understanding as may grow out of the study of the forces producing domestic discord. The first task is that of science, and may best be performed if all presumptions regarding social policy be left out of account for the time being. The second task belongs in the fields of ethics or applied sociology and may best be performed by workers in that field. The scientist often makes himself as ridiculous

ments in every period of history or in every cultural area. It is assumed, however, that the processes are universal for all groups of "modern intelligence,"[1] and that accordingly an adequate definition may be found to cover all cases, whether or not the definition here offered is found to be satisfactory.[2]

FAILURE OF PRIMARY-GROUP CONTROL

The method relied upon in the past for the control of family disorganization has been what Thomas[3] has called the "ordering-and-forbidding" technique. It is the technique of the primary group whereby the family, the church, and the community regulate behavior by repressing that which is not desired and commanding that which is wanted.[4]

The primary-group technique of control reaches its highest development in control by law, in which it takes on some of the impersonal characteristics of the secondary group inas-much as the enforcement of its rights and obligations is left to delegated groups, such as the police and the courts. Unfortunately, these delegated groups are not so impersonal as is often assumed, and therefore the transition from the

---

when he tries to formulate what is desirable as does the reformer or the moralist when he attempts to discover the forces involved in a given situation which he desires to reform. Both stand to gain, however, if the division of labor indicated here is recognized as it is in the so-called "natural sciences."

[1] I.e., belonging to man as he is known historically rather than to some group of simian ancestors.

[2] See p. 142 for this definition.

[3] Thomas and Znaniecki, *The Polish Peasant*, I, 3.

[4] Thomas and Znaniecki say: "The oldest but most persistent form of social technique is that of "ordering-and-forbidding"—that is, meeting a crisis by an arbitrary act of will decreeing the disappearance of the undesirable or the appearance of the desirable phenomena, and using arbitrary physical action to enforce the decree. . . . . A good instance of this in the social field is the typical legislative procedure of today."—*Loc. cit.*

"ordering-and-forbidding" to a secondary-group technique based upon science is not as rapid as might be expected.

The movement for divorce-law reform in the United States has been one of the ways in which control through law has been attempted. This movement has been directed for the most part toward making divorce more difficult, but partly through attempts to prevent hasty marriage. In general, the western states have placed upon their statute-books more liberal laws with respect to divorce than have the eastern and southern states. The result has been that many people in these states with more liberal laws have wished to modify these earlier statutes and have advocated reforms accordingly, while groups in those states with limited grounds for divorce have advocated a more liberal policy.

Besides these suggestions for less stringent divorce laws, several states have tried out the divorce-proctor system in various forms. The essential elements of this system consist in having some impartial person, usually an attorney, investigate the case preceding the court hearing and report his findings with recommendations to the court. In view of the fact that divorce cases are heard by courts according to the usual chancery procedure, it is contended by advocates of the proctor system that by the intervention of an impartial investigator into the contentious process between attorneys representing the complainant and the defendant, facts of prime importance to the court are brought out which would be neglected otherwise. This is, of course, especially true where only one party is represented in court, which is the situation in about three-fourths of all divorce-court hearings.[1]

---

[1] Kansas, for example, provided in its divorce law that the county attorney shall act as a divorce proctor in each suit for divorce, investigating the case and submitting a report to the judge before whom the case is to be tried.

Another approach to reform has been through the state marriage laws. Reformers have presented, and have had accepted in a few states, laws requiring the physical examination of one or both parties, publication of advance notices, etc.[1] Illinois for a long time forbade remarriage of divorced persons within one year after divorce upon all grounds except adultery, for which the ban continued for two years. But that law was repealed in 1923, when it became generally recognized as allowing persons who had been married contrary to law a loophole for terminating the union by having the marriage annulled.

The method of control through law most highly indorsed by professional reformers has been the family court. This plan usually consists in having a special court hear all cases involving family relations, though it may leave to another court the cases of juvenile delinquency. Chicago in 1911 established the first court, calling it the Court of Domestic Relations. Since that time similar courts have been established in a number of cities. The usual procedure in such a court is to have workers interview the complainants and then try to work out an adjustment outside of court—the court itself being utilized only in such cases where no adjustment can be made without the force of the law. Unfortunately, the workers in such courts generally are both overworked and seldom especially trained for this difficult and delicate task.[2]

[1] Wisconsin, Alabama, Louisiana, North Carolina, North Dakota Oregon, and Wyoming require that all males applying for marriage licenses present certificates showing the absence of venereal infection; advance notice is required in Maine, Massachusetts, New Hampshire, New Jersey, and Wisconsin; of non-residents in Connecticut, Rhode Island, and Vermont. See Hall, *Medical Certification for Marriage;* Hall and Brooke, *American Marriage Laws;* Schouler, *Marriage, Divorce, Separation, and Domestic Relations.*

[2] In Chicago, for example, several workers have previously been connected with the complaint department in the capacity of clerical workers,

Each of these types of attempt to control family disorganization by law assumes that the legal technique is an effective method for controlling human behavior. From the genetic point of view, law may be characterized as representing the desire of the group to promote its own orderly functioning by coercion through the application of punishment by impartial representatives of the group upon those persons who commit acts which are regarded as injurious to group welfare.[1] The legal technique thus implies a formal conception of family disorganization, and its control which seems hardly to conform to the facts for even a most casual study of the results of legislative efforts will convince one of the ineffectiveness of this technique. The constant stream of new proposals in technique of the sort just mentioned is sufficient testimony that the "right combination" has not yet been found.

INADEQUACY OF SOCIAL-WORK TECHNIQUE

Another form in which the "ordering-and-forbidding" technique is to be found is in the functioning of social agencies. The National Desertion Bureau assists Jewish agencies in locating deserters, and so facilitates the operation of law as a technique of control. The family-case-work organizations themselves attempt likewise to control family relations.

---

and have been promoted without further training to interviewing cases. Further, the chief justice of the Municipal Court, under whose jurisdiction is the Court of Domestic Relations, believes that all marital discord can be adequately explained in terms of heredity and therefore holds that the work of the court is only palliative. In view of this attitude he is opposed to any attempt to study the problem further.

[1] Cf. G. H. Mead, "Psychology of Punitive Justice," *American Journal of Sociology*, XXIII, 577–602.

From the standpoint of social control, social work in the city attempts to perform certain functions which, under rural conditions, are left to the community. This institutionalization of community control takes the form primarily: (1) of an extension of the governmental or legal processes, and (2) of organized gossip. The theory of the law is that everyone knows what it is, and is therefore equally able to defend himself against injustice. Under urban conditions, however, large numbers of persons do not know what the law is, or how to avail themselves of the protection afforded even though they are aware that such protection is guaranteed. The service of lawyers is, of course, always available but many people do not have the funds necessary to employ a lawyer.

Furthermore, the law assumes that the citizenry of a community are interested in the enforcement of the law, and will report violations to the police and to the courts even though such violations do not directly injure them. In the city, however, this function is being delegated more and more to the police. But, obviously, the police cannot be present always. The result is that social work has come in as an agency to perform these functions for certain social classes and therefore act as an extension of governmental processes, both in assisting the individual to obtain justice before the courts and to assist the police and the courts to enforce the wishes of the community.

But social work has taken over from the community other means of control than that of the more formal extension of the governmental processes. Social work operates also as a form of organized gossip in defining the situation for the individual in terms of community standards. "Gossip is a mode of defining the situation in a given case and of attaching praise and blame. It is one of the means by which the status of the individual and of his family is fixed."[1] Under rural conditions the gossip performed, gratis, the function of controlling the behavior of those who took the mores too lightly. In the urbanized community today, the social worker performs much the same function.[2]

One of the chief means the social worker has at her command for bringing pressure upon individuals is to go to relatives and attempt to make them feel some responsibility for the welfare of the "dependent" family. In the rural community if there was any occasion for such coercion the village gossips took care of it. Relatives did not allow their kin to want for things below the minimum standards of the community if they were themselves in a position to help for fear of being talked about. In the city, however, this fear breaks down, and needs to be revived by the social worker.

Then there is the matter of employment. The social worker is constantly exerting pressure upon employers to prevent exploitation, loss of employment, and to obtain employment. In the rural community the individual was protected from exploitation by his employer by gossip. Again, if the employer wished to dispense with the services of a laborer, he had to take into consideration the attitudes of the rural community. The social worker in the city attempts also to bring into the foreground personal factors which have no part in the efficient operation of economic production. Much the same thing might be said for the obtaining of employment.

[1] Thomas, *op. cit.*, p. 49.

[2] The most effective method the community has for regulating the behavior of its members is by talking about them. Gossip has a bad name because it is sometimes malicious and false, but in the main it is true and therefore an organizing force. It is in this latter sense that it is used here.

The social worker acts further in the capacity of the village gossip in formulating and organizing the attitudes of the community with reference to the conduct of individuals and groups. In this relationship she often serves as a means of communication between relatives, neighbors, school authorities, etc., keeping them informed with regard to the conduct and problems of the individual or family and thereby setting into motion the natural control which emanates from such sources. This even goes to the extent of making known to a part of the community the undesirable conduct of those who come within the range of the social worker's activities. Control in this way may take the form, even, of formulating rationalizations to explain the behavior of certain individuals as "queer"—psychopathic, mentally deficient, neurotic, etc.—and so to be given an inferior status in the community in much the same way in which village gossip fixed the status of the queer individual.

If a formulation of the attitudes of the neighborhood is not possible because behavior norms do not have local acceptance, the social worker attempts to widen the range of community influence by organizing the attitudes of the larger community toward misconduct and so extend the informal control exerted through gossip. And while the social worker gives much more attention to other family problems than to those of marital conflict, her technique in dealing with the latter is the same. Thus, whether as an extension of the governmental processes or as organized gossip, the function performed by social work in the control of family disorganization is more in keeping with the point of view of the primary group than with that of science.[1]

[1] It is true that social work aspires to be the application of scientific principles to the problem of the control of human behavior, but as yet that

DECLINE OF CHURCH CONTROL

A third institution through which reform has been advocated is that of the church. This institution has functioned as a control organization in three ways: (1) by incorporating into its creed adherence to certain standards of family life, such as the monogamous family, lifelong marriage unions, etc.; (2) by defining the situation in given cases of family disorganization; and (3) by attempting to adjust marital discord through the personal ministrations and advice of pastors and priests.

Control in the Protestant church has been indirect rather than direct and in the hands of the congregation rather than within the province of the minister. In the Catholic church the situation has been somewhat different. Here the control has been more direct and almost exclusively in the hands of the priesthood. The technique by which standards were maintained, however, has been essentially the same in both churches. It has consisted in bringing to bear the entire weight of the religious system in support of the traditional standards of family relations. This has been accomplished by insistence upon the coherence and unity of the whole system, to reject any part of which was to reject all. In this way, both in the minds of the clergy and the congregation

---

is only an aspiration. If it should ever become an applied science it would have that objectivity common to all arts utilizing scientific principles and become truly a secondary-group technique. So far, however, social workers have failed, for the most part, to utilize even those principles of human behavior which have been adequately demonstrated. It must be admitted, of course, that up to the present the social sciences have contributed few principles which are of value to social work. Nevertheless, social workers, like most artists, tend to fall into the conventional routine and in so doing depend more upon common sense than upon science for their principles of procedure.

has been built up the feeling that the entire set of religious attitudes is more or less involved whenever the individual has to choose between a socially sanctioned definition and one not having social sanction.[1]

The failure of this system of control is due largely to the fact that the chief emphasis has been upon "sins" rather than upon "merits." That is, the system tries merely to counteract the tendency to perform certain acts rather than attempting to develop the wish to perform only acts which are socially sanctioned.

Beyond this adherence to certain standards of family life the Protestant church has done little directly to control family disorganization. In fact, harmony in family relations has been implicit in the practices of Protestant churches. The emphasis upon faith and righteousness generally made these appear to be the way to the solution of all worldly problems. That is, the assumption has been that if one were truly religious, "right with God," such problems as family conflict would not arise, or if they did arise would furnish their own solutions.

The Catholic church, on the other hand, has not only attempted to define the situation in certain cases of family disorganization but it has also tried to work out adjustments. This has been done primarily through the technique of the confession.

The Catholic confession, according to the intention of the Church, is not only a disclosure of sins for the sake of remittance, but also a means of directing the believers, regulating their every day life according to the Christian principles as they are exposed by the Catholic Church.[2]

[1] Cf. Thomas and Znaniecki, *op. cit.*, IV, 135–36.

[2] See Document 77, Thomas and Znaniecki, *op. cit.*, IV, 103–4.

Through the confession the Catholic church has been able to modify to the degree which seemed necessary under unique conditions the categorical imperative involved in the traditional definition of standards of conduct in terms of the negation of sin. At the same time the priest has been able to offer solutions of personal problems to the penitent. It is true, of course, that these solutions have been of the "rule-of-thumb" sort, but nevertheless they have represented a more satisfactory method of control of family discord, probably, than the strict dependence upon emphasis of the importance of an "inner life."[1] The Protestant church, on the other hand, is just beginning to give more attention to this phase of church activity.

Unfortunately, what has been done by both priests and ministers to adjust family conflicts through advice and suggestions has been based upon rule-of-thumb procedures rather than upon scientific principles. The orthodox church has tended to regard science with suspicion in the training of persons for the pastorate and priesthood. And especially has this been true of those sciences which have the most to contribute to the understanding of human behavior, social and individual psychology, psychiatry, and sociology. In showing reluctance to accept a mechanistic view of human behavior, however, the church has only reflected the attitudes of the majority of people, whether churchmen or not.[2]

[1] To the extent that the Protestant church has been able to redefine marital relations in terms of an "inner life," however, it has been an instrument in the adjustment of family conflicts. It is because this technique is becoming less and less effective that the Protestant church is turning more to something similar to the Catholic confessional.

[2] It should be understood, of course, that the so-called conflict between the church and science is more adequately described as the conflict between urban and rural theology. The "orthodox" churchmen represent the theology which developed under rural conditions in which there was little science.

This attitude, fortunately, is becoming slowly modified, as will be pointed out later (see p. 285). We have seen, then, how the primary group has attempted to control family disorganization through law, social agencies, and the church. In so far as these attempts have been unsuccessful it has been due to the failure of the "ordering-and-forbidding" technique to function in the secondary group. This method of control is highly effective in the rural community where it was developed. There everyone knew everyone else, and the status of individuals and families was constantly being fixed by the degree to which one conformed to the standards of the group. In the urbanized community, however, there is no loss of status to the individual who does not conform. He is known much less intimately than in the rural community or not known at all. Contact is at one or two rather than at all points as in the rural community. The result is that the old "ordering-and-forbidding" technique ceases to function or becomes less effective. Another method of control is therefore necessary—one which fits the needs of the secondary group.

Some people have advocated the revival of the primary group as a cure for the present failure of the "ordering-and-forbidding" technique to function.[1] The program for the re-

---

Unaccustomed, therefore, to scientific methods, these churchmen have been frightened by the rapid demands for change made by their more liberal brother-churchmen of the cities who would dispense with much of the metaphysical theology of the past and reformulate religious principles in keeping with present-day advancement in science. But the conflict in religion is in no wise unique, for it is to be found in many types of human relations where rural and city interests diverge, such as in politics, in business, and in trade.

[1] Cf. Cooley, *Social Organization*, with Thomas, "The Persistence of Primary-Group Norms in Present Day Society," in Jennings, Watson, Meyer, and Thomas, *Suggestions of Modern Science Concerning Education*.

vival of the neighborhood has ordinarily taken the form of organizing community centers of various sorts. But such programs run counter to the currents of city life and can have under the most favorable conditions only a brief success. People who have become urbanized do not want to return to a primary-group organization of their activities. Such a reorganization of life upon a primary-group basis would deprive them of the freedom which they desire and which furnishes the chief motivating force drawing a greater proportion of them into the cities. The only alternative, therefore, lies in the development of a technique of control which "fits" the changed social situation. This technique is to be found in the control afforded through science.

SCIENCE AND THE SECONDARY GROUP

It is well known that science has developed in the city rather than in the country. The scientist is and always has been the arch-heretic. If he refused to consider new ways of doing things he could never develop the habit of experimentation which is necessary for the development of scientific principles. In the city he has found freedom for the progressive development of his "heresies." In view of his successes in the material world it seems reasonable to believe that he will be as successful in dealing in the same way with human behavior, and that control based upon the principles developed will constitute an efficient technique for the secondary group. In fact, if we turn to such fields as juvenile delinquency and psychiatry we find effective demonstration of the usefulness of the principles of science in the control of human behavior.

While all other courts are still operating upon the assumption that the individual is entirely responsible for his criminal acts and should therefore be punished, the juvenile court is attempting to control conduct through a scientific understanding of human behavior.[1] Here the individual delinquent is not brought into court solely for the purpose of determining his responsibility, but rather to determine his "irresponsibility," in the sense that the thing of chief concern is to find out what can be done to modify circumstances in a way that will prevent a repetition of delinquency. The tendency here is to take a mechanistic attitude toward the

[1] Perhaps Sutherland (*Criminology*, p. 283) has pointed out this antithesis between the criminal and the juvenile courts most clearly in the following comparison:

CRIMINAL COURT	JUVENILE COURT
1. Trial characterized by contentiousness; two partisan groups in conflict.	1. Hearing characterized by scientific methods of investigation.
2. Purpose of trial to determine whether defendant committed a crime with which he is charged.	2. Purpose of hearing to determine the general condition and character of the child.
3. No machinery for securing information regarding the character of the accused.	3. Elaborate machinery for securing information regarding character of the child.
4. Such information, if secured, may not be introduced as a part of the evidence.	4. Such information is the basis on which a decision is made.
5. Punishment if convicted.	5. Protection and guardianship of the state if the existing conditions show the need.
6. Treatment in a specific case determined not by the needs of the particular individual but by the legislature in advance, for all who violate the law in question, with reference primarily to other actual or potential delinquents.	6. Treatment in a specific case determined by the needs of the particular individual without reference to other actual or potential delinquents.

Obviously, as Sutherland points out, the juvenile court in many places falls far below this standard, while in some respects certain criminal courts approach the standard of the juvenile court. Nevertheless, the procedure of the juvenile court indicates a tendency to take a mechanistic point of view toward human behavior. Thus, while its handling of cases is largely dependent upon the skill and intuition of its workers, the court has incorporated into its procedure much more of scientific principle than have any other of the political processes.

behavior of the delinquent and attempt to solve his problems for him, often along lines recommended by experts in human behavior.

Fortunately, the juvenile court has had the benefit of research into the mechanisms of behavior found in delinquency. Though the study of delinquency has often consisted primarily in the application of psychological principles to the interpretation of the behavior of juvenile delinquents, in not a few instances have the students in this field contributed principles to the science of human behavior.[1] The method of approach throughout has shown a complete break with common sense and an acceptance of the point of view of science with its mechanistic outlook upon life, whether in the realm of the physical or the psychical.

Psychiatry as well has shown the effectiveness of the scientific approach. One school, psychoanalysis, has, by its successes in the treatment of cases, revolutionized in many respects not only the whole field of psychiatry, but of psychology and sociology as well, by contributing to the science of human behavior a great fund of concrete data in addition to a method of research.[2] The result is that in the control of human behavior in which mental disintegration is a significant factor, there is at hand a definitely formulated and effective technique of treatment for many cases. And whether or not one accepts the explanations offered by the psychoanalysts for their results, one must admit the effectiveness of their technique.

[1] See, for example, Healy, *Mental Conflicts;* Van Waters, *Youth in Conflict;* Thomas, *op. cit.*

[2] It is true that psychoanalysis has contributed a number of principles also, but these have not yet been generally accepted, at least not in the form proposed by the psychoanalysts, and therefore are of minor importance in comparison to the concrete data and the method of research.

The whole field of psychiatry is not represented by psychoanalysis, of course, even though that particular school has done much to revolutionize the approach even of the orthodox psychiatrist. But the orthodox school also has found its technique greatly improved by the introduction of more objective methods into its investigative procedure and by the utilization of such principles as have been developed in whatever field has had something to contribute to the general science of human behavior.

In fact, so successful has the psychiatrist been in controlling human behavior that much of his contribution has been incorporated into the technique of so-called "psychiatric case-work."[1] To the degree, then, that social workers are utilizing psychiatric principles they are becoming more scientific.

A similar tendency toward the utilization of science in the treatment of "problems in personality" may be observed in the field of religion. While it is true that the church is reluctant to modify its philosophy of life, which assumes the freedom of the will and the innate depravity of man, nevertheless a great many ministers are beginning to realize that their work requires some training in the science of human behavior for effective handling of the many personal problems which are brought to them. The result is that several of the leading seminaries are offering courses in case-work problems of the minister.[2]

[1] Psychiatric training for social workers undoubtedly will soon give way to a broader training based upon a more inclusive science of human behavior. Nevertheless, the demand for psychiatric training indicates a trend toward more objectivity and greater utilization of the scientific method in case-work.

[2] See, for example, the announcements of courses at the Union Theological Seminary, New York City; the Divinity School, University of Chicago, Chicago; and the Divinity School, Harvard University, Cambridge, Mass.

Control of family disorganization, however, still proceeds in harmony with the "ordering-and-forbidding" technique. Little has yet been done to study the forces bringing about marital discord, and nowhere except in child study is there any attempt to control the situation scientifically. Those who are dealing with cases, such as judges, court workers, social workers, are still trying to make adjustments by resorting to common sense and magic.[1] Moreover, for the most part they are blind to the defects of their own technique or else consider the situation wholly hopeless.

This unfortunate situation, of course, is largely attributable to the lack of any concrete method of approach to the study of family disorganization. Studies in the past have been concerned primarily with the analysis of cases in terms of common-sense attributes without determining whether or not these attributes were in any way different from those characterizing families which were not disorganized.[2] Even when care was taken to rule out such characteristics as were

[1] An example of the programs offered by the juristic mind. is Judge Sabath's "recipe," reported in the *Chicago Tribune*, September 24, 1925, as follows:

"If no one under 25 years of age was allowed to marry—if the law required that a period of six weeks elapse between an engagement and a wedding—if married couples were required to explain their differences to an impartial arbiter before being allowed to file suit for divorce—

"Then, according to Superior Judge Sabath, who yesterday returned from a study of the divorce courts of Europe, there would be only one divorce suit where four now occur.

"Judge Sabath, who has heard more divorce cases than any other American jurist, visited France, Switzerland, Germany, and Czecho-Slovakia. In the latter country he found conditions that were nearly ideal so far as the laws concerning marital relations are concerned, he said.

"The European system of a conciliation court, where man and wife must argue their differences before an arbitrator, was also commended by the judge. Such a court would cut divorces by 75 per cent, he declared."

[2] See chaps. ii, iii, iv, vii, and viii.

common to normal families, explanations were given in common-sense terms which prohibited prediction of the ultimate outcome of any specific case.

A second difficulty, furthermore, lay in the study of family disorganization as a general behavior pattern rather than as the typical ways in which individuals find interests and wishes clashing in their marriage contacts. Studies of the relationship between family disorganization in general and the business cycle, for example, are useful only when accompanied by studies of the processes of change in the attitudes of individuals in certain types of marriage relations.[1] For it is only in terms of the latter process that prediction can be made with reference to specific cases, which is primarily what control demands.

A concrete method of approach suitable to the demands for control will be concerned, then, with social co-ordinations, i.e., with the interaction of husband and wife under certain conditions. This method will have to be developed in detail in the course of many particular investigations, as has been the case in the physical sciences.[2]

It is obvious, of course, that the problem of family disorganization is too large to be studied as a whole to the greatest advantage. It must be broken into parts and approached with all the care and precision with which the chemist conducts his experimentations in the laboratory. A few of the more outstanding problems involved may be indicated.

1. *Problem of rural to urban movement.*—How do family attitudes change when a family moves from the country to

[1] See Hexter, *Social Consequences of Business Cycles*, for an elaborate statistical analysis of the relationship between divorce and business cycles.

[2] For a detailed outline of significant factors in the case-study method of investigation into the causes of family disorganization see Appendix B.

the city? Under what conditions does this change from country to the city make for instability or stability of the organized family and how?

2. *Problem of immigrant adjustment.*—What change in family relations results from the transference of a family from one country to another? How do these changes differ for different cultural or national groups?

3. *Problem of the changed status of women.*—How has the changed economic status of women changed family relations? What has been the effect of romanticism upon marital relations?

4. *Problem of sex.*—How has sex education and sex discussion changed the organization of the family? What is the effect of birth control upon family attitudes? Does the tendency for families to have few children, and therefore of only one sex, change the organization of attitudes between husband and wife?

5. *Problem of individual differences.*—How has the modern emphasis upon individual differences—mental, temperamental, and cultural—modified the possibilities of family adjustment? How do conditions, such as deficient mental capacity and psychoses, affect family life?

6. *Problem of economic adjustment.*—How does the economic independence of women, particularly the gainfully employed wife and mother, affect family relations? Under what conditions do economic factors seem inevitably to undermine family relations? What are the chief factors in this process?

7. *Problem of selection of mates.*—Upon what bases are selection of mates made? How do present methods of selecting mates promote or prevent domestic accord?

8. *Problem of mobility.*—How does the mobility of city

life affect family relations? What is the correlation between other forms of disorganization and that of the family?

9. *Problem of urban areas.*—How does the differentiation of city areas affect family organization? What are the neighborhood forces producing the differential rates of family disorganization?

10. *Problem of control.*—How do primary-group methods of control, such as gossip, the church, the school, the neighborhood, public opinion, social agencies, and the family, break down in secondary society? How do secondary methods, such as the courts, the press, and the police, function in the urban environment? How can present scientific knowledge of human behavior be utilized by these control groups in promoting domestic accord and preventing family conflicts? What experiments for observation and treatment of family discord, such as family clinics, family councilors, etc., are feasible and practicable at the present time?

The study of these problems and the many more which would develop out of them should result in an understanding and control of family disorganization in a much more thoroughgoing way than has been possible in the past. Upon the basis of such knowledge it would be possible to venture upon the clinical treatment of family discord in much the same fashion that disease is treated by the medical fraternity.

APPENDIX A

STATISTICAL DATA PRESENTED IN CHARTS

Chart I.—Table included in the text.

Chart II.—Divorces per 100,000 population in the United States, 1870–1924:

	YEARS							
	1924	1922	1916	1906	1900	1890	1880	1870
U.S...........	151	136	112	84	73	53	39	28

Chart III.—Number of marriages to one divorce in the United States, 1887–1924:

	YEARS						
	1924	1922	1916	1906	1900	1890	1887
U.S.................	6.9	7.6	9.3	11.8	12.3	16.2	17.3

Chart IV.—Number of divorces per 100 marriages for rural and urban areas in the United States, 1887–1924:

AREAS	YEARS							
	1924	1922	1916	1906	1901	1896	1891	1887
Urban.........	15.0	12.5	8.5	6.1	6.6	5.9	4.4	4.7
Rural.........	7.7	7.2	7.3	6.6	6.6	5.6	5.0	4.4

SELECTED AREAS
Urban

New York State
 Kings County
 Bronx County
 New York County
 Queens County
 Richmond County
Illinois
 Cook County
Pennsylvania
 Philadelphia County
 Allegheny County

Ohio
 Cuyahoga County
Missouri
 St. Louis City
Maryland
 Baltimore City
Massachusetts
 Suffolk County
California
 Los Angeles County
Michigan
 Wayne County

Rural

New York State
 Delaware County
 Hamilton County
 Lewis County
 Livingston County
 Orleans County
 Putnam County
 Schoharie County
 Schuyler County
 Wyoming County
 Yates County
Illinois
 Calhoun County
 Gallatin County
 Hamilton County
 Hancock County
 Henderson County
 Johnson County
 Kankakee County
 Kendall County
 Pope County
 Scott County

Ohio
 Adams County
 Brown County
 Geauga County
 Harrison County
 Holmes County
 Morgan County
 Morrow County
 Paulding County
 Pike County
 Vinton County
Missouri
 Crawford County
 Douglas County
 Hickory County
 Knox County
 Ozark County
 St. Clair County
 Schuyler County
 Stone County
 Taney County
 Worth County

Pennsylvania
  Adams County
  Clarion County
  Forest County
  Fulton County
  Juniata County
  Perry County
  Pike County
  Snyder County
  Sullivan County
  Wyoming County
Michigan
  Alcona County
  Arenac County
  Gladwin County
  Kalkaska County
  Lake County
  Missaukee County
  Montmorency County
  Ogemaw County
  Oscoda County
  Roscommon County

Maryland
  Calvert County
  Caroline County
  Charles County
  Garrett County
  Howard County
  Kent County
  Queen Annes County
  St. Mary's County
  Somerset County
  Worcester County
Massachusetts
  Barnstable County
  Dukes County
  Franklin County
  Nantucket County
California
  Amador County
  Calaveras County
  Del Norte County
  Lake County
  Mariposa County
  Modoc County
  Mono County
  Plumas County
  Sierra County
  Trinity County

Chart V.—Number of divorces per 100 marriages in Illinois, 1887–1924:

	YEARS							
	1924	1922	1916	1906	1901	1896	1891	1887
Illinois........	16.0	14.7	12.2	11.1	10.5	8.9	7.6	7.5
Cook Co.....	20.4	17.2	13.3	12.3	12.3	9.4	7.4	7.6
Remainder...	11.9	12.0	11.6	10.1	9.4	8.6	7.7	7.5

Chart VI.—Number of divorces per 100 marriages in Cook County and ten most rural counties, Illinois, 1887–1924:

	YEARS							
	1924	1922	1916	1906	1901	1896	1891	1887
Cook Co.......	20.4	17.2	13.3	12.3	12.3	9.4	7.4	7.5
Rural counties..	10.6	10.3	11.5	8.6	9.6	6.9	6.1	5.7

Chart VII.—Proportion of total number of decrees granted to each party of five-year periods of married life, Chicago, 1919:

DURATION OF MARRIED LIFE IN YEARS	PERCENTAGE OF ALL DECREES		
	Total	To Husband	To Wife
All cases.................	100.0	26.4	73.3
0– 4....................	51.9	14.6	37.3
5– 9....................	24.8	6.0	18.8
10–14....................	12.3	2.9	9.4
15–19....................	5.7	1.4	4.3
20–24....................	3.1	0.9	2.2
25–29....................	1.2	0.4	0.8
30–34....................	0.4	0.2	0.2
35–39....................	0.2	....	0.2
40–44....................	.01	....	0.1

Chart VIII.—Percentage distribution of cases by five-year periods with respect to children for (1) divorces to husbands and (2) divorces to wife, Chicago, 1919:

DURATION OF MARRIED LIFE	DECREE TO HUSBAND		DECREE TO WIFE	
	Children Percentage	No Children Percentage	Children Percentage	No Children Percentage
All cases.....	100.0	100.0	100.0	100.0
0– 4.......	64.3	33.8	61.5	34.8
5– 9.......	19.6	29.9	21.8	31.2
10–14.......	7.3	19.0	9.5	17.5
15–19.......	3.9	8.5	3.6	9.4
20–24.......	1.5	5.8	2.0	4.5
25–29.......	1.3	1.8	0.7	1.6
30–34.......	0.6	0.8	0.3	0.3
35–39.......	0.2	0.2	0.4	0.1
40–44.......	0.1	....	0.1	0.1

Chart IX.—Desertion cases in the Court of Domestic Relations by yearly totals and by moving averages, Chicago:

Year	No. of Cases	Moving Aver.	Year	No. of Cases	Moving Aver.
1907.........	861	....	1915.........	1,931	2,053
1908.........	1,063	....	1916.........	2,114	2,177
1909.........	1,432	1,335	1917.........	3,591	2,489
1910.........	1,548	1,485	1918.........	2,094	2,588
1911.........	1,769	1,567	1919.........	2,717	2,670
1912.........	1,612	1,512	1920.........	2,425	....
1913.........	1,472	1,588	1921.........	2,525	....
1914.........	1,157	1,657			

Chart X.—Family areas in Chicago (see text).

Chart XI.—Areas of family disintegration in Chicago, 1920 (see Table XXXIII).

Chart XII.—Percentage of women ten years of age and over gainfully employed in the United States, 1870–1920:

	YEARS					
	1920	1910	1900	1890	1880	1870
All occupations..	21.1	23.4	18.8	17.4	14.7	13.2

Chart XIII.—Percentage of women in domestic and personal service of all women ten years of age and over gainfully employed in the United States, 1870–1920:

	YEARS					
	1920	1910	1900	1890	1880	1870
Domestic and personal service............	25.5	31.7	39.3	41.5	44.7	53.0

Chart XIV.—Increase in population in Chicago by decades, 1860–1920:

Year	Total Population	Year	Total Population
1920.............	2,701,705	1880.............	593,185
1910.............	2,185,283	1870.............	298,977
1900.............	1,698,575	1860.............	109,260
1890.............	1,099,850		

Chart XV.—Increase in average daily newspaper circulation per 100 population in Chicago, 1884–1923:

Year	Population	Total Circulation	Circulation per 100 Population
1923...................	2,888,122*	2,409,547	84.0
1920...................	2,701,705*	2,085,412	77.4
1915...................	2,443,494*	2,128,545	86.8
1910...................	2,185,283	1,668,634	76.3
1906...................	1,990,600*	1,638,492	82.4
1900...................	1,698,575	1,104,800	64.6
1895...................	1,398,712*	955,253	68.3
1890...................	1,099,850	481,118	43.6
1884...................	741,850*	243,990	32.8

*Estimated

APPENDIX B

FACTORS IN FAMILY DISORGANIZATION

For the present at least, the following factors seem to be of particular importance, and need therefore to be taken into account in the study of family disorganization where the chief method utilized is that of the study of cases.

1. *Cultural background.*—What have been the educational, intellectual, social, political, recreational, and religious interests of husband and wife both before and after marriage? How did these interests change? How do husband and wife explain these changes? What are the outstanding characteristics of the cultural groups, including their respective families, from which each came? What were the conceptions of sex relations of each? Financial relations? To what degree did premarriage contacts continue after marriage? How did these contacts change? Why?

2. *Ecological factors.*—What were the professional interests and training of husband and wife? What is their economic philosophy? In what economic areas have they lived both before and after marriage? What communities have they lived in both before and after marriage? How did these communities change while they were there? What effect did these changes in community forces have upon their behavior?

3. *Personality traits.*—What were the early ambitions and enthusiams of husband and wife and how have they changed? What rôles did each play in his or her own family before marriage? What are the philosophies of life of each? What are the principal antipathies of each? What does each fear most? What are the strongest wishes of each?

4. *Conception of family life.*—What was the conception of family life carried over by each from his own home? What love stories were read by husband and wife prior to marriage? Had there been previous love affairs? How were these terminated, and how did they change the love attitudes of husband and wife? What were the conflicting conceptions of family life with which each came into contact?

5. *Rationalizations.*—How do husband and wife account for their conflicts? Under what circumstances do conflicts arise? What about? How have these conflicts changed their attitudes toward each other? If they married again what would they do to prevent conflict?

THE QUESTIONNAIRE

In securing data from the persons themselves, the first step in the method proposed, the following questionnaire is offered tentatively as an outline of questions to be asked and order of procedure in interviewing:

I. HISTORY OF EARLY MARRIED LIFE

1. What subjects or points always create friction and misunderstanding?
2. Have there been any conscious attempts at accommodation? Why did they fail?
3. What intimacies are allowed in marriage relations? Did the romance of marriage seem to die? Why?
4. What does each consider to be the fundamental difficulty? How does each explain why he failed in choosing a mate?
5. Were children wanted? Who are favorites? Who disciplines the children? Have the children been a source of accord or conflict?
6. What has been the frequency of sexual relations? What is the reaction of the wife toward this experience? Is there mutual understanding or disagreement? Have there been any attempts to prevent conception? What conflict of attitudes here?
7. What was the first quarrel about? What disillusionments have there been in marriage?
8. How has the conception of marriage relations of each changed? What forces produced these changes?

II. HISTORY OF COURTSHIP

9. What were the motives for marriage?
10. Was there any opposition to the marriage? Of what nature? How was adjustment made to it?
11. Under what circumstances did the man and woman meet? What drew them together? What was the reaction of each? Did courtship begin immediately or later and under what circumstances?
12. What problems were discussed before marriage? (a) Sex? (b) Financial? (c) Religious? (d) Cultural? (e) Temperamental? (f) Disagreements? What attempts to adjust them?

13. What intimacies were allowed before the engagement? After the engagement, but before marriage? What was the reaction of each?

14. Had there been previous love affairs? How were these terminated? Engagements? Disillusionments? How did these change their conceptions of family relations?

III. HISTORY OF EARLY LIFE

15. What were their early conceptions of family relations? What were considered the essential features? Sources of these conceptions?

16. Had there been discord between father and mother of either? How did this influence their attitudes toward marriage?

17. Were there early love affairs? What is remembered about them?

18. What love stories were read during adolescence? What impressions did these make?

19. What was the early religious training of each? What impression did it make?

20. What were the early interests, ambitions, and enthusiasms of each? Who were their early playmates?

21. How many children were there in their respective families? Sex of each? Were they oldest or youngest? Which parent was the favorite of each? What were the relations between the children in each family?

APPENDIX C

A SELECTED BIBLIOGRAPHY[1]

I. THE FAMILY IN MODERN SOCIETY

I. HISTORY AND ORGANIZATION OF THE FAMILY

Bosanquet, Helen. *The Family* (London, 1906).

Calhoun, Arthur W. *A Social History of the American Family* (3 vols.; Cleveland, 1917-19).

Dealey, James Q. *The Family in Its Sociological Aspects* (Boston 1912). (I, 2, 3.)

Ellis, Havelock. *Man and Woman: A Study of Human Secondary Sexual Characters* (London and New York, 1894 and 1914).

———. *Studies in the Psychology of Sex* (6 vols.; Philadelphia, 1900, 1901, 1903, 1905, 1906, 1910, 1913, and 1915).

Flügel, J. C. *The Psycho-Analytic Study of the Family* (London, 1921).

George, W. L. *The Intelligence of Woman* (Boston, 1916). (I, 3.)

Gillette, John Morris. *The Family and Society* (Chicago, 1914). (I, 2, 3.)

Goodsell, Willystine. *A History of the Family as a Social and Educational Institution* (New York, 1915). (III, 1.)

Howard, G. E. *A History of Matrimonial Institutions, Chiefly in England and the United States with an Introductory Analysis of the Literature and the Theories of Primitive Marriage and the Family* (3 vols.; Chicago, 1904).

International Eugenics Congress. "Eugenics, Genetics and the Family," Vol. I, *Scientific Papers of the Second International Congress of Eugenics* (Baltimore, 1923). (I, 3.)

Knight, M. M., Peters, Iva Lowther, and Blanchard, Phyllis. *Taboo and Genetics: A Study of the Biological, Sociological and Psychological Foundations of the Family* (New York, 1920).

Letourneau, Ch. *The Evolution of Marriage and of the Family* (trans., New York, 1891).

[1] Numbers in parentheses after titles refer to other topics in the classification of the literature upon which the work cited has bearing.

Malchow, C. W. *The Sexual Life* (St. Louis, 1923).

Myerson, Abraham. *The Nervous Housewife* (Boston, 1920).

Robie, W. F. *Rational Sex Ethics, Further Investigations: A More Intensive Study of Sex Histories, and Dreams, with Therapeutic Suggestions and Philosophical Deductions* (Boston, 1919).

Thomas, W. I., and Znaniecki, Florian. *The Polish Peasant in Europe and America* (5 vols., Boston, 1918–20). (I, 2; III, 1, 2; IV, 2.)

Thwing, Charles F., and Carrie F. B. *The Family: An Historical and Social Study* (Boston and New York, 1887). (I, 2.)

Tridon, André. *Psychoanalysis and Behavior* (New York, 1920).

Westermarck, Edward. *History of Human Marriage* (3 vols.; London, 1891 and 1921).

White, W. A. *Mechanisms of Character Formation: An Introduction to Psychoanalysis* (New York, 1916).

Williams, James Michel. *Principles of Social Psychology as Developed in a Study of Economic and Social Conflict* (New York, 1922).

Van Waters, Miriam. *Youth in Conflict* (New York, 1925).

2. SOCIAL CONTROL OF FAMILY RELATIONS

Grant, Robert. *Law and the Family* (New York, 1919).

Hall, Fred S. *Medical Certification for Marriage: An Account of the Administration of the Wisconsin Law as It Relates to the Venereal Diseases* (New York, 1925).

Hall, Fred S., and Brooke, Elizabeth. *American Marriage Laws in Their Social Aspects: A Digest* (New York, 1919).

Howard, G. E. "Social Control and the Functions of the Family." *Congress of Arts and Sciences* (Boston and New York, 1906).

Jennings, H. S., Watson, John B., Meyer, Adolph, and Thomas, W. I. *Suggestions of Modern Science Concerning Education* (New York, 1920).

Lofthouse, W. F. *Ethics and the Family* (London and New York, 1912). (I, 1, 3.)

Post, Louis F. *Ethical Principles of Marriage and Divorce* (Chicago, 1906).

Richmond, Mary E. *Social Diagnosis* (New York, 1917).

———. *What Is Social Case Work? An Introductory Description* (New York, 1922).

Richmond, Mary E., and Hall, Fred S. *Child Marriages* (New York, 1925). (I, 3.)

Schouler, James. *Marriage, Divorce, Separation, and Domestic Relations* (2 vols.; Albany, 1921).

Stelk, John. *Report of the Domestic Relations Court* (Chicago, 1917).

3. SOCIAL REFORM AND THE FAMILY

Coolidge, Mary Roberts. *Why Women Are So* (New York, 1912).

Densmore, Emmet. *Sex Equality: A Solution of the Woman Problem* (New York, 1907).

Gilman, Charlotte Stetson. *The Man Made World or Our Androcentric Culture* (New York, 1911). (I, 1.)

Key, Ellen. *Love and Marriage* (trans.; New York and London, 1914).

Martin, Mr. and Mrs. John. *Feminism: Its Fallacies and Follies* (New York, 1916).

Meisel-Hess, Grete. *The Sexual Crisis: A Critique of Our Sex Life* (trans.; New York, 1917).

Nearing, Scott and Nellie M. S. *Woman and Social Progress: A Discussion of the Biologic, Industrial and Social Possibilities of American Women* (New York, 1912).

II. STATISTICAL ANALYSIS OF FAMILY DISORGANIZATION

Brandt, Lilian. *Five Hundred and Seventy-four Deserters and Their Families: A Descriptive Study of Their Characteristics and Circumstances* (New York, 1905).

Colcord, Joanna. *Broken Homes: A Study of Family Desertion* (New York, 1919).

Hexter, Maurice B. *Social Consequences of Business Cycles* (Boston and New York, 1925).

Lichtenberger, J. P. *Divorce: A Study in Social Causation* (New York, 1909).

Mowrer, Ernest R. "The Variance between Legal and Natural Causes for Divorce," *Journal of Social Forces*, III (March, 1924), 388–89.

Patterson, S. Howard. "Family Desertion and Non-Support," *Journal of Delinquency*, VII (September and November, 1922), 249–82, 299–333.

Quinn, James A. *Family Desertion in St. Louis* (unpublished manuscript).

United States Bureau of the Census. *Marriage and Divorce, 1867–1906* (Washington, 1908–9).

———. *Marriage and Divorce, 1916* (Washington, 1919).

———. *Marriage and Divorce, 1922* (Washington, 1924).

———. *Marriage and Divorce, 1923* (Washington, 1925).

———. *Marriages and Divorces in the United States, 1924* (press statements).

Wilcox, W. F. *The Divorce Problem*, "Columbia University Studies in History, Economics and Public Law," Vol. I (New York, 1891).

III. THE CASE-STUDY METHOD OF STUDYING FAMILY DISORGANIZATION

1. SOCIAL FORCES IN SOCIAL AND FAMILY DISORGANIZATION

Babbitt, Irving. *Rousseau and Romanticism* (Boston and New York, 1918).

Chapin, F. Stuart. *An Historical Introduction to Social Economy* (New York, 1917). (I, 1.)

Groves, Ernest R. "Social Influences Affecting Home Life." *American Journal of Sociology*, XXXI (July, 1925), 227–40. (I, 1.)

Hulme, Thomas E. *Speculations: Essays on Humanism and the Philosophy of Art* (London and New York, 1924).

Knowles, L. C. A. *The Industrial and Commercial Revolutions in Great Britain during the Nineteenth Century* (London and New York, 1921).

Lee, Porter R. "Changes in Social Thought and Standards Which Affect the Family," *Family*, IV (July, 1923), 103–11. (I, 1.)

Ogburn, William Fielding. *Social Change with Respect to Culture and Original Nature* (New York, 1922).

2. CASE ANALYSIS

Bennett Arnold. *Our Women: Chapters on the Sex Discord* (New York, 1920).

Breckinridge, Sophonisba P. *Family Welfare Work in a Metropolitan Community: Selected Case Records* (Chicago, 1924).

Eubank, Earle E. *A Study of Family Desertion* (Chicago, 1916). (II.)

Healy, William, and Bronner, Augusta F. *The Judge Baker Foundation Case Studies*, Series I, Nos. 1–20 (Boston, 1922).

Kammerer, Percy G. *The Unmarried Mother: A Study of Five Hundred Cases* (Boston, 1918).

Sherman, Corinne. "Racial Factors in Desertion," *Family*, III (October–January, 1922–23), 143, 165, 197, 222.

IV. METHODOLOGY

1. GENERAL

Columbia Associates in Philosophy. *An Introduction to Reflective Thinking* (Boston, 1923).

Hobson, E. W. *The Domain of Natural Science*, "The Gifford Lectures Delivered in the University of Aberdeen in 1921 and 1922" (Aberdeen, 1923).

Jevons, W. Stanley. *The Principles of Science: A Treatise on Logic and Scientific Method* (London, 1907).

Keynes, J. M. *A Treatise on Probability* (London, 1921).

Pearson, Karl. *The Grammar of Science* (London, 1900 and 1911).

Ritchie, A. D. *Scientific Method: An Inquiry into the Character and Validity of Natural Laws* (London and New York, 1923).

Yule, G. Udny. *An Introduction to the Theory of Statistics* (London, 1910, 1912, 1915, and 1919).

2. SOCIOLOGICAL

Burgess, Ernest W. "The Family as a Unit of Interacting Personalities," *Family*, VII (March, 1926), 3–9. (III, 2.)

Chapin, F. Stuart. *Field Work and Social Research* (New York, 1920).

Cooley, Charles H. *Human Nature and the Social Order* (New York, 1902, 1912, and 1922).

———. *Social Organization: A Study of the Larger Mind* (New York, 1909).

———. *Social Process* (New York, 1918).

Giddings, Franklin H. *The Scientific Study of Society* (Chapel Hill, N.C., 1924).

Healy, William. *Mental Conflicts and Misconduct* (Boston, 1917). (III, 2.)

Lindeman, Eduard C. *Social Discovery: An Approach to the Study of Functional Groups* (New York, 1924).

Park, Robert E., and Burgess, Ernest W. *Introduction to the Science of Sociology* (Chicago, 1921).

Park, Robert E., Burgess, Ernest W., and Others. *The City: Human Behavior in the Urban Environment* (Chicago, 1925).

Simmel, Georg. "Die Grossstadt und das Geistesleben," *Die Grossstadt* (Dresden, 1903).

Thomas, William I. *The Unadjusted Girl: with Cases and Standpoint for Behavior Analysis* (Boston, 1923). (I, 2; III, 2.)

INDEX

INDEX

Abandonment. *See* Desertion

Adultery: and children, 76–79, 84; cause for divorce, 58, 60; and number of children, 82–84, 88; and sex of children, 81; tensions resulting in, 66–67; an undifferentiated term, 66–67

Advertising, increase in, index of secondary contacts, 170

Airplane, the, characteristic of modern culture, 267

Arizona, divorce rate in, 53 n.

Arkansas, divorce rate in, 53 n.

Astronomy, advance in, 267

Atomization, of individual in city life, 23, 228

Attitudes: analysis of, 256–60; conflict in, 257, 261; in desertion, 178; flow of, 220; and ideals, organization of, 3; life-history of, 229; primary *vs.* secondary, 45–46; relation to behavior, 228–29; and sentiments, 218–19

Australia, divorce trend in, 33–34

Autobiographies, as case materials, 230

Automobile, the: characteristic of modern culture, 267; increase in use of, 170

Babbitt, Irving, cited, 159

Bargelt, Louise, cited, 90 n.

Behavior: description of, 220; distinction between types, 219; overt in desertion, 177–78; students of human, 230; thinking as form of, 219; units of or events, 219. *See also* Human behavior

Behavior patterns: confusion of, in city life, 22, 23 n.; in family disorganization, 287

Belgium, divorce trend in, 33–34

Biology, advance in, 267

Blake, Doris, cited, 9

Blanchard, Phyllis, and Knight and Peters, cited, 19 n.

Bosanquet, Helen, cited, 136, 137, 138

Brandt, Lilian, cited, 92, 96, 99, 100, 103, 174, 176–77, 178, 180–81

Bronner, Augusta F., and Healy, cited, 194 n.

Brooke, Elizabeth, and Hall, cited, 273 n.

Burgess, Ernest W.: cited, 194 n.; and Park, cited, 133 n., 218–19

Business cycle, and family disorganization, 287

Cabot, Hugh, and Smith, cited, 200–203

Calhoun, Arthur W., cited, 133, 134, 147, 148, 149, 167

California: divorce rate in, 53 n.; selected rural areas in, 292; selected urban areas in, 291

Case-studies: offer materials, 262; often superficial, 230; need for, analyzed, 260

Case-study method: and analysis of behavior sequences, 216–29; in analysis of family tensions, 195–215; as analysis of social forces, 145–73; and casual observation, 145 n.; limitations of, 172–73, 192–94, 286–87; and records of social agencies, 174–94; and social diagnosis, 184–85; and statistical analysis, 146 n., 262–63; from two sources, 143–45; use of, by social agencies, 174

309

Family in America

AN ARNO PRESS / NEW YORK TIMES COLLECTION

Abbott, John S. C. **The Mother at Home:** Or, The Principles of Maternal Duty. 1834.

Abrams, Ray H., editor. **The American Family in World War II.** 1943.

Addams, Jane. **A New Conscience and an Ancient Evil.** 1912.

The Aged and the Depression: Two Reports, 1931–1937. 1972.

Alcott, William A. **The Young Husband.** 1839.

Alcott, William A. **The Young Wife.** 1837.

American Sociological Society. **The Family.** 1909.

Anderson, John E. **The Young Child in the Home.** 1936.

Baldwin, Bird T., Eva Abigail Fillmore and Lora Hadley. **Farm Children.** 1930.

Beebe, Gilbert Wheeler. **Contraception and Fertility in the Southern Appalachians.** 1942.

Birth Control and Morality in Nineteenth Century America: Two Discussions, 1859–1878. 1972.

Brandt, Lilian. **Five Hundred and Seventy-Four Deserters and Their Families.** 1905. Baldwin, William H. **Family Desertion and Non-Support Laws.** 1904.

Breckinridge, Sophonisba P. **The Family and the State:** Select Documents. 1934.

Calverton, V. F. **The Bankruptcy of Marriage.** 1928.

Carlier, Auguste. **Marriage in the United States.** 1867.

Child, [Lydia]. **The Mother's Book.** 1831.

Child Care in Rural America: Collected Pamphlets, 1917–1921. 1972.

Child Rearing Literature of Twentieth Century America, 1914–1963. 1972.

The Colonial American Family: Collected Essays, 1788–1803. 1972.

Commander, Lydia Kingsmill. **The American Idea.** 1907.

Davis, Katharine Bement. **Factors in the Sex Life of Twenty-Two Hundred Women.** 1929.

Dennis, Wayne. **The Hopi Child.** 1940.

Epstein, Abraham. **Facing Old Age.** 1922. New Introduction by Wilbur J. Cohen.

The Family and Social Service in the 1920s: Two Documents, 1921–1928. 1972.

Hagood, Margaret Jarman. **Mothers of the South.** 1939.

Hall, G. Stanley. **Senescence:** The Last Half of Life. 1922.

Hall, G. Stanley. **Youth:** Its Education, Regimen, and Hygiene. 1904.

Hathway, Marion. **The Migratory Worker and Family Life.** 1934.

Homan, Walter Joseph. **Children & Quakerism.** 1939.

Key, Ellen. **The Century of the Child.** 1909.

Kirchwey, Freda. **Our Changing Morality:** A Symposium. 1930.

Kopp, Marie E. **Birth Control in Practice.** 1934.

Lawton, George. **New Goals for Old Age.** 1943.

Lichtenberger, J. P. **Divorce:** A Social Interpretation. 1931.

Lindsey, Ben B. and Wainwright Evans. **The Companionate Marriage.** 1927. New Introduction by Charles Larsen.

Lou, Herbert H. **Juvenile Courts in the United States.** 1927.

Monroe, Day. **Chicago Families.** 1932.

Mowrer, Ernest R. **Family Disorganization.** 1927.

Reed, Ruth. **The Illegitimate Family in New York City.** 1934.

Robinson, Caroline Hadley. **Seventy Birth Control Clinics.** 1930.

Watson, John B. **Psychological Care of Infant and Child.** 1928.

White House Conference on Child Health and Protection. **The Home and the Child.** 1931.

White House Conference on Child Health and Protection. **The Adolescent in the Family.** 1934.

Young, Donald, editor. **The Modern American Family.** 1932.